W9-DEC-065

DOWN the NIGHTS
and DOWN the DAYS

THE IRISH IN AMERICA

Studies Sponsored by the Ancient Order of Hibernians and the Cushwa Center for the Study of American Catholicism

DOWN THE NIGHTS AND DOWN THE DAYS

Eugene O'Neill's Catholic Sensibility

Edward L. Shaughnessy

University of Notre Dame Press

Notre Dame, Indiana

Manufactured in the United States of America

Library of Congress Cataloging-in-Publication Data

Shaughnessy, Edward L., 1932–
    Down the nights and down the days : Eugene O'Neill's Catholic sensibility / Edward L. Shaughnessy.
      p. cm. — (Irish in America)
    Includes bibliographical references and index.
    ISBN 0-268-00882-5 (alk. paper)
      1. O'Neill, Eugene, 1888–1953. 2. American drama—Catholic authors—History and criticism. 3. Dramatists, American—20th century—Biography. 4. Drama—Religious aspects—Christianity. 5. O'Neill, Eugene, 1888–1953—Religion. 6. Catholics—United States—Biography. 7. Catholic Church—Doctrines. 8. Irish Americans—Religion. I. Title. II. Series.
PS3529.N5Z79696   1977
812'.52—dc20
[B]   96-27117
                                 CIP

Once again, of course, for Janet,
and for Peg, Katie, Molly and Kevin—
Pax et felicitas.

Out of the depths I cry unto you, O Lord,
  O Lord, hear my voice.
Let thy ears be attentive
  To the voice of my supplication.

—Psalm 129

I fled Him, down the nights and down the days;
I fled Him, down the arches of the years;
I fled Him, down the labyrinthine ways
Of my own mind; and in the mist of tears
I hid from Him, and under running laughter.

—Francis Thompson

"Life's a tragedy—hurrah!"

—O'Neill

Contents

Acknowledgments

IT IS DIFFICULT TO SAY how or when this project began. I remember a saintly Benedictine monk who once cautioned that reading Eugene O'Neill was asking for trouble. Perhaps he was right, although the same might be said about reading Shakespeare and Dostoevski. Over the years dozens of other good men and women have provided counsel and, happily, encouragement. I wish to thank some who have been especially generous. Without their support I could not have traveled very far along the road of this enterprise.

I extend thanks to the following individuals: Scott Appleby and Barbara Lockwood of the Cushwa Center for the Study of American Catholicism, who have been exceptionally supportive; Professors Thomas E. Porter and Paul R. Valliere, for their useful suggestions after reading an early version or section of the manuscript; Lewis Miller and Nancy Everett, Director and the Collection Management Supervisor, respectively, of Irwin Library, Butler University; fellow O'Neillians Travis Bogard, Margaret Loftus Ranald and Frederick C. Wilkins, for advice and encouragement; Fr. Thomas J. Daly of the Boston Chancery Office, for recollections of diocesan attempts to be put in touch with Eugene O'Neill when the playwright was dying; Sr. Regina Shaughnessy, S.P., for keeping me in mind; and for others who should be named, in justice and affection—Irving Fine, George Hoffmann, James McCaslin, and Francis Quinn.

To archives and archivists (every researcher's best friends) I extend gratitude: the Special Collections Division, Lauinger Library, Georgetown University, for permission to quote from letters of Daniel Lord, S.J., to Martin Quigley and from Eugene O'Neill to Martin Quigley; the Memorial Library Archives, Marquette University, for use of materials in the Dorothy Day and Catholic Worker collections; to the Hesburgh Memorial Library, University of Notre Dame, for photographs and a letter, Eugene O'Neill to Laurence Lavanoux; the Cushwa-Leighton Library, St. Mary's College, for a letter from Louis Sheaffer to Sr. M. Madeleva, C.S.C.; to the Dinand Library, the College of the Holy Cross, for letters exchanged between Michael Earls, S.J., and Richard Dana Skinner.

For permissions to quote passages from *The Plays of Eugene O'Neill,* volumes 1, 2, and 3 (1983) and from *A Moon for the Misbegotten* (1952), I should like to thank Random House; from *Long Day's Journey into Night* (1956), *A Touch of the Poet* (1957), and *More Stately Mansions: The Unexpurgated Edition,* Martha Gilman Bower, ed. (1988), I acknowledge with thanks to Yale University and the Yale Collection of American Literature, Beinecke Library. I am grateful for permission to reprint excerpts from *Eugene O'Neill in Ireland: The Critical Reception* (1988), an imprint of Greenwood Publishing Group, Inc., Westport, Conn.

The Cushwa Center for the Study of American Catholicism at the University of Notre Dame supported this project in the form of a stipend that accompanied the 1994 Hibernian Research Award.

My deepest gratitude to Janet and our children for their constancy and cheerful support.

Prologue

IN THE THREE quarters of a century leading up to Vatican Council II, the world of American Catholicism was massively established. It is not surprising, then, that we are staggered by its later undoing. For that world is no more. When John XXIII threw open the windows of the Vatican, not zephyrs but a hurricane swept through the church. Indeed, the consequences of that heroic gesture defy easy summary: not only has the institution itself been radically transformed, but the very character of our times has been altered by the Council. In 1900 the American Catholic church was a phenomenon quite different from that same communion as it exists today. To many of its faithful it was the very center and focus of life. If we fail to recognize that essential fact, we cannot begin to estimate its influence on the life of yesterday's everyman, including that of the apostate genius, Eugene O'Neill.

Many Catholics of that earlier period saw their church as this world's chief repository of truth. In that community one felt secure in the accepted definitions of reality (of good and bad, that is). For a Catholic coming of age in the first half of the twentieth century, certain words carried a theological plausibility that today seems positively quaint. *Sin* and *redemption* were such words. For some outsiders, Roman Catholicism itself must have seemed an anachronism. Here was an institution that commanded loyalty and obedience, even as it had in the Middle Ages. But to its members, the church's promise to endure until the end of time was taken as a very article of faith. For Holy Mother had transformed the tragedy of suffering into the salvific mystery of the *via dolorosa*. Who could deny her stunning appeal? In defining its role, this church invoked both the law of love and the symbols of authority. Her mission was to console the dispirited, a work of mercy named in the Sermon on the Mount. But the church could play equally well the role of stern patriarch, whose icy glare of disapproval could paralyze the soul of dissenter or rebel. One might love the church or leave it (or both). Its claims, however, would remain deeply etched in the Catholic psyche. Such was the power that formed the moral vision of the faithful. It played no small part in forming the worldview of James and Ella O'Neill and that of their sons, James, Jr., and Eugene Gladstone.

Eugene left the church as an adolescent. Asked in 1946 if he had returned to Catholicism, he responded, "Unfortunately, no." None, then, should attempt to make of him something that he was not. The aim here is to see the something that he was. In addition to his (anyone's) impenetrable mystery, O'Neill was sometimes a fearful, intimidating presence. In his searing honesty he often startled his interlocutors. Thus, he no doubt raised eyebrows when he remarked at a final rehearsal for *The Ice Man Cometh*, "*In all my plays sin is punished and redemption takes place.*"[1] Most students of O'Neill will agree that this is an astonishing declaration. What did it mean?

When he used such language, O'Neill understood full well its power and nuances. But there is absolutely no reason to think he accepted the doctrinal authority the words conveyed to believing Christians. That given, an even greater mystery attaches to his utterance. For, whatever he meant, we may be certain that he was neither joking nor playing the card of obscurantism. Not O'Neill.

Those who turn in sorrow or anger from early faith no doubt suffer deep spiritual trauma. We are not surprised, therefore, when they seek to flee all reminders of the soul-scalding experience. Eugene O'Neill knew such an experience, yet his life offers something quite remarkable among biographies of modern artists: he did not, thereupon, give up his search for God. Rather, he seems to have been haunted by the very idea of God. Seen in this context, then, his well-known obsession with Francis Thompson's poem about the "hound of heaven" suggests a certain logic. Indeed, the very image of the hound connected with O'Neill's sense of life as a mystery.

His teenage rejection of Catholicism, born first of disappointment and then of fury, only intensified his search for the "answer." He was determined to locate it. O'Neill gave his attention and short-term fealty first to this, then to that, philosophy—eastern and western, ancient and modern. It is interesting to note, therefore, that his most prolonged allegiance derived from inspirations old and new: Greek dramatic ritual, given latter-day relevance in the works of Friedrich Nietzsche. In this philosopher he found a celebration of classic forms that made the theater a kind of temple and tragedy a religion. Thus it seems fitting to speak of O'Neill, even after he severed ties to Catholicism, as a religious man.

He had said that *The Iceman Cometh* was "a denial of any other experience of faith in my plays."[2] Yet we are transfixed by some inner logic that moves through the O'Neill canon. How was it possible for him to speak of sin and redemption in his plays, after the explicit denial of faith? It would be difficult to imagine language more conspicuously or traditionally Christian.

Sin and *redemption*: the very words recall the central mystery of Christianity. But if O'Neill's words cannot be construed to have a theological explanation, what can they mean? Was his remark nothing more than a sentimental characterization of his life's work? Was he indulging a penchant for irony? We cannot be certain, of course, but we know that O'Neill was little given to the sort of irony practiced by absurdists and self-satirists. No, his words tend more to betray habits (a sensibility) formed by training and culture. By the time he wrote his final plays he had, it seems clear, settled the question of his identity. And, while it would seem perverse to speak of him then as a doctrinal or practicing Catholic, it seems perfectly reasonable to speak of him as a man formed in the crucible of Irish Catholicism. So it was that Eugene O'Neill could remark without self-consciousness about sin and redemption. This grounding had taken place in the final decade of the nineteenth and earliest years of the twentieth centuries. It undoubtedly affected his personality formation. Thereafter, his psychological-spiritual profile becomes more and more difficult to interpret. Perhaps no one's becoming can be fully fathomed. The clues appear to be in part traceable but in larger part enigmatic.

Two basic issues are at the core of this study. I wish to define "Catholic sensibility," for I believe O'Neill carried this value over from childhood into adulthood and that its presence contributed much to his moral vision. Second, I attempt to follow O'Neill's sin-and-redemption theme where it leads. I think it does not lead to the sweeping inclusiveness of "all my plays." My focus is therefore as much biographical as it is critical. I see evidence of a cultural memory that gives his plays the authority of lived experience.

Part 1 of this study addresses several interrelated issues, biographical-historical and literary. That is, it takes up connections between O'Neill's personal life and art and certain developments in Catholic intellectual history. It thereby provides a background against which to read the meaning of his Catholic sensibility. It traces the years of his initiation and training in the milieu and his intellectual-spiritual rebellion in adolescence and young manhood. Chapter 2 offers an examination of the powerful forces in the Catholic ethos that established themselves deeply in his psyche, the teachings on sin and guilt, for example, which he later disclaimed but whose imprint remained in certain ways indelible in his memory. These presences, I believe, were carried over into his understanding of tragedy itself.

In chapter 3 I attempt to describe the climate of opinion that characterized American Catholic intellectual life from the mid-nineteenth century until the years just prior to Vatican Council II (1962–1965). There can be no doubt, of course, that the reception of O'Neill's plays in the Catholic community was affected adversely in this climate. Pius X's condemnation of modernism in 1907, with its chilling effect on the development of Catholic literature, has considerable relevance to the problems of many artists with the church. Indeed, the heavy-handedness of the Pope's gesture damaged prospects for Catholic intellectual life well into the next half century and, consequently, impaired the reception of O'Neill's plays in the Catholic world.

Yet a too protracted examination of such issues in modern church history can distract our attention from an immediate concern with O'Neill's Catholic sensibility. Therefore, I have chosen to offer limited discussion of this background in the endnotes and an appendix ("The Immigrant Church Press and the Catholic Writer, 1920–1950"). The appendix carries (1) a brief review of the Pope's censure of modernism that so discouraged the development of a lively Catholic intellectualism; and (2) an account of the hostility often directed by the American Catholic press toward Catholic writers in this country. These materials will explain a great deal, I believe, about the playwright's attitude toward the institutional church.

But O'Neill's work is in part the history of an artist's "search for God." (He himself used this phrase more than once, as we shall see.) Indeed, his attempts to find a substitute for his lost faith were exceptionally intense, especially in the 1920s. Of course, this history demands attention here; therefore, in the final subsection of chapter 3 I treat, in rapid review, three "search-for-God" plays from the twenties: *The Great God Brown, Lazarus Laughed,* and *Strange Interlude.* Fascinating and brilliant as they are in their contributions to the modern theater, however, these plays do not place before us protagonists who are involved in deep human relationships, as do the plays examined in part 2. Another way of putting this is to say that the major characters do not "sin," since sin is an act committed in human interconnectedness. In these plays "big subjects" overshadow character and character development.

The very concept of sin implies relationship. One person wounds another—out of spite or anger or envy. The tissues of love or friendship are scarred; the integrity of connection is violated. The plays chosen for discussion in part 2 are chiefly those that treat the dynamics of human relationships, especially familial and marital ties. Here the sin-and-redemption thesis is put to the test in eleven plays. Included among these is *The Iceman Cometh,* a work some will insist cannot fairly be called a family play. I hold to precisely the opposite view: familial and marital dynamics operate very powerfully in it.

In certain O'Neill plays, however, no such connections exist, or they are merely implied. As a general rule expressionistic plays do not examine interpersonal exchanges. Thus, *The Emperor Jones* and *The Hairy Ape* are not taken up in this study. One thinks also of the *S. S. Glencairn* plays, powerful mood pieces but not plays of complex human relationships. Not all one-act plays need be disqualified, however: *Ile* stands the test.

I examine plays from O'Neill's three major periods. From the early years (1916–1923), I have chosen *Ile, Beyond the Horizon,* and *All God's Chillun Got Wings.* In the middle period (1924–1933) *Desire Under the Elms, Mourning Becomes Electra,* and *Ah, Wilderness!* offer the excellent examples of the theme under consideration. But I choose the greatest number of titles from the late period (1939–1943): *The Iceman Cometh, Long Day's Journey into Night, A Touch of the Poet, More Stately Mansions,* and *A Moon for the Misbegotten.*

These were the years of O'Neill's most universally acclaimed achievements. The reader will not be surprised, therefore, that the most striking illustrations of my theme are to be found in the plays of this period. *Days Without End* (1934), the "Catholic play," is taken up separately in chapter 6.

Some may question the inclusion of *Ah, Wilderness!*, O'Neill's only comedy. I examine this question at length further along, of course. For the moment, perhaps it is enough to say that the play offers a model of marriage and the family. This means that it deals, as does *Long Day's Journey*, with issues of relationship. Its value, then, lies in the idea of example by contrast.

In sections that take up ideas of tragedy, I frequently cite commentators who were O'Neill's near contemporaries: Joseph Wood Krutch, George Jean Nathan, Richard Dana Skinner, Lionel Trilling, et al. I intend by this no slight to scholars of my own generation, born between the world wars, and those younger still. As a matter of fact, many of the older critics held strong reservations about O'Neill's intellectual depth: Eric Bentley, Bernard De Voto, Francis Fergusson, Trilling. Nevertheless, they were usually alive to assumptions dealt with in his plays, whether or not they agreed with them. Some may feel that Krutch's views are too often invoked. I know very well that, even as *The Modern Temper* (1929) made a brilliant contribution to intellectual history, its influence has long since paled. As Edwin H. Cady noted over two decades ago,[3] Krutch himself seemed later to downplay the pessimism of his study. I call attention to Krutch's views for three reasons, however. First, in the years before World War II, when many distinguished critics (De Voto and Fergusson among them) addressed O'Neill's "weaknesses" in *ad hominem* terms, Krutch tried to render a scrupulously fair judgment. Second, although he was himself compelled to accept the assumptions of the modernist movement in the arts, the venerable critic recognized spiritual dimensions in the equally pessimistic work of O'Neill. Third, in my judgment, Krutch's ideas on tragedy carry into the present with considerable authority.

Richard B. Sewall has written on O'Neill and tragedy with refreshing modesty and clarity. In "Eugene O'Neill and the Sense of the Tragic," Professor Sewall recalls that in his "career-long fumbling with the idea of Tragedy, I have come to at least one conclusion. If the set of your mind is not tragic, you'd better not try to write a tragedy."[4] O'Neill, he said, had the tragedian's mind-set.

When the truth is told, most of us "fumble" on this field. This is so because, if it implies anything, tragedy implies mystery. In discussing it, therefore, we cannot know (entirely) what we are talking about. But we should try to clarify our intentions. Take Sewall's elementary distinction between *tragedy* and *tragic*: " . . . [T]ragedy as a term in criticism is in danger of becoming exclusive and academic. I have found the adjective more useful."[5] The latter term suggested to him the "great tragic temperaments" that connected O'Neill with such figures as Shakespeare and Hawthorne, Melville and Conrad, Dostoevski and Strindberg. "Great tragic temperaments" may strike us as a bit sonorous, but the words create a context and give us a sense of the direction the critic will take. So long as the characterization is valid, we will feel comfortable in the discussion.

One matter may require a special word. Should even limited reference be made to the post–Vatican II Catholic sensibility that has evolved? After all, O'Neill died in 1953, nine years before the convening of the Council in Rome. Therefore, this later evolution in Catholic teaching and "style" may appear to be irrelevant to any discussion of his life work. At first this position seems entirely plausible. Yet, in the end, I reject its absolute imposition for this reason. The Council was born of dynamic forces that had been abuilding for decades, both inside and outside the monolith of Roman Catholicism. The conclave marked, of course, the church's coming to terms with long-standing issues of authority and freedom. Indeed, the phenomenon took on the patterns of earlier upheavals in intellectual and cultural history.

Standing at the remove of four or five centuries, we today can see the patterns that were then forming but that were too blurred to be discerned by that earlier "man in the street." Perhaps the chaos of our moment will be better understood by others who may look back upon it as we now look back upon those centuries of Renaissance and Reformation. The tensions born in such "episodes" inevitably challenge the reigning authority and unsettle the fixed opinions of the majority. In time, however, resolution occurs and the changes (in definition and doctrine and in the organization's understanding of its role) become themselves a part of the tradition. Thus, the very issues that once burned white hot lose their vitality and immediacy.

Occasional but necessary reference to post–Vatican Council II conditions, then, can give us a clearer view, by contrast, of earlier times and tensions. That point is especially relevant here, for, by reminding ourselves of those cultural values O'Neill accepted and those he rejected, we gain some understanding of Catholic influence on his life and work.

* * *

Endlessly, obsessively, O'Neill dealt with the same three themes, all interconnected. First was the question of belonging: Where do I fit in? In this he spoke for many of his fellow artists and friends and for many other men and women of our time. A second and equally haunting theme was that one he announced to Krutch (and which has been, perhaps, cited with irritating frequency): "I am interested only in the relation between man and God."[6] The third was his obsession with the past, for the past held the mystery of his fate. He could never break its code.

To many commentators his work, especially after the mid-1920s, had become self-absorbed and irrelevant to the great issues of the day. Indeed, his entire canon offers titles that appear to have little connection with the workaday struggles of the proletariat: *Beyond the Horizon, Lazarus Laughed, Strange Interlude, Mourning Becomes Electra, Ah, Wilderness!, Days Without End, The Iceman Cometh, Long Day's Journey into Night.* And even in those works that deal with questions of prejudice, social justice, or workers' rights (e.g., *Anna Christie, The Hairy Ape, All God's Chillun Got Wings*), the greater issues are existential-philosophical. "O'Neill is least interesting when he occasionally concerns himself with social realism. His tradition is that of *Lear* and *Faust*."[7] Even if he called himself "a philosophical anarchist," he may have been, like his own Larry Slade in *The Iceman Cometh,* unable to conquer his own ambivalence: "When man's soul isn't a sow's ear, it will be time enough to dream of silk purses" (III, 590).

Was O'Neill, then, merely playing at the revolution with such true believers as Jack Reed and Louise Bryant, Max Eastman and Hippolyte Havel? Did he choose to ignore the causes that bound them all in a common mission? Perhaps the one best qualified to offer an opinion was Dorothy Day, apostle to the poor, a revolutionary who remained faithful to social causes to the end. Some years after his death, she seemed to suggest that he had a different battle to fight, one that consumed his artist's soul:

> . . . she disagreed with Agnes Boulton and with O'Neill's last wife, Carlotta Monterey, that O'Neill had no interest in religion or the idea of God. To this proposition, Dorothy said, she could "only disagree." She thought of her discussions with O'Neill on Baudelaire and Strindberg, and what O'Neill had said about their art. O'Neill had not dismissed the God idea as so much trivia. "Gene's relations with his God was a warfare [*sic*] in itself. He fought with God to the end of his days. He rebelled against man's fate."[8]

He was not, like Clifford Odets and Arthur Miller a little later, formed in the wake of Sacco-Vanzetti and the paralysis of the American 1930s. Political conscience is not the spine of O'Neill's work, Depression era or any other period. He had given that up long before Odets had come on the scene: "Time was when I was an active socialist, and, after that, a philosophical anarchist. But today [1922] I can't feel that anything like that really matters."[9]

Spiritually he was a classicist. The absurdist has an eye on the present, for what else is there? That is his tragedy. The writer with a political agenda, often a profound ethicist (Shaw and O'Casey; Miller, Hellman, Hansberry), places greatest value on the future: "Awake and sing!" But to be transfixed as O'Neill was is to be bound to the past.

> I do not think you can write anything of value or understanding about the present. You can only write about life if it is far enough in the past. The

present is too much mixed up with superficial values; you can't know which thing is important and which is not. The past which I have chosen is one I knew. . . . [10]

That was to be both the torment and the glory of his tragic vision.

O'Neill's past proved to be a heavy burden: a history of loss. He lost faith and family and fellowship. Prudence argues against confronting matters of such gravity. The challenge is daunting, especially if one lacks, as I do, the theologian's training that seems to be called for. Yet I take heart: "Tillich said that anyone who had a degree of ultimate concern was a theologian."[11] I add to this a belief that those who hold something of the cultural memory are responsible for preserving it. To that end I undertake this formidable task.

PART ONE

The Reluctant Apostate

> *. . . I must confess to you that for the past twenty years almost, (although I was brought up a Catholic, naturally, and educated until thirteen in Catholic schools), I have had no Faith.*

> —*Eugene O'Neill to Sr. Mary Leo Tierney, O.P.*

1 | The Lad, the Rebel, the Artist

The O'Neills: Cradle Catholics

EARLY AND OFTEN Eugene O'Neill had been reminded of his Irish heritage. That, it is probably fair to say, was not much different from being reminded of his Catholic heritage.[1] If one's ethnic and religious origins often shape one's identity, this principle surely held true in the case of O'Neill. The Celtic background appealed to him. Indeed, he took considerable pride in the history of the O'Neills, especially that of the second Earl of Tyrone, Hugh O'Neill.[2] But the Catholic influence of his formative years produced lifelong anguish. He could neither forget his past nor live comfortably in the knowledge of it. Down the years he fled his fate. When he sketched the scenario for a "miracle play," *Days Without End*, the playwright described the hero's dilemma in words that undoubtedly carried autobiographical overtones: "[O]nce a Catholic always a Catholic." To O'Neill, moreover, whatever touched upon identity became ineluctably charged with mystery. A complex fate, Henry James might have called it.

The near reflex response to religious authority that once obtained among the Catholic laity has been forgotten by many and never experienced by other contemporary Catholics. Earlier devotional habits of daily living are now so long forgotten that their renewed practice would seem the starkest eccentricity in this late day of the twentieth century. The overused word *ambience* may be the only fair characterization of the pre–Vatican II state of Catholic consciousness. An entire vocabulary has been lost to a generation. Not only has liturgical Latin been preempted by the vernacular, but a very catalog of phrases, formulae, and objects is no longer stored in the memory bank. Over a century ago James Joyce recorded some of these terms in his first novel: *genuflection, thurible, chasuble, tunicle, paten, dalmatic, monstrance.*

Unfamiliarity with these words cannot be measured merely by our chronological distance from them, however. Separation is psychological and intellectual as well as temporal. The contemporary Catholic's understanding of himself is something very different from that of his counterpart a century ago. The institution's earlier customs might well seem, to today's believer, something very close to superstition. Some appreciation of the older forms can be gained from novels like those of Patrick A. Sheehan (1852–1913), Irish author and priest, or from the American, J. F. Powers (1917–   ). And yet, Canon Shee-han's stories are altogether out of vogue today, and Powers's work is less and less read. Here is the nub of the thing: without direct contact, one lacks expe-riential insight. To have lived in an institution's presence, even if one is con-temptuous of its power, is to sense something of its culture. One will then know its diurnal hum and rhythms by acquaintance (*connaître*).

What is fading is a memory of the ethos that animated American Catholi-cism as it was *practiced,* let us say, from 1870–1960. The institution, on the eve of the twentieth century (it is hard to overemphasize the point) had been formed by a hierarchy whose roots were Irish. And for another three score years, the American Catholic Church would retain this decidedly Irish charac-ter. This meant that its administrative style was authoritarian. In the life of both its professed (priests, nuns, and brothers) and its lay Catholics, we will discover a faith in the institution as the living embodiment of mystery.

Laws of fasting and abstinence were built into the calendar, constant re-minders of the need to do penance: the forty days of Lent, introduced by the stern lesson of Ash Wednesday; meatless Fridays; the Easter duty (a require-ment to confess one's sins and to receive the Eucharist between Easter Sunday and the feast of the Ascension). Arranged by the calendar, the gospel stories were retold every year. No human activity could stand unregulated. The rules of relationship were enforced with paternal authority; all moral deviance was considered sinful and was punished. The laws were clear and unequivocal: no divorce, no sex outside matrimony. The most egregious offenses were called mortal sins (death to the life of grace in the soul; death until the sinner con-fessed, received absolution, and did penance). Even to place oneself in prox-imity to temptation was called an "occasion of sin." It should not be hard to see how these negative assessments of one's own nature (puritanical, Jansenis-tic, even Manichaean) might induce overscrupulosity among the timid.

Some called it all a mindless program of rote recital. Its practitioners, how-ever, internalized its symbolism and therewith learned to read "reality." If a person's training were solid enough to carry her through adolescence and young adulthood, she might even find it possible to speak without shuddering about her own imminent demise. Indeed, at their first communions, a moment of ineffable joy, children whispered the "prayer for a happy death." The senti-ment would be reinforced thousands of times over a lifetime in the Ave Maria: "Pray for us, now and at the hour of our death." Thus, there was no incon-gruity on Ash Wednesday, when one heard the reminder, *Memento mori* (Re-member death). At home and on the playground children used this vocabulary.

Indeed, they spoke of things doctrinal and liturgical with such confidence that one might have thought of them as elfin theologians or infant mystics.

> There is not an uncertain moment in the young Catholic's acceptance of established creed. Before he has completed his years of adolescence, every fundamental truth of his Church has become a part of him; the articles of the Apostles' Creed are the steel uprights in the process of his religious thought. The truths his whole life is founded upon are dogma, and he spurns the liberality of open Bible and free interpretation. There is not an elastic idea in the structure of his belief.
>
> Hence it is that the Catholic's attitude toward life in all its phases is fundamentally theological. And the more his mind grows in capability to grasp ideas for the superstructure of his dogma, the more does it become theological in attitude.[3]

Strange beyond all was that this parochialism existed in America, where the stolid Protestant was both worthy citizen and wary neighbor. In the streets of New York, Chicago, Detroit, and scores of other cities one saw nuns in a hundred different habits, priests wearing Roman collar at the ball game, altar boys in cassock and surplice and marching in public procession. It is a picture worth imagining. We are not speaking here of life in the capitals of medieval Europe; we are recalling a phase of life amid the buzz of twentieth-century American cities. The strangeness of it all seemed even greater, moreover, because this openness appeared not to be self-conscious. Thus oriented, one might remain confident, even joyful, on life's pilgrimage. There was the other side of things, to be sure: the sense of sin, a crippling legacy for many. That is another chapter, however, to be taken up at length further along. The point to be stressed here is that a child coming into awareness in this elemental Catholic world would bear until death its indelible character, its mark on the soul: a complex fate indeed.

It was into this view of the natural and supernatural that James, Sr., and Ella entrusted the winsome and hopeful Jamie and, a decade later, the impressionable Eugene. The latter, after boyhood, came to realize that he shared with his parents and brother a fate impossible to avoid: Life was a tragedy.

James and Ella O'Neill were "cradle Catholics," persons baptized, as their sons would be, in infancy. They would immerse these "lads," James, Jr., and Eugene Gladstone, into the ethos they knew and revered. Here was the classical operation of tradition, literally the handing on of a way of life and a set of beliefs, a sense of the world's and the self's reality as formed by religion. To fail in this rite would constitute a serious dereliction. A parent's life was blighted whose child should abandon his faith. Thus, in O'Neill's family drama, James Tyrone chides his sons for their betrayal: "You've both flouted the faith you were born and brought up in—the one true faith of the Catholic Church—

and your denial has brought nothing but self-destruction."[4] The parents were legion who, like James and Ella O'Neill, committed their children to an intellectual and spiritual regimen that they themselves had experienced and honored.

If parents could afford, as the O'Neills could, to place their offspring in the best Catholic grammar and prep schools, they could insulate the children from threats to their cultural identity that would surely be encountered in daily exchanges in the urban public schools. When reinforced by ritual practice in church and school, the stern lessons of the catechism became things so fixed in memory that their echoes might be recalled, even after faith itself had been discarded. "What will it profit a man if he gain the entire world yet suffer the loss of his own soul?" Even more sombre: "Remember, man, that thou art dust and unto dust thou shalt return."[5]

It is important to realize that O'Neill's prepubescent years coincided exactly with the final dozen years of the nineteenth century. The times themselves offered far fewer challenges to parental authority than are fronted in today's cacophony of distractions. Moreover, in their earliest years children seem little inclined to challenge authority figures in value-conflicts. Indeed, the child will probably wish to please her adult protectors and models. At no time in later life will all matters seem so clear. When one has experienced this protected childhood, she remembers forever the language and impressions of these early years, when other ideals had not yet surfaced to conflict with what one knew to be true.

Whether such a regimen is at bottom efficacious is a question beyond consideration here. We do know, however, that religious memory can produce powerful effects on adult perception. Memory can offer a retreat from the trauma of the moment. We know this in part because the playwright has, with unusual authority, recorded many such instances. So it is that Mary Tyrone mourns her fall from innocence: "I was brought up in a respectable home and educated in the best convent in the Middle West. Before I met Mr. Tyrone I hardly knew there was such a thing as a theater. I was a very pious girl. I even dreamed of becoming a nun" (*LDJ*, 102). Her husband also recognizes his failures in virtue. "It's true," he says, when his sons challenge his fidelity, "I'm a bad Catholic in the observance, God forgive me. But I believe" (77).

The Church had called this world a vale of tears. One should not expect to be happy. The world was not a playground, children were told. The liturgical calendar itself, in its annual cycle of feasts and seasons, was intended to remind the faithful of that sombre injunction: Take up your cross. Life is a kind of war in which one mystery (evil) contends with another and greater mystery (love). When the Church bade adieu to one of its sojourners, it had completed its mission in relation to that soul and now entrusted the departed one to other spirits: *In paradisum, deducant te, Angeli* (May the angels lead you into paradise). The faithful were taught to believe in the superiority of the "other," as it sanctified the here-and-now.

James O'Neill had climbed from galling poverty onto the plateau of fame and wealth. Ella, on the other hand, had known the security of a pampered childhood. The fragile Miss Quinlan, christened Mary Ellen, had not been brought up to take a place in the somewhat racy world of the professional theater. Ella (the name she came to prefer) had been prepared to participate in a life of high culture. Thus she had been trained in music and languages, first by the Ursuline Nuns of Cleveland, and then by the Sisters of the Holy Cross at St. Mary's Academy, South Bend, Indiana. Ella proved to be docile, talented, and modest. She was happy in an environment far removed from the hurly-burly of an expanding America in the decades following the Civil War. Later Ella O'Neill would recall her years in those semicloistered precincts as a time of peace and happiness. In the 1870s, however, her life was transformed. By the time she returned to Cleveland, her father had been dead one year.

James, who also grew up in Ohio, had been protected from nothing. With his brothers and sisters he had, like thousands of others, come from an Ireland of famine only to join in a hardscrabble campaign to survive. His family would live a catch-as-catch-can existence. After a few bitter years in Buffalo, where his father had apparently abandoned them, James moved with his mother and siblings to Cincinnati.

The young James O'Neill was nothing if not resourceful and eager to make his way. At age twenty or so, passing an idle evening at the billiards table, he was invited to come next door onto the boards of Cincinnati's National Theatre. Extras were needed to fill small parts in Dion Boucicault's immensely successful melodrama, *The Colleen Bawn*. The year was 1867. By 1874 James was playing with Edwin Booth, in one production alternating with the tragedian in the parts of Iago and Othello. He had already behind him an impressive list of important roles with other major stars: Joseph Jefferson, Barry Sullivan, and Edwin Forrest. He had played Romeo to Adelaide Neilson's Juliet and Macbeth to Charlotte Cushman's Lady Macbeth. He had been leading man in John Ellsler's Cleveland stock company and achieved a similar prominence at McVicker's and Hooley's in Chicago. By the end of the seventies he had played the nation's greatest theaters in the full range of parts from Boucicault to Shakespeare.

Along the way James had hit it off with Thomas J. Quinlan of County Tipperary, who had settled in Cleveland with his wife, Bridget (Lundigan) and their two children, Mary Ellen and William. With a partner, Quinlan had built a successful business, retailing tobaccos, candies, liquors and newspapers. His store was located near Ellsler's Academy of Music, where James often performed. Before long the young actor had become a frequent guest in the Quinlan home, where he came to know the retailer's shy daughter, eleven years his junior. He probably saw her infrequently in the years she attended St. Mary's (1872–1875).

But the young lady had, withall, a certain measure of assertiveness. After completing her course at St. Mary's, Ella convinced her widowed mother to move to New York, where she became reacquainted with James O'Neill. Bridget Quinlan, who had no high opinion of actors, hoped to discourage her daughter's ardent response to the handsome actor, but to no avail. The couple were married at St. Anne's Church in Manhattan on June 14, 1877, the new Mrs. O'Neill not quite twenty years old.

The bride and groom shared a love that was anchored in their devotion to the faith of their Irish forebears, a faith that would carry them through a long life and to the consecrated ground of St. Mary's Cemetery, New London, Connecticut. In the beginning, however, the joy of this beautiful match was diminished somewhat by a paternity suit that was brought against James. The charge was made by a Miss Nettie Walsh of Cleveland, with whom the actor had lived for a brief time. The case was eventually dismissed. In the long years of their marriage, Ella had no reason to doubt James's fidelity, but the premarital insult to her sensibilities could never be entirely forgotten. At any rate, the couple soon left for San Francisco, where James had been signed on and where, on September 10, 1878, James O'Neill, Jr., was born.

Over the next decade the first scars of married life were etched into the tissues of their relationship. James drank, probably too much, even if he kept a tight rein on his habit and never missed a cue or a line. Nevertheless, his habitual post-performance unwinding had not been anticipated by the sensitive convent academy graduate. She soon came to tire of travel by trains, inelegant lodgings, and in general the men and women who made up the acting company.

In 1883 James made a decision that would bring on his greatest professional tragedy. He agreed to replace Charles Thorne, Jr., in the part of Edmond Dantes in Charles Fechter's adaptation of the Dumas romance, *The Count of Monte Cristo*. Eventually O'Neill bought the rights from John Stetson, manager of Booth's Theatre in New York. He made from it a fortune but became its slave. For a quarter century James O'Neill was chained to this lumbering vehicle that eventually carried him down a road to theatrical oblivion. He played Dantes everywhere, finally ending the fiasco in 1912, when he made a film version of it. James O'Neill had by then come to rue the day he'd ever heard of *The Count of Monte Cristo*. He knew what he had done: "I'd lost the great talent I once had through years of easy repetition," laments James Tyrone in Eugene O'Neill's family tragedy.[6] A paralyzing fear of poverty had built in him a desire for financial security, a security that he gained, but at the cost of his genuine promise as artist of the stage.

In 1885 the O'Neills lost their second son, Edmund Burke, aged two. In this case it was Ella who would forever carry the heavy burden of guilt. In order to be with James on tour, she had left the baby in the care of her mother, who was also caring for Jamie. The older brother, who had measles, had been told not to enter Edmund's room. But Jamie did, and the smaller boy died as a result of the infection he contracted. Ella always suspected her first son of deliberately infecting his brother, but she blamed herself more for neglecting her motherly responsibilities. Later that year Ella would accompany Jamie to South Bend, Indiana, where he would be left as a boarding student in the Notre Dame Minim division. There he was placed in the charge of the same Holy Cross sisters who had guided Ella at St. Mary's across the road. Two years later Bridget Lundigan Quinlan died and was buried in St. Mary's Cemetery in New London, where the O'Neills had established their summer head-quarters only a few years earlier. (James and Ella, taking the Grand Tour in Europe, were unable to be present for the funeral.) One further major event occurred in the decade of the 1880s, a moment that produced very mixed blessings indeed. Eugene Gladstone O'Neill was born on October 16, 1888.[7] Ella had hoped the baby would be a girl.

Eugene O'Neill would be endlessly reminded of his parents' high reputation as practicing Catholics. Throughout the first decade of their marriage James and Ella had reinforced one another's faith. Even in the morally shabby theater world, James had come to be known for benevolence toward his fellow actors, for an uncommon civility, and for an admirable fidelity in the practice of his faith. Brandon Tynan, his young colleague in *Joseph and His Brethren*, said of him: "I was proud to be in that show, and enjoyed getting to know 'the Governor.' We used to go to Mass together every Sunday, even on the road."[8] Among his friends James counted many priests. (He himself had once been mistaken for a priest.) His reputation as a model Catholic was well established: "James attended Mass every Sunday at St. Joseph's Church [in New London], contrary to Eugene O'Neill's description of James Tyrone, who is pictured as being negligent about his formal observance of religion. Ella's relatives, in fact, were constantly after James to bring Ella with him to church. They had long since given up on Eugene."[9] George M. Cohan later recalled that his own father and James O'Neill had been very instrumental in founding the Catholic Actors Guild.

Ellen Quinlan would always be known for her piety. She is, of course, the model for Mary Tyrone.

> The nuns praised her schoolwork and her piety. Ellen wore a large cross on a heavy gold chain around her neck, and she took a grave delight in praying in the Holy House of Loreto, a replica of the Santa Casa in Italy, exotically beautiful with its flickering candles. Sometimes she and her friend Daisy Green talked of becoming nuns like Mother Elizabeth Lilly, head of the Conservatory of Music.[10]

Years later, basking in the glow of James's fame, she would slip away from their Manhattan hotel to attend morning Mass. And, it is said, she repaired to a convent in 1914 where, nearly desperate, she conquered her morphine addiction.

Training and Education

James and Ella O'Neill had no doubt about the kind of education their sons would receive. The lads would be sent to Catholic schools: Jamie to Notre Dame (minim division), Georgetown Preparatory, and then to Fordham; Eugene to St. Aloysius, the minim at Mount St. Vincent in Riverdale (the Bronx) and later to De La Salle in Manhattan. Given James's loyalty to Ireland[11] and both parents' devotion to Catholicism, neither Jamie nor Eugene could have remained unaffected by these powerful cultural influences. The Gelbs note that Eugene read the novels of "the Irish romantic, Charles Lever, and the volumes of Irish history with which James's library was studded. . . . "[12] The playwright-to-be had been born into a milieu, a climate of opinion, a rich religious and cultural tradition that would leave lasting marks on his identity.

Like so many of his characters (Smitty in the *Glencairn* plays, Dion Anthony in *The Great God Brown,* and Edmund Tyrone), O'Neill always saw himself as something of an alien in an unfriendly zone, a "stranger." His feelings of estrangement began to develop very early, no doubt, when father and mother were touring with *Monte Cristo.* Of course, they sometimes took him along with them before he went to school and while Jamie was at Notre Dame. The earliest terror came when he was sent off to the Sisters of Charity, at age seven, to St. Aloysius (Mount St. Vincent). This was in the fall of 1895.

Because he was quiet and introspective, not many teachers and classmates suspected the intense pain Eugene felt in his "abandonment." In this early period religion, with its promised rewards for developing a pious interior life, appealed to his already contemplative nature. Religion asked and promised love. Still, he felt betrayed. Slowly he began to lose confidence in the promise: " . . . Eugene burrowed into himself. In the depths of his being, below all conscious thought and decision, he began to armor himself against love."[13] The teachings of the catechism had seemed beautiful, but hopes alone could not satisfy his need for the closeness and warmth of his beloved mother and hero brother. (Jamie had himself felt abandoned a decade earlier when his mother left him in the Indiana winter.) Years later Eugene would recall to Carlotta Monterey his terrifying memories of being abandoned.

> . . . he talked of his pain each fall, when, after a summer of secure love, the whole terrible betrayal was repeated, and again he was sent away in spite of

all the tears. Whatever he suffered from the other frustrations of childhood, this was the experience of which he always talked with the greatest bitterness—never forgetting the shock to his love for his parents and his trust in them when they banished him to school.[14]

If life for the lads at Mount St. Vincent was rather spartan, this posed no great problem for young O'Neill. He would always be able to adapt to physical hardship. Like the others, he was called upon to serve early Mass in the Chapel of the Immaculate Conception. One supposes that, in his own way, he took solace from these rigors. On her occasional visits to the school, Ella hinted that he should give some thought to a vocation as priest. Not all his classmates, however, saw O'Neill as especially pious: "He didn't seem particularly religious to me," Joseph A. McCarthy recalled. "He went to church every Sunday because we all had to go."[15] His polite manner stood as a model of decorum, even if he was looked upon as something of a loner.

In his five years at Riverdale he would encounter the typical Catholic mode of religious instruction that obtained in the United States from the years after the Civil War until the fourth or fifth decade of the twentieth century.

> Nowhere else in the world were so many Catholic children drilled in the catechism as thoroughly as in American parochial schools; nowhere did the notion of Catholicism as embodying a tidy system of rules and regulations covering practically every aspect of life gain stronger hold on the faithful. . . . But by no means was the defensive posture wholly beneficial. For example, theology was taught as a series of ineluctable syllogisms rather than a delve into mystery, and the "siege mentality" the schools inculcated was often carried over to life outside the classroom.[16]

Even so, the grown man would have recollections of spiritual joy experienced in these childhood days. First Communion day may have been the happiest.

> On May 24 [1900], Ascension Thursday, after confession, penance, and mortification to prepare himself for a state of grace, he received for the first time the sacrament of Holy Communion. It all was familiar to him through his regular attendance at Mass, his countless times as an altar boy: the Offertory preparations, the solemn Canon with the elevation of the Sacred Host and the chalice, the ringing of the bell, the "*Memento*" for the dead and "*Nobis quoque peccatoribus*" for the living, all climaxed in the Communion. But for all his familiarity with the ancient prayers and rituals, they took on a new solemnity and mystical significance this day as he first partook of the Eucharist, the sanctified bread and wine that had been transmuted into the Body and the Blood of the Redeemer. He was now one with Christ.[17]

The memory of such an experience was certain to be carried throughout the long journey. Never would the cords that tethered him to this Catholic world be entirely severed.

At Mount St. Vincent his teachers were nuns. Their punishments were something to recall in more or less good humor, as he did when he wrote to former classmate McCarthy: "Do you ever think of Sister Martha who used to knuckle us on the bean? And Sister Gonzaga? They often come back to me."[18] When he enrolled at De La Salle in the fall of 1900, however, he was introduced to the "manly" style of the Christian Brothers. This school, in the heart of Midtown on 59th near 6th Avenue, celebrated the man in motion. But the horseplay and aggressive athleticism did not appeal to Eugene. In this portrait we may be reminded of Joyce's Stephen Dedalus, who was offended and frightened by the boys' rough play at Clongowes. In his first year at De La Salle, however, O'Neill lived "at home," that is, in an apartment near Central Park. In addition, Ella herself seemed to be making an effort to spend time with him. In his second year there he was placed in the boarding department, for his mother had fallen back into the snare of her morphine addiction. Nevertheless, he did well enough on the academic side, although his record never equalled Jamie's at Notre Dame and Fordham. Nor did he make any sort of outward show, again unlike his brother, who had excelled in dramatics and elocution. Indeed Jamie was only too visible. It was in his senior year at Fordham (December 1899) that he was "asked to leave" the Rose Hill campus for "indiscretions."

Eugene's faith was diminishing; he was losing heart, although he did not know just why. It seems now that his view of life as tragic may have had its roots in his mother's sickness and consequent aloofness. Eugene could not hold her; she drifted from his grasp. Depressed and sullen, he found it harder and harder to keep faith. He asked his father to withdraw him from De La Salle. James had had enough of moving a son from one school to another, but he reluctantly granted Eugene's wish, and the boy entered Betts Academy in Stamford, Connecticut, in the fall of 1902. When, in the summer of the following year he witnessed a demonstration undeniable that his mother was "a dope fiend," the boy gave up all pretense of fidelity to religion. After learning that her addiction began as a consequence of his birth (morphine administered to ease Ella's pain), he would forever be haunted by this guilt. For the moment, however, he argued violently with his father about "practicing" his religion. The rebellion had begun. Soon he would move hellbent toward undoing himself.

Jamie's course to self-destruction was more "classic": booze, wenching, and a failure to take responsibility for his acts. Yet he seemed on the surface such a merry fellow in a sort of extended adolescence. Even when people saw the danger of his behavior, they enjoyed his company, but his life over the next two decades may be described as slow self-immolation. Eugene turned inward, a young man nearly blinded with bitter fury in his discovery of how "rotten" life was. His capacity for self-annihilation was more ominous than his older brother's, however. Indeed, in his loss of hope there is, perhaps, something of a mystery. How great is the fall of the idealist turned angry, the poet who finds himself for a season in hell! Eugene O'Neill, whose boyish vision had been edifying and beautiful, was beginning a long journey toward melancholy. In manhood, no matter how often he struggled to rekindle faith, the sparks would be each time extinguished. As one of his characters says, "Be god, there's no hope."

O'Neill became a restless spirit, an individual who is both intimidating and vulnerable. He frightens family and friends because his disaffection is not pretended. He can damn God and religion with a power unknown to those who play at alienation. In a few years O'Neill would meet a woman who was herself something of a rebel. Her name was Dorothy Day. She too stopped at the "Hell Hole," as if it were one of the stations along the *via dolorosa*. Like his, her life would be remembered more for works than days. At the moment of their meeting, however, each had come to a standstill. They would love each other in spirit and memory. As we shall see further along, she carefully recorded her anguish for his sorrow.

He never identified with the lads at Betts or the men of Princeton. Eugene took no part in team sports but liked better the solitary exercise of swimming. Some days he would swim so far out into the literal deep as to place his life in danger. He took greater and greater risks—risks with alcohol, absinthe, and "chorus girls." He flaunted mere rules. Eugene began to read the mordant poets: Dowson, Swinburne, Wilde, Rossetti, Baudelaire, and Poe ("whoremongers and degenerates," old Tyrone calls them). His heroes were the white-hot intellectuals: Ibsen, Shaw, Nietzsche, Rousseau ("atheists, fools, and madmen"). He read Emma Goldman's *Mother Earth,* while he was forging his first links to anarchism and socialism. For a time these ideas held him, but he would come to believe that no mere political or socialist scheme could undo the tragedy that life is.

> . . . any victory we *may* win is never the one we dreamed of winning. The point is that life in itself is nothing. It is the *dream* that keeps us fighting, willing—living! Achievement, in the narrow sense of possession, is a stale finale. The dreams that can be be completely realized are not worth dreaming.[19]

The year at Princeton (1906–1907) only accelerated the dizzy spiral. Embarrassed by the rah-rah pastimes of most undergraduates, Eugene glared at his "fellow" freshmen as fools hopelessly ignorant of life's dreary reality. What Louis Sheaffer said of him may remind us again of James Joyce, six years O'Neill's senior: "Eugene yearned to be part of something larger than himself;

he both felt superior to and envied those who belonged, he wanted friends and did not want them, he wanted most of all the strength to stand alone."[20] In the spring he attended classes with less and less regularity and by the end of the term he had nearly quit. Recognizing his plight, he made no objection when his name was quietly dropped from the class (of 1910) roster.

Establishing a lifetime pattern, he could not or would not fit in. Few artists have confronted with more acute insight than O'Neill the problem of "not belonging." But his alienation was not altogether personal and, therefore, was not merely self-indulgent. He came to see estrangement as the very condition of modern man. It is quite true that others had seen it before him: Baudelaire for one, T. S. Eliot for another. If the later existentialists and absurdists have promulgated a colder variety of pessimism, their basic premises seem hardly to have differed from O'Neill's.

Of course, his loner personality contributed to O'Neill's estrangement; and the situational matters of his childhood intensified his fear of being abandoned. He learned from the *Rubaiyat* that no one can rewrite what has been set down. We are forced to wonder, even so, what life might have been for both James, Jr., and Eugene O'Neill had the tragedy of their mother's morphine addiction not befallen this talented family. We speak, often without much confidence in our assumptions, of the combination of givens, accidents, and choices that make the personal equation of one's "fate." But some, like O'Neill, speak of the mystery of individual destiny. No one can know it in advance. Nor can one ever fathom it entirely, even looking back.

When he became obstreperous, morose, and opinionated, his fellow students and teachers could hardly be blamed for viewing Eugene as conceited and his behavior as outrageous. If O'Neill later came to be regarded as a genius, nothing suggests that he was looked upon as a prodigy in his school years. Although he was remembered with his "nose in a book," his teachers and fellow students did not think of him as brilliantly gifted. Later, having already been mortified by Jamie's colossal waste of talent and the scandal of his public carrying on, James and Ella had good reason to fear that Eugene might visit upon them another disappointment. To see the older brother's baleful influence on the younger no doubt frightened all those who cared for him. O'Neill knew, moreover, as anyone does who treats his own life without respect, what effect his rebellion was having on others. He knew that his parents were frozen with fear by the parallels they could see developing, his life to Jamie's. The one man, after all, was a full decade older, his talents already squandered. When he transferred these years to autobiography, the playwright took care to place the blame where it belonged.

> I'd like to see anyone influence Edmund more than he wants to be. His quietness fools people into thinking they can do what they like with him. But he's

stubborn as hell inside and what he does is what he wants to do, and to hell with anyone else! (*LDJ*, 35)

This passage established Eugene O'Neill's own part in wrecking his youth. Even in those years he understood what he was doing and the price he would surely pay.

He was heading into an extended period (1909–1912) of wandering, working, and adventuring. None of it was established on much of a plan, of course, nor could his activities be defended as constructive. If some of his experiences could be used later as material for his plays, that was his good fortune, not the dividend of prudent investment. The best that might be said about the years of adventuring was that he gained a greater love for the sea and earned a certificate as able-bodied seaman. But a great many things turned out badly. He entered into a hopelessly ill-advised marriage which produced a son, Eugene O'Neill, Jr. (He would not see the boy until the latter was twelve years old.) James managed to get his Eugene lined up with a gold-prospecting team heading for Honduras. He found there not gold but malaria. He joined his father's acting company for a short time, signed aboard a ship bound for Buenos Aires, knocked about, returned to America, was divorced from his first wife (Kathleen Jenkins O'Neill) on the grounds of his admitted adultery, and moved into a flophouse on Fulton Street. He remained there for some time in a sort of boozy fog. After another sea voyage (to England) O'Neill returned to New York and apparently hit bottom. Early in 1912 he attempted suicide by veronal, a drug easily accessible without prescription. That summer he moved in with his family and worked as a reporter for the *New London Telegraph*. The protracted period of self-destructive behavior ended at Christmas time of that year, when he was admitted into the Gaylord Farm Sanitorium in Connecticut. He would remain there until early summer of 1913, a tuberculosis patient. In the "san" he read and wrote, inspired in large part by the Irish Players of the Abbey Theatre, who had made their first American tour the previous winter.

Greenwich Village, Radicals, and the Provincetown Theatre

O'Neill's dissolute days were far from ended. By now, however, he had come to see, not just in anger but with a critical eye, the actual problems of his father's theater and to fathom somewhat the significance of the new drama. He read now with intellectual attention all the modern playwrights. Moreover, having access *carte blanche*, via James, to all the Broadway playhouses, he began to appreciate what gifted and serious writers might accomplish: Ibsen, Strindberg, Hauptmann, Wedekind, Yeats, and Synge: "It was seeing the Irish

Players . . . that gave me a glimpse of my opportunity. . . . I went to see everything they did."[21]

He had still to complete his course in the hard knocks curriculum. In Greenwich Village he formed lifetime friendships and associations—political, intellectual, and theatrical. Having determined "to be an artist or nothing," in the Village O'Neill found himself among a group of idealistic writers, actors, and political activists. Both by accident and by design, they took the lead in forming a mature American theater to keep pace with developments in the other arts, philosophy, and psychology.

The story of O'Neill's association with the Provincetown Players has been many times told.[22] The story includes the emergence of a new philosophy of American drama. George Cram ("Jig") Cook, who with Susan Glaspell was chief founder of the Provincetown Theatre, would make an act of faith in the *amateur.* He wished to provide the playwright a place to experiment and thereby to learn. Paradox was built into his ideal, however: commercial success would constitute failure. Yet even radical ideas can be as much the result of accident as they are of planning: "Quite possibly there would have been no Provincetown Players had there not been Irish Players. What he saw done for Irish life he wanted for American life—no stage conventions in the way of projecting with humility of true feeling."[23] Cook saw what O'Neill saw and was in a position to do something about it.

Nevertheless, Eugene O'Neill stands as the central figure in this story. He ran with Jig Cook's idea of a theater liberated from the shackling sentimentalism of his father's day. Yes, he needed the Provincetown but, as history shows, he became its resident genius. Glaspell said as much in describing how the first members felt when they read a play submitted by O'Neill, who was summering on Cape Cod in 1916 with his anarchist friend, Terry Carlin. "So Gene took 'Bound East for Cardiff' from his trunk and Freddie Burt read it to us. . . . Then we knew what we were for."[24] *Bound East* headed the first bill of the fall season in 1916–1917. Between 1915–1922, the seven years when Cook was in charge, the Provincetown introduced fifteen O'Neill plays.[25] His success marked a strange watershed: "The tempting offers that came on the heels of the Provincetown's success had drawn them to other theaters. O'Neill, their outstanding playwright, was also committed to uptown producers. The Provincetown had fulfilled its mission so well that he no longer needed it; his days of apprenticeship were over and his last play, *The Hairy Ape,* had swept away the final timidities of commercial managers."[26] Cook's ideal had undergone a transformation, the inevitable result of his leaguing with other idealists and revolutionaries. Of course, O'Neill's part in this history constitutes yet another form of his personal rebellion: not only against the shallow American theater of the day but, by implication, against his father. James O'Neill had supported Eugene as well as he thought he could. He paid for the publication of his son's first book of plays in 1914. He took a box with Ella for the opening of *Beyond the Horizon* at the Morosco Theatre the night of February 3, 1920. The elder O'Neill had been both defeated and redeemed by the American theater. For, irony within irony, his greatest vindication was wrought by his rebel son, who had set out to destroy his father's "hateful" theater.

We have gotten slightly ahead of the story. Eugene O'Neill's rebellion via the Provincetown had to do not only with the drama (and his father) but with an entire set of values, social and political. In these years (1916–1923) he came to know in Provincetown and Greenwich Village an assortment of radicals, bohemians, anarchists, and free-thinkers. Involved in sometimes harrowing associations, he began to sift through his values. If his lifestyle and ideological preferences seemed to express contempt for religious values, especially Catholicism, he did not truly elude religion's nets. O'Neill was haunted by the idea of God (a condition examined in both chapters three and six). The entries in his log of spiritual anguish, however, suggest that this part in the rebel's forming constituted a period of immense and painful growth and development.

In the Village gathered talented practitioners in the arts and politics. Among this group of young socialists and anarchists was a fiery immigrant named Hippolyte Havel. His native brilliance never fully realized, Havel had been fellow-traveler and lover of Emma Goldman,[27] whose *Mother Earth* magazine O'Neill had begun reading in 1906. She preached the evil of all institutional authority, especially that of religion and all agencies of capitalism. As he came upon these leftists and free thinkers, O'Neill's own beliefs were still forming. That he learned much from them hardly seems contestable.

Many of the young radicals wrote for or took part in the dramatic productions of the Provincetown Players. They performed at the Wharf Theater in Provincetown in summers and in two theaters on Macdougal Street in the Village. But, since the majority of the "players" were amateurs, most made their living in other areas, especially journalism. Many have become well known names in American intellectual history: Michael Gold, Floyd Dell, and Max Eastman of the *Masses;* John (Jack) Silas Reed and Louise Bryant. Reed, who was dazzled by the Bolshevik Revolution in 1917, traveled to Moscow to cover that explosive moment in Russian history. Out of this came his powerful account, *Ten Days that Shook the World* (1919) and Bryant's *Six Red Months in Russia* (1918).

O'Neill admired Reed's idealism and was captivated by Louise Bryant's beauty and liberated spirit. Bryant, pledged to Reed, seems to have initiated an affair with O'Neill in 1916 by suggesting that she was denied relations with Jack owing to his kidney ailment. She suggested further that Reed would not be offended by her liaison with Eugene. (O'Neill's capacity for guilt could hardly have been diminished by this betrayal of his friend.) Reed returned to Russia in 1919, followed by Louise in 1920. In August they met in Moscow, where Reed died of typhus. On October 24, 1920, his body was interred in the Kremlin wall. He is the only American ever to be so honored by the Soviet government.

The daring young women who contributed to the Provincetown project made life exciting in the Village: Edna St. Vincent Millay, Ida Rauh, Nina Moise, and others. Among them was a journalist and short story writer named Agnes Boulton.[28] Some accounts suggest that she looked like Louise Bryant. Both were beautiful. But this factor no doubt complicated her relations with O'Neill: "This resemblance had rather an obnoxious effect on me. The main thing I wanted to find out was what she looked like. Perhaps I felt it was a good thing. For if each man carries in his heart an image of the woman he can love, then at least I bore some resemblance to that woman! Actually no two women were ever more unlike than Louise Bryant and myself."[29] In the bitterly cold winter of 1917–1918, they had met in a bar called the Golden Swan, and the playwright fell in love with her almost immediately. For some years after their marriage in April of 1918, they seemed happy with one another: in Provincetown, in Greenwich Village, in Bermuda, and elsewhere. Ella and James liked Agnes and became proud grandparents of Shane Rudraighe, who was born in Provincetown in October of 1919. Eugene and Agnes had another child, Oona, who was born in Bermuda in 1925.

Many other "steadies" came into and out of the Golden Swan, or "the Hell Hole," as it was more often called. A gang of Irish toughs, the "Hudson Dusters," seemed to respect O'Neill's "values" and his introspective genius. The Golden Swan, whose memory O'Neill fused with another place like it ("Jimmy the Priest's" at 252 Fulton Street), was owned by an ex-Tammany Hall politician named Tom Wallace. The list of patrons included Jig Cook and Susan Glaspell, Dorothy Day, journalists Max Eastman and Michael Gold, and Terry Carlin—socialists all. Some of these Hell Hole "regulars" were memorialized in *The Iceman Cometh,* O'Neill referring to them in an interview as "the best friends I've ever known."[30] His memory of them was clear: "I knew 'em well. I've know 'em all for years. . . . Harry Hope, and all the others—the Anarchists and Wobblies and French Syndicalists, the broken men, the tarts, the bartenders."[31] Yet O'Neill could not maintain a white-hot zeal for causes and programs. That he was clearly sympathetic to the idealism of his friends is given some proof in the political views that surface in *The Hairy Ape, All God's Chillun Got Wings,* and *The Iceman.* But socialist activism was never O'Neill's primary theme. As early as 1922 he offered the following *apologia:* " . . . as we progress, we are always seeing further than we can reach. I suppose that is one reason why I have come to feel so indifferent toward political and social movements of all kinds. Time was when I was an active socialist, and, after that, a philosophical anarchist. But today I can't feel that anything like that really matters."[32]

Many reasons for this detachment suggest themselves. The first is that O'Neill's temperament did not allow him to function very well as part of a team in the way that Jack Reed, for example, could: that is, he found it difficult to submerge his individuality in the group identity. The closest he came to joining anything may have been the Provincetown of Cook, Glaspell, et al. His chief professional companions in the twenties were, besides George Jean Nathan, Robert Edmund Jones and Kenneth Macgowan (the latter two designer and producer respectively, his exact contemporaries, with whom he made up the well known "Triumvirate"). Over the years his closest friend was probably Saxe Commins, nephew of Emma Goldman, who became O'Neill's confidant, typist, and editor. If a trace of hauteur occasionally colored his attitude, that posture more than likely constituted a defense, just as Jamie's wit and repartee parried attempts by others to get too close to him. In each case we see a man who had been made vulnerable and who wished not to be hurt further in relationships. If he shared something of the radicals' idealism, O'Neill was in truth less enthusiastic in his estimate of human nature. Several of his characters manifest similar attitudes: Dion Anthony, Con Melody, and Larry Slade among them.

His deeper concerns hinged on questions of an existential nature: *Where is home? How does the individual fit in? How shall we meet the fundamental tragedy that life is?* His heart was not in the Movement, as philosophical anarchism was called.[33] Perhaps a useful way to approach O'Neill's complexity is to study what was perhaps the most singular relationship of his spiritual journey.

Dorothy Day

She would always march to a different drummer. It was in service to the poor and troubled that she would eventually find her vocation. In time she became a friend of living saints like Jacques Maritain, Thomas Merton, and Peter Maurin.[34] With Maurin she founded the Catholic Worker Movement in 1932 and its megaphone, *The Catholic Worker,* in 1933. Dorothy Day became something of a gadfly to the privileged, especially powerful antiliberal and voices in the Catholic Church: for example, "the radio priest," Fr. Charles Coughlin, and Francis Cardinal Spellman.[35] "Hospitality houses," which the movement established, mark a high moment in the history of American private charities. The Catholic Workers have operated these havens to shelter and feed the down-and-out (today called the homeless) in New York and other large American cities. In later years Dorothy and her volunteer colleagues joined with Martin Luther King, Cesar Chavez, and the Berrigan brothers in support of civil rights for the exploited and in protests against the Vietnam War. Dorothy remained a lifelong pacifist.

Nine years O'Neill's junior, Dorothy Day was born in Brooklyn on November 8, 1897. By the time she arrived in the Village, she had made only a modest impact as a student at the University of Illinois (1914–1916). But her socialist proclivities had been incubated there. When she moved back with her family to New York City, she went to work for Socialist and Communist journals: *The Call, The Masses,* and *The Liberator.* Dorothy was a worker: she worked for the cause and worked with fidelity. The decade 1920–1930 proved to be very difficult. For a time she had rather brutalizing relationships that included marriage and divorce. Her daugher, Tamar, was born out of wedlock. Day had the child baptized a Catholic; shortly thereafter, she herself took the formal step to conversion. For a time mother and daughter moved from place to place while Dorothy worked as journalist and as dialogue writer for the new "talkies." She also accepted commissions from *Commonweal* and *America,* Catholic journals of opinion.

There was nothing of the coquette about her. Even in her youth she was direct and unequivocal. "Dorothy was beginning to be accepted [in the Hell Hole] . . . because of her songs and her complete lack of fear about anybody or anything. It was odd, because she looked and dressed like a well-bred young college girl. But I believe it was also that she had a sort of desperate quality beneath her extremely cool manner."[36] She had established herself, of course: as a journalist and leftist, even something of a formidable drinker. At any rate, she was not cut from the common cloth. One frequent customer in the Hell Hole was Jamie O'Neill, who apparently could not figure her out: " . . . when Dorothy appeared he would gaze at her with silent, baffled curiosity."[37] She appears now to have been involved, perhaps unknown to herself at the time, in some sort of undefinable spiritual quest.

Dorothy Day's conversion to Catholicism and her life thereafter stand as one of the century's major spiritual biographies. And her establishing, with Peter Maurin, the Catholic Worker Movement, must be regarded as an important entry in American social activism. (Here was another movement O'Neill did not join.) At the same time Dorothy was moving toward Catholicism and activism in the twenties and thirties, O'Neill seemed to be running harder and harder in the opposite direction. So far as we know, he never saw her again after 1918. Her name is not mentioned in any of O'Neill's published correspondence. Therefore, our best insights into their relationship derive from what she herself has placed on the record.

If Dorothy Day has left any impression on those who knew her or who love her memory, it is that of a hard saint. She loved and served the people, yes, but she would not sentimentalize them. She did not deny that sin is the scourge of mankind in this world. What follows is an attempt to suggest that Dorothy and O'Neill gave each other something—vital, basic, and unalloyed. In her Village days she had come upon him and had sensed, in his great rebellion, a heart that pined for God. Anyone who knows her life, or his, has read of her listening transfixed to O'Neill's recitations of "The Hound of Heaven."[38]

> One evening she went with Mike Gold to the Provincetown Playhouse on MacDougal Street (*sic*), and there Gold introduced her to Eugene O'Neill. She may have fancied his glowing eyes and sunken cheeks, and perhaps thought she might replace the gall in his soul with honey. But in those night-long sessions, as she sat with him in the back room of Jimmy Wallace's "Golden Swan," he gave her something of greater substance than a trembling hand to hold or a recitation of his misspent youth. When O'Neill heard Dorothy's own story of her restlessness and of the call she sometimes felt she heard from God, *he urged her to read* St. Augustine's *Confessions*. It was here, said Father John Hugo at the Dorothy Day Memorial Mass at Marquette University on November 5, 1981, that "she heard the unforgettable words which summarize the whole burden of the saint's story: 'You have made our hearts for yourself, O God, and they will never rest until they rest in you.' "
>
> Late one night in the "hellhole," as Wallace's back room was called, O'Neill, quite drunk, recited Francis Thompson's poem "The Hound of Heaven." "Gene could recite all of it," said Dorothy, in *From Union Square to Rome*. "He used to sit there, looking dour and black, his head sunk on his chest, sighing, 'And now my heart is as a broken fount wherein tear-drippings stagnate.' " It was, she continued, "one of those poems that awaken the soul, recalls to it the fact that God is its destiny. The idea of this pursuit fascinated me, the inevitableness of it, the recurrence of it, made me feel that inevitably I would have to pause in the mad rush of living to remember my first beginning and last end." When she heard O'Neill's recitation, she said, neither O'Neill nor Mike Gold "knew . . . how profoundly moved I was. I did my best to hide it, but I was again 'tormented by God.' "[39]

O'Neill's brief period of contact with Dorothy reveals a great deal about his own search. Much of her social consciousness seems to have been formed during her days with the Village radicals, artists, and journalists. For a brief time her closest friend, with whom she spent many hours, must have been Eugene O'Neill.

> I used to sing to Eugene O'Neil [*sic*] in the Hell's Kitchen. It was a harmless son[g] and I was accused of singing lewd songs to him. It went like this:
>
> > In the heart of the city
> > where there is no pity
> > the city which has no heart.

> I would come home to my apt. and he would put his head on my shoulder.
> . . .
> [T]he same ending in several of his plays.
> [H]e looked upon me as a mother;
> [I] was companionship that he needed[.]
> [H]e must have seen something maternal in me—even though I was bu[t] 18.
>   . . . Eugene would come to the apt to keep warm. During the war[,] to conserve fuel[,] we had what they called heatless Mondays.
>   Gene and I would love to walk down West St. and then up the [E]ast Side. We would stop in saloons to keep warm. . . . The saloons would close at one o'clock and Gene and I would wa[l]k the waterfront and then on to Romany Marie's [a small restaurant on Washington Place]. . . . Gene was terribly influenced by Strinberg [*sic*]. He used to talk a lot about him to me.[40]

> What I got personally from Eugene O'Neill was an intensification of the religious sense that was in me. I had never heard The Hound of Heaven before [*sic*], and Gene knew it by heart and could recite it in his grating, monotonous voice, his mouth grim, his eyes sad.[41]

Dorothy Day's reminiscences about O'Neill's spiritual sensibilities carry considerable authority, she having been virtually beatified since her death in 1980. His love for Thompson's profoundly Catholic poem suggests much about his sensibility. Dorothy saw this. She saw that his personality in effect precluded his engagement with "the people." If his manner had been arrogant, she would have found it contemptible. But Dorothy had known O'Neill in those brutally cold months of 1917-1918, when both were wrestling with their own idealism and vulnerability. She probably learned from him that he had discovered Thompson's poem in his period of recovery from tuberculosis. Doris Alexander provides an interesting interpretation of what "The Hound of Heaven" meant to him.

> In Thompson's flight from love and God, in his search for meaning, in his urgent images of running and hiding, always pursued by what he fled until he came full circle back to faith, O'Neill saw his own flight from his parents' love and from his boyhood religious faith, saw all his years of wandering and intellectual searching, his despair in a hall bedroom of Jimmy the Priest's rooming house after his witnessed bedding with a prostitute for his divorce, his suicide attempt, and his return to his family just before the tuberculosis got him.[42]

More and more often that winter Dorothy Day found herself dropping into St. Joseph's Church on Sixth Avenue. Her intention was to get warm and to do . . . *she knew not what*. In looking at pictures of Dorothy Day in her later life, one gets the impression that she was no longer vulnerable, at least not as she had been in her youth. We learn something by comparing them with earlier portraits. "Her wandering gaze was caught in an early picture by John Stier, which more than any other image suggests the continuity between her early radicalism and her later dedication."[43] She remembered O'Neill as a man who carried the terrible cross of loneliness, a cross she too had borne. Without condescension or presumption, she could speak about his spirituality as most biographers cannot. In her austere and noble charity, Dorothy remembered O'Neill as a difficult young intellectual. He had created a mask to conceal his mysterious vulnerability. Only when "liberated" from his nearly paralyzing inhibitions could he carry off the "performance." He did this in his recitations of "The Hound of Heaven." It was a performance such as his father could not have given, one that riveted the hangers-on and the house cynics in the Hell Hole, the Hudson Dusters, and Dorothy Day.

Both Dorothy and Eugene loved the poor, albeit they showed this in different ways. And both hated the vulgarity of commercialism that sweeps the soul into oblivion. She was truly a prophet, one who calls down a judgment on the times.[44] Whether they ever spoke to each other about it, Dorothy Day and O'Neill had in common a belief in the reality of sin. Her response to his recitations of "The Hound of Heaven" offers only part of the proof. Everything says that they were kindred spirits, but persons who could never have given themselves unconditionally to one another: "Eugene couldn't make up his mind who to marry. I was too independent—not the type of woman that would have waited on a man."[45]

In "Told in Context" (1958) Dorothy recalled the man she had known forty years earlier.

> If ever a man had the tragic sense of life it was Eugene O'Neill. If ever a man was haunted by death it was Gene. . . . But he never would have taken his life because he felt too keenly his own genius, his own vocation, his capacities as writer to explore and bring to light those tragic deeps of life, the terror of man's fate.
>
> To me, he portrayed more than any other, what life without God is like. "Without the redemption, how great a tragedy ever to be born," Newman wrote.
>
> But did he admit to believing in the redemption. Like Ivan [Karamazov] he wanted to reject, he wanted to turn back to God his ticket. His whole life seemed to be like that terrible dialogue of Ivan with Alyosha, about the problem of evil, and God's permissive will.
>
> Gene seemed always to be setting his will against God.
>
> Since he brought to me such a consciousness of God,—since he recited to me "The Hound of Heaven," I owe him my prayers. There is no time with God and I would be sinning against hope, faith and charity if I did not believe that my prayers, and whoever else is praying for the soul of Gene, are not heard.[46]

For the brief time they were in contact, it was the other's company each wanted. Speculation about sexual communion seems futile, is worthless, unless it can be proved. And what then? Companionship is what each treasured in the other. "She was one of the rare people who could pull O'Neill out of his night-long bouts of despondency, and the two saw a good deal of one another in the winter of 1917–1918. Nothing came of the relationship, but O'Neill, like others, recognized Day as a strong and attractive character."[47] Could there be anything to challenge in this splendid observation? Just this: In truth, much came of the relationship.

*   *   *

After his early triumphs with the Provincetown and on Broadway (*The Emperor Jones, Beyond the Horizon, The Hairy Ape*), O'Neill's star was in ascendancy for the remainder of the twenties. He suffered defeats, to be sure, both personal and professional: among them, the deaths of his parents and brother in less than three years, the breakup of his marriage to Agnes Boulton, the colossal failures of *The First Man* and *Welded*. But the awards and successes at home and abroad were also stunning: *Desire Under the Elms, The Great God Brown, Lazarus Laughed, Strange Interlude,* and *Mourning Becomes Electra*. Such an ambitious agenda filled many canvasses and made O'Neill an international celebrity. All of this seemed somehow to match the hum and dizziness of the American decade: Henry Ford's assembly line; Prohibition, speak-easies, and the establishment of the Federal Bureau of Investigation; the rise of professional and intercollegiate athletics; and the flowering of great novelists and poets. But, as the nation headed into depression at decade's close, O'Neill's own vision was turning more and more inward, his plays less disguised in their autobiographical inventory. Moreover, although he would be honored by the Nobel Prize in 1936, at home he was becoming a forgotten force. As Travis Bogard puts it, "He passed into that degrading limbo of lost dramatists: the academic reading list."[48]

In certain ways O'Neill seemed to will his own eclipse, so brilliantly had his star burned in the 1920s. After the failure of *Days Without End* in 1934, O'Neill offered nothing again until World War II had been ended for more than a year. If he had pulled back from the bright lights of Broadway, however, O'Neill had been steadily working against the ever-growing shadows of his own depression. Having achieved fame, he sought to avoid the tensions and intrusions that attend it; indeed, he preferred to live as a near hermit in his California sanctuary, Tao House, with his third wife, Carlotta Monterey. She was his staunch ally in this. From the late 1930s until 1944 she defended his privacy with such fierce loyalty that both his children and his friends were often hurt and angered.

Thus began and ended one of the most remarkable reclusions in the history of American art. In California O'Neill would relive his life in memory. He would suffer intense psychological loneliness. In that period he conceived but lacked the energy to complete a cycle of plays intended to cover the whole of American history. Its individual parts would be connected not only by the logic of chronology but by visionary scope: *A Tale of Possessors, Self-Dispossessed.* Its theme was to be the effects of unbridled materialism and the denaturing of the American soul. Only two of the projected units were ever produced, *A Touch of the Poet* and *More Stately Mansions.*[49] His health failing, O'Neill ended his thirty years of writing in 1943. In the decade that remained to him, he suffered all the infirmities and insults of premature aging. His longevity would fail to match that of his father, who died at age seventy-four.

But 1939–1941 were also his *anni mirabiles.* In his removal from the world's traffic, O'Neill wrote the masterpieces *Long Day's Journey into Night* and *The Iceman Cometh* and the one-act gem called *Hughie.* In these works he distilled the story of the Tyrone family; called onto the stage, under the veil of fiction, the community of "Brothers and Sisters" in the Village; and probed the dynamics of simple relationship established between two strangers in the course of one hour. Into these works O'Neill poured the full measure of his insight and the knowledge gained in harrowing experiences of an earlier day. In them he represented with a fidelity to truth that shrinks before nothing human, the awful comedy and tragedy that life is. His understanding of sin, guilt, and redemption is revealed with such power that we cannot deny the authority of his moral vision. Of course, he had long since left the Catholic Church. He was not a believer. Yet O'Neill had internalized the catechism of sin-guilt-redemption so completely that he could see the dimensions of reality only through a lens ground in the laboratories of youth and rebellion. The vision rendered is frighteningly clear. Caligula cries out in despair at the end of *Lazarus Laughed,* "Men forget." O'Neill did all that he could to keep men from forgetting. He forgot nothing, and from his plays he omitted nothing that counts.

2 | Catholic Memory, Classic Forms

Catholic Sensibility: A Brief Definition

ON THE QUESTION of how we employ certain literary terms, Edwin H. Cady has made an important contribution. As he sought to understand *romanticism, realism,* and *naturalism,* Cady concluded that, in the end, the terms defy precise definition. Thus, " . . . it is probably true that there are not finally any naturalists. I am not aware of a work of fiction which will stand adequately and consistently for the naturalistic sensibility. There was only a *sensibility* to be fragmentarily, inconsistently, or occasionally expressed."[1] If we accept Professor Cady's conclusion, we shall not be forced into that familiar cul-de-sac: the choice between the absolutes of free will and determinism. In fiction, for example, if a character's life patterns are beyond her capacity to shape, then she is denied significant freedom to choose her own course. Such givens would always limit the artist in creating characters. He could, strictly speaking, produce only literary robots. O'Neill himself once expressed frustration in the difficulty of making useful distinctions between realism and naturalism.[2] What he may have wanted was the concept Cady had fashioned.

> Deeper in the psyche than ideas, perhaps a source for them, certainly a major determinant of our choice of one possible idea in favor of another, sensibility is more than "feelings," emotion. It connotes tact, a feeling for life, a way of taking events and making experience, a ground for life-style and at last for morality.[3]

A Catholic *sensibility,* I suggested in chapter one, grows out of an *ethos* (the former term being somewhat harder to define than the latter). *Ethos* calls to mind something more generalized, a pervasive condition that characterizes the spirit of an entire community. *Sensibility* suggests a personal response, an individual's own psychological experience in receiving the worldview and the established values of the group. If these descriptions be accepted, then we will probably agree that the experience of Eugene O'Neill stands as something irregular yet quite plausible. On the one hand, he said that *The Iceman Cometh* denied "any other experience of faith in my plays"; on the other hand, he claimed that in his work sin is punished and redemption occurs. But does this surface contradiction, necessarily, undermine the truth?

In what may appear at first a gratuitous strategy, I should like to bring another figure briefly into the discussion. For in his experience certain parallels to Eugene O'Neill's can be discovered. This second figure is the philosopher-poet, George Santayana, who also cast off his allegiance to Roman Catholicism as a young man but who retained a lifelong sympathy for that religion. A comparison of their experiences can prove instructive. Their personalities and life situations were immensely different, of course. Furthermore, Santayana was more ironical but also less anxious than O'Neill about his "Catholicism."

> Like my parents, I have always set myself down officially as a Catholic: but this is a matter of sympathy and traditional allegiance, not of philosophy. In my adolescence, religion on its doctrinal and emotional side occupied me much more than it does now [at age sixty-seven]. I was more unhappy and unsettled; but I have never had any unquestioning faith in any dogma, and have never been what is called a practising Catholic. . . . [Even so] my sympathies were entirely with those other members of my family who were devout believers. I loved the Christian epic. . . . [4]

The "Christian epic" was his *afición*. Late in life Santayana could devote an entire volume to *The Idea of Christ in the Gospels*. He took up residence in Rome, where pagan and Christian traditions fuse. He elected to live out the last decades of his life in a convent, and he insisted on burial in a Catholic cemetery. Yet this charming eccentric wished to be understood: He did not believe that Catholicism held any truth on her doctrinal side. He loved the church, he said, because it shared in a tradition of spiritual freedom: "The incidental esoteric discipline, which is all that I respect in Catholicism, terminates in the same inward liberation and peace that ancient sages attained under all religions or under none."[5] In retaining this connection, he was retaining his identity, I should say.

In ethnicity and proclivities they had little in common. Santayana (1863–1952), who suffered a kind of spiritual deracination, had been brought from Avila to America as a child of eight. Educated at Boston Latin School and Harvard, he chafed under Brahmin disdain for his "exotic" difference. Thus he made thirty-eight "fussy [Atlantic] crossings" in annual retreats to his beloved Spain and stations on the continent. Until he could support himself by other means, Santayana took his place, reluctantly, in the professoriate. Patrician and somewhat aloof, he cultivated few intimate relationships. O'Neill, an American-Irishman, was the son of an immensely popular and gregarious actor. And, although he too grew up in New England, he had been firmly planted in Catholic soil. Indeed, his mother urged him to consider a priestly vocation. His brother had lived and studied at Notre Dame, Georgetown, and Fordham.

O'Neill himself was educated, until age thirteen, by the Sisters of Charity and the Christian Brothers.

How different he was, in his late adolescence and young manhood, from the fastidious and urbane Santayana. Embittered by God's "failure" to rescue his beloved mother from her tragic morphine addiction, Eugene responded with chilling eagerness to brother Jamie's corrosive influence. He soon became the kind of man who is more dangerous to himself than to others. Dorothy Day saw him as a tragic loner and compared him to Dostoevski's Ivan Karamazov, who "wanted to turn back to God his ticket."[6] Yet, in their love of "essences," both O'Neill and Santayana described their similar plights: " . . . I will always be a stranger who never feels at home . . . ," says Edmund Tyrone (*LDJ*, 153). And the philosopher in "Cape Cod":

> O, I am far from home!
>
> And among the dark pines, and along the flat shore,
> O the wind, and the wind, for evermore!
> What will become of man?[7]

Differences in temperament and experience notwithstanding, both men retained a religious ideal.

We can see in their lives sensibilities and responses to religion formed by a Catholic background. Santayana late in life recalled his boyhood dreams, but dreams chastened by skepticism.

> I thought how glorious it would have been to be a Dominican friar, preaching that epic eloquently, and solving afresh all the knottiest and sublimest mysteries of theology. . . . For my own part I was quite sure that life was not worth living; for if religion was false everything was worthless, and almost everything, if religion was true. . . . I saw the same alternative between Catholicism and complete disillusion: but I was never afraid of disillusion, and I have chosen it.[8]

Writing at age forty to his friend, Sr. Mary Leo Tierney, O.P., Eugene O'Neill stabs the heart with his combined idealism and despair.

> There is nothing I would not give to have your faith—the faith in which I was born and brought up (as a good O'Neill should be)—but since I may not know it, since belief is denied to me in spite of the fact that my whole adult spiritual life is that search for a faith which my work expresses in symbols, why then my thwarted search must have its meaning and use, don't you think, for whatever God may be? Perhaps they also serve who only search in vain! That they search—and not without knowing at times a black despair that believers never know—that is their justification and pride as they stare blindly at the blind sky! The Jesus who said, "Why hast Thou forsaken me?" must surely understand them—and love them a little, I think, and forgive

them if no Savior comes today to make these blind to see who may not cure themselves.[9]

Could Santayana find truth in Catholicism? Never, after adolescence. Did O'Neill return to the church? "Unfortunately, no."

Nevertheless, Eugene O'Neill accepted *sin* and *redemption* as realities. For him such language was neither figurative, nor, strictly speaking, theological. With the reader's permission, let us recall Croswell Bowen's memory of O'Neill's searing words: "In all my plays sin is punished and redemption takes place." Some scholars have questioned Bowen's reliability as a careful worker,[10] but it seems unlikely that a remark such as this could have been improvised; it carries a too authentic ring. Of course, as Raleigh has observed, the three major biographies before Louis Sheaffer's (including Bowen's) are undocumented accounts, often based on "interviews with people who knew O'Neill, and were thus depending on memory, a notoriously unreliable repository for facts. . . . "[11] Even without Bowen's record, however, O'Neill's sin-and-redemption views could in any case be inferred. Nothing in his life and works, of course, suggests sympathy for a religious fundamentalism that such words might call to mind ("the sawdust trail to salvation," as Larry Slade calls it in *The Iceman Cometh*). The first priority, then, is to blow away every whiff of smoking brimstone. O'Neill was a modern sophisticate, the type least likely to traffic in anti-intellectualism (religious, political, or other). He was Mencken's hero, not one of the boob.oisie. Moreover, O'Neill was neither philosopher nor theologian. Thus, to give his words their fair weight will prove difficult for two reasons.

In the first place, O'Neill can in no sense be seen in the role of preacher. Indeed, the very suggestion would have made him and his older brother fall into paroxysms of laughter. Furthermore, because he loathed whatever posed as pedigreed, he enjoyed puncturing balloons of pious hot air. His very lifestyle from ages fifteen to thirty-five constituted a standing offense against accepted behavior. He could hardly have been taken as an apologist for "clean living." In company with the waggish Jamie, he committed every possible prank to embarrass their father's sense of decorum. He incurred the lethal risks of alcoholism and debauchery that ended in suicidal depression. Cynical, angry, and blasphemous, Eugene sought out the companionship of the world's drop-outs: drifters, losers, whores, and hoodlums. Still, he never lost his affection for his friends, nor would he have given up the memory of his days with them. We shall want to come back to these relationships, for they have to do with his concept of the dignity of the person (of the sinner, if you will). When he graced their company with poems he had learned by heart, he recalled a Lover from Whom he had sought to escape: "I fled Him, down the nights and down the days; / I fled Him, down the arches of the years."[12] The poem's speaker, even as he seeks to hide his lusts, is transfixed by his stalker. The mystery of this lyric forever haunted O'Neill.

> Agnes Boulton says that Dorothy [Day] listened "in a sort of trance" when O'Neill would recite ["The Hound of Heaven"]. She even managed to get him to recite . . . [it] one night from beginning to end . . . while the Hudson Dusters listened admiringly.[13]

Here was no Elmer Gantry or circuit-riding con man who traded on other people's vulgar fantasies, a mere entertainer who can put on a tent-and-Bible show as splashy as that given by any other carnival barker. O'Neill seems to have been accepted because he did not ask to be accepted. As he has been sketched by Agnes Boulton, Dorothy Day, and others who knew him before he had achieved fame, his melancholy was self-evident. (George Jean Nathan could hardly recall O'Neill's laughing.) He knew the loneliness that anyone feels who has lost his way home. Sin is separation.

To a Catholic sensibility, the idea of sin was plausible. To one for whom mystical experience was real, the metaphor of the Hound does not seem improbable. In his catechism of values are etched one's earliest moral paradigms. This does not mean that his beliefs cannot be "corrected" by intellectual processes. They can be. Yet their influence will never be entirely erased. For life's tragic plunge had become, to persons like O'Neill, part of the nature of things. Men and women who may have no other dignity could, in this view, be seen to participate in their own fate. The idea of sin was not only plausible, but necessary. As men wounded themselves and one another, they might hope, however feebly and ineffectually, to rescue one another. That was *redemption* (also plausible, and necessary). As Agnes Boulton recalled, O'Neill was by inclination prepared to discover some invisible force that would complement his nature: "I think . . . he was striving for some perfection in his own life; some dream or hope of a relationship with 'one other'—that *other* of whom he had spoken to me one day in the back room of the Hell Hole. . . . There was that in him which desired this—and that in him which denied it. I suppose he was haunted by the God whom he had discarded."[14] Because O'Neill knew what sin was, he would not undervalue it or call it by lesser names.

If many today do call sin by lesser names and find it impossible to register personal culpability, others complain of a general permissiveness that dilutes the sense of mystery that religion fosters. At any rate, the modern rejection of the idea of sin constitutes, to traditionalists, a rejection of the darker side of mystery.

> The Superego has been banished; the ego trip has supplanted the guilt trip; the pursuit of happiness has devolved into the pursuit of pleasure. The Greeks believed the goal of human life was *eudaimonia,* "being good." In our day, human fulfillment has been quicksanded into 'feelin' groovy."

When "anything goes," there's nothing to rebel against. As Christopher Lasch says so well, we've exchanged guilt for formless anxieties, and the therapeutic voyage to the interior "discloses nothing but a blank."[15]

To a Catholic sensibility, the idea of sin was plausible. This is but another way of saying that mystery is plausible.

O'Neill the Traditionalist

No matter how much the loner he was by preference, O'Neill recognized the claims of the community. It is this recognition, in the end, that explains his attention to classic themes. We sometimes call them universals, questions that seem to defy resolution. We should not be surprised, then, if his typical narratives have to do with those personal and familial struggles that have preoccupied women and men throughout the ages. These themes inevitably involve such fundamental problems as self-knowledge and identity, loyalty and rebellion. They are dramatized in certain perennial antagonisms: the *polis* and the person, love of other and love of self, Oedipal and Electra complexes. Since such issues have obsessed all tragic playwrights, the motives that drive their characters are as old as storytelling: lust, greed, ambition, jealousy, pride, anger: the "deadly sins." If they are exploited in contemporary soap opera, the same subjects are found in biblical, Greek, and Elizabethan tragedy. It is the manner of their treatment that distinguishes the classic from the vulgar. High drama differs from the tabloids not so much in the deeds it names as in its tone, emphases, honesty, and tragic intention. The one medium seeks to provide insight, the other to manipulate our emotions. O'Neill's interest "in the relation between man and God" tells us something of his high intention. He did not squander his powers on ephemera. His approach was traditional.

How strange it sounds: O'Neill the traditionalist. Everything in his personal life history seems to argue against such an idea: everything but the O'Neill canon. A tragic writer is, by heart's inclination and in relation to the aim of his work, a *conservative:* Such a term is difficult to separate from narrowly political connotations, however. Let us be very clear about what I mean here.

O'Neill was not in sympathy with political or social attitudes that are sometimes associated with such writers as Eliot, Yeats, Evelyn Waugh, even Robinson Jeffers, whose philosophical and political points of view tended toward the right and whose social preferences might be called antipopulist. His social and political views were certainly not those of Ezra Pound, whose anti-Semitism and fascist sympathies fairly called the poet's honor into question. Of course, O'Neill's admiration for Nietzsche should not prompt comparison to the ruggedly individualistic philosophy of, say, Ayn Rand. Let us recall that as late as 1946 the playwright still confessed himself a philosophical anarchist. His roster of friendships and intellectual associations had always been "left of center": Terry Carlin, Jack Reed and Louise Bryant, Hippolyte Havel, Dorothy Day, Michael Gold, Emma Goldman, Paul Robeson, and Saxe Commins.

It is true that his relationship with Carlotta Monterey strikes a discordant note in this connection. We must suppose that his love for her, while deep and lasting, evolved not for reasons of ideological compatibility. The third Mrs. O'Neill was often ungenerous, both in spirit and deed, to his friendships and political beliefs. And the tensions caused by their differences on these and other issues sometimes brought to O'Neill acute pain and embarrassment. Little of this, however, was related to his philosophy of art.

His traditionalism as artist is demonstrated in his nearly obsessive mission to find a replacement for "the old God," as he put it and his devotion to the tragic ideal and classic themes. O'Neill's plays are not fundamentally topical. Lionel Trilling, never his most enthusiastic reader, spoke of his plays in the same breath with *Lear* and *Faust*. In noting O'Neill's "tragic sense," he could hardly have described a more thoroughgoing traditionalist.

> Eugene O'Neill, if only by reminding us of death and the not wholly rational nature of man, has rendered a service to the very positivistic philosophies which he rejects. For positivism is always in danger of falsifying and vulgarizing its own best ideals. . . . the tragic sense of life, springing from the remembrance of death, is an invaluable safeguard. And nowadays, when our philosophies do not remind us of death and when religion does not feel strong enough to consider what was once a favorite subject, it is a scientist, Freud, and some few artists like O'Neill who speak of it. Death is connected with all that is irrational in life. . . . Tragedy is the recognition of the irrational nature of things which puts so large a discrepancy between man's desire and his accomplishment. The knowledge of the tragic basis of life makes us more nearly complete men; in our time there are few who stand with O'Neill as propagandists of that knowledge.[16]

Egil Tornqvist claims that "O'Neill . . . thought of himself as primarily a religious playwright."[17] Even with his qualification ["not, of course, in the strict sense with which such a designation can be bestowed on Eliot or Claudel"], Tornqvist has made an astute observation and a daring assumption.

Once he cut formal ties with religion, around 1903, Eugene O'Neill never again practiced the faith of his youth. It is far from the aim of this study to deny that fact. Such a denial would serve truth no more than James Tyrone's ludicrous insistence that Shakespeare was an Irish Catholic. However, that Eugene suffered a lifetime of guilt and anxiety after severing the links to Catholicism seems a truth beyond contention. His spiritual crisis was surely intense, but it was also something quite familiar in the experience of modern intellectuals.

The term "modern" is used here as it was employed by Joseph Wood Krutch in *The Modern Temper* (1929) and *"Modernism" in Modern Drama* (1953). The intellectual community had pretty much given over the "faith of [its] fathers" by the end of the nineteenth century. E. A. Robinson's "two fond old Enormities" [heaven and hell] no longer registered as plausible. Like many of his contemporaries, O'Neill saw that the old gods had fallen and that pining for their return was futile. One had to conclude that God was dead. What else can be inferred from reading *The Great God Brown, Lazarus Laughed, Strange Interlude, Dynamo,* and *The Iceman Cometh?*

Thus, O'Neill's loss of faith resulted in the same sort of spiritual deracination as that experienced by many of his immediate forerunners and fellows. But, if their dilemma was philosophical, the devastation was psychological: one's very identity was at stake. Yet he seems to have met the crisis differently in one crucial respect. Eliot's poet-intellectuals (e.g., Prufrock and Gerontion) become spiritually timid and ineffectual. O'Neill, on the other hand, faced the terror with the bit in his teeth: "Life's a tragedy. Hurrah!" Perhaps his meeting this spiritual dilemma head-on derives from his having had a clearer sense of what he came from. He placed great importance, for example, in the fact that he had been formed in the mold of Irish Catholicism. Indeed, he saw this background as the very foundation upon which his identity had been erected.

The agony of deracination was only compounded for the modern poet-mystic (who is different from the poet-intellectual). This woman or man, born of a believing tradition but everywhere encountering modernist skepticism, finds no deliverance from sorrow. One was born with the sensors of the poet-ascetic yet could find nothing worthy of his allegiance. Thus does Edmund Tyrone speak for the poet, Catholic and other, who feels himself a stranger in time but who cannot locate the source of his alienation: "It was a great mistake, my being born a man. I would have been much more successful as a sea gull or a fish" (*LDJ*, 153).

O'Neill was an ambivalent modernist, a man who could not come to terms with the death of God. He had always been inclined to mysticism but in a way that juxtaposed oddly with his philosophy. For, while he felt the urge to unite with the sublime, he questioned whether there was in truth anything beyond the horizon, anything to unite with. Yet he was also convinced that to believe we belong is our necessary pipe dream, a supportive illusion without which we cannot live. Man's modern tragedy, then, is to seek a higher life but to know that it cannot be attained. Still, this impossible condition, the playwright held, gives modern drama its stature. It represents the closest imitation of the Greeks he could conceive.

His themes never really changed. Announced as early as 1922 in *The Hairy Ape,* they would be rendered frequently over the next two decades. One can state the core theme very simply: Modern man can no longer integrate with his universe. He has lost his old harmony with nature and can find no viable substitute for his lost faith. The individual seeks to know, "Where do I fit in?" As he becomes more articulate (e.g., Larry Slade), this modernist now knows that he does not fit in. Thus defeated by his "fate," he creates a life lie, the dream that he counts on and upon which he builds the shaky structure of his existence. Is it heroism or madness? In the end we are defeated by the impossibility of knowing the answer (*madness*). But one must also accept the need to act, even to act irrationally, if he chooses to go on (*heroism*).

Despair and exaltation, have they not always fused paradoxically in tragedy? In this later period, however, O'Neill stands as an anomaly: the classicist who said he accepted the melancholy assumptions of modern philosophy. Again and again we find his characters sick and poorly integrated with their time and world. Defeated and dodging self-knowledge, they seek escape in pipe dreams. Yet they experience guilt caused by having embraced the illusions in the first place. Such self-deception requires deft rationalization, precisely Larry Slade's point when he says that chasing happiness is a great game. Turning a deaf ear to the ancient maxim, "Know thyself," each feels humiliated in his weakness and becomes, like Edmund, "a little in love with death."

If some today see guilt as an unhealthy vestige of superstition, O'Neill could not so easily dismiss it. In his world guilt compels the individual to seek dignity in spite of a sense of his own insignificance. Psychologically his characters cannot accept that insignificance, even if they claim to accept it "rationally." This is a matter of the highest importance because, stripped of his sense of worth, the person becomes merely pathetic. Thus, in the end, his guilt contributes to his tragic humanity. (There is nothing new in this idea; it had always been that of the tragedian.) Moreover, a sense of guilt, as judged in the Christian view, permits the individual to long for redemption. O'Neill's lack of faith in the doctrine would not necessarily preclude his recognizing the human capacity for guilt.

O'Neill knew that even Greek drama fostered illusion, yet he functioned as dramatist in the western intellectual and philosophical traditions. Thus, he embraced the Greek idea, conceding that it was "very much of a dream, but where the theatre is concerned, one must have a dream, and the Greek dream in tragedy is the noblest ever."[18] In this view he is claiming that the tragedian is by definition a visionary. (O'Neill probably heard about an Irish production of *The Emperor Jones* given at the *Taibhdhearc Na Gaillimhe* [Galway] in 1941. If so, he might have been pleased to know that *taibhdhearc* means "the place for seeing visions.") He had inherited in full measure the sensibilities of the Hellenic-Hebraic-Christian tradition. It is especially important here to stress *sensibilities* over beliefs. For in his professional mode, O'Neill was an artist, not a philosopher or theologian.

As an innovator, he was daring. However, even the genius owes something to the past, to tradition. And he was, in heart and bone, a man of the theater. If he rejected such absurdities as those practiced in his father's workshop, O'Neill set about to rescue, not destroy, the institution, and to reform what had been debased as it had been passed down to him. He needed the religious and theatrical inheritance conferred by his parents, with its full share of western content. He built on the past. In this sense he was a traditionalist of the theater. This identification gave him a wider potential appeal than, say, that of the undeviating Marxist or an absurdist playwright. His more universalist vision makes him plausible simultaneously to both an urbane and a provincial world. Vincent Dowling has reflected on O'Neill's appeal to the rural Irish of *Long Day's Journey into Night.* Consider Dowling's remarks on a celebrated Abbey production of 1967 that toured the provinces. "Strong Connemara men, Gaelic speaking, whose families knew America better than they knew Dublin, not only wept at the play, many of them would weep years after to think of it and talk of it, with us, again. Oddly enough, *Ah, Wilderness!* in which I was lucky enough to play Richard . . . seemed to touch the same chords in artists and audience in Dublin and Belfast, even though the tune was, apparently, more mellow."[19] This capacity to connect widely makes O'Neill relevant to a far vaster world than provincial and urban Ireland alone. Something important is involved here. In their perennial appeal these works remind us that O'Neill was a traditional Irish wordsmith, the *shanachie:* the storyteller.

O'Neill and the Timeless Issues of Sin and Guilt

Here O'Neill came up against the problem that eventually stalks any modern dramatist who posits an idea of tragedy. If one takes as given "the death of the old God" or that "we are here as on a darkling plain," what reason would he have to speak of *sin?* The very notion would constitute an absurdity. To call life tragic would be to indulge a sense of the "injustice" of our situation. Moreover, simply saying that this is tragic or that unjust does not make them so. *Tragedy* and *injustice* are merely terms that men and women take comfort in, for they assign value to human existence. Of course, if the very grounding of existence is meaningless, if one's intentions can change nothing, then one need not be burdened by a sense of responsibility. This given, of course, one's life is robbed of tragic significance. What then is sin but a word, an affective encumbrance, archaic and useless? The idea of sin is merely a burden. How did the self-proclaimed unbeliever-yet-tragedian (O'Neill) meet such a dilemma?

Sin presupposes some moral presence in the universe, something outside men and women that they can please or offend. If God has "died," that presence seems to be negated. One need not be trained in philosophy to understand Nietzsche's meaning. Indeed, without a philosopher's credentials, one might venture a limited observation: To say that "God is dead" is a thing very different from saying that "God never was." Perhaps what the great German meant was that *faith is dead,* or dying. Given the erosion of traditional certainty in modern times, given the ascendancy of rationalism and the duty to doubt, it has become ever more difficult to believe in the "old God." (This seems to be O'Neill's point.) The baggage ought to be overthrown, says the absurdist. But what is to be the plight of the thinker who accepts certain premises of literary modernism yet rejects its conclusion that tragedy is no longer possible? What shall we make of this same person who says that the theme of sin, punishment, and redemption enters all his plays? His dilemma is unlike that of the absurdist.

The old theological explanations (e.g., Catholic teachings on sin) just didn't work anymore for O'Neill. To accept church doctrine would be to confess faith in the sacramental system, what he said was not possible for him after adolescence. Even so, the lessons from childhood haunted his Catholic memory. The very terms *sin* and *redemption* evoke doctrinal echoes. So powerful were these presences, it seems, that they influenced O'Neill's interpretation of human motivation: his psychology. In other words, the catechetical model provided his first and, perhaps, deepest understanding of the dynamics of guilt. Thus, his reading of the human heart continued to suggest a Christian sensibility (but not an acceptance of Catholic doctrine). G. K. Chesterton made an observation that may be helpful in this context: "We are psychological Christians even when we are not theological ones."[20] Because O'Neill understood the efficacy of forgiveness, the propriety of absolution remained vital in his creative imagination.

This takes us back to O'Neill's concern about relationship: "Most modern plays are concerned with the relation between man and man, but that does not interest me at all. I am interested only in the relation between man and God." This attitude may seem to exclude the cosmic significance of mere human associations. But it doesn't. It can't. Let us try, without becoming enmeshed in nets of theological disquisition, to sketch a possible logic in O'Neill's statement about sin and punishment.

We are dealing with an idea of human relationships, an idea that on one level is not difficult to understand, even if the quotidian experience is. It has to do with the manner in which men and women treat each other and the principles that motivate their deeds and intentions: unkindness, hatred, ruthlessness, niggardliness, on the one hand; grace, love, pity, generosity, on the other. We violate one another, or we treat each other with virtue. If the effects of violation are sin, then guilt may be a symptom. Perhaps we can say that guilt is itself the punishment. Redemption is brought about by those deeds and sentiments whose motivating principle is the intention to "save" each other. We could not conceive the concepts of sin, guilt, and redemption except in terms of relationship. Nowhere are these connections more basic (and vulnerable) than in the individual's first crucible, the family. Jacques Maritain has provided a splendid insight into this state of things.

> . . . from the very start, I say from childhood on, man's condition is to suffer from and defend himself against the most worthy and indispensable support-ers whom maternal nature has provided for his life, and thus to grow amidst and through conflict, if only energy, love, and good will quicken his heart.[21]

Because relationships are *dynamic and not static,* they become in turn en-nobled and befouled. In O'Neill they may be (and often are) characterized by ambivalence, he knowing that love is experienced first and last in the family. Like Maritain, he might have seen in this most elemental human form the in-dividual's greatest tormentor and most perfect redeemer. "A tragic writer," Krutch said, "does not have to believe in God, but he must believe in man."[22]

The artist wishes to give his work the highest possible significance, an ob-jective all applaud. But, in the absence of God, if it is argued that he is dead, one can dramatize human fate *only* in terms of human interactions. Even if he suggests, as O'Neill did, that visionary experience alone is worth recording, one wishes to communicate that experience to another human mind. From his earliest through his final full-length plays, Eugene O'Neill repeatedly demon-strated this point. The only way for Robert Mayo in *Beyond the Horizon* to communicate his belief that there is something "beyond the horizon," is to tell his brother. But Andrew, without a vision, thinks Robert is "nutty." Edmund Tyrone's "stammering eloquence" affords the only bridge to his father and thus a way to include the father in the intimacy of the son's "other" world. All rests in relationship.

What model of successful relationship had Eugene been offered? He knew the example of his parents' love, beautiful but frail. The doctrine of the Trinity advanced in the catechism offered another image, but he could no longer ac-cept as valid any Christian teaching. Yet, even if the concept of the Trinity was implausible to the adult man, it might have suggested to O'Neill a paradigm for human imitation. For, in the language of his Catholic youth, God was de-scribed as an entity of persons united as one. "The immanent Trinity is God actively *inter-relating* through the divine processions—God the personal com-munity in itself. . . . God has 'opened up' for us—made it possible for abso-lutely significant things to happen."[23] But how, we ask, can this unattainable perfection be emulated, since our sinful disposition cancels realization at every moment of life? We can only cite the gospel exhortation to do the impossible: "Be ye perfect, even as my father is perfect." The ideal is contained in the in-terpersonal nature of the Trinity.

> . . . [S]in principally is lovelessness. Lovelessness often shows itself as a preju-dicial sourness that can abort colleagueship. . . . Tuck away in your mind's

side corridor, then, the notion that sin often shows itself as a lack of *community*. Socially, it is at work in the disorder, the fractiousness, the antagonism of people who refuse to cooperate. One advantage of this reading is that it links up nicely with traditional reflections on evil. For a line of Catholic thought that goes back at least as far as Augustine sees evil as the privation of good. . . . Sin essentially is moral evil—evil that we choose. . . . Socially [in relationships], then, much of our sin is a culpable privation of good. We refuse to go out to others in the love that would bring community, cooperation, justice, and mutual support. We refuse to be humane as we ought to be.[24]

In the connecting tissues of relationship alone are the possibilities for sin (and for love). Since relationship is conducted in a zone wherein we may honor or wound one another, individuals hurt each other and themselves spiritually, in ways that other creatures cannot (e.g., Dion Anthony to Margaret, John Loving to Elsa, Jamie Tyrone to his mother). But our relations are also given potentially sacred character, if we see them founded on a theological basis ("the relation between man and God"). In this light, violating the mystery of self or others can be seen as sinful.

In *The Role of Nemesis* Chester C. Long looked at these dynamics, but in terms of the models of Greek tragedy. We can hardly study O'Neill without these models in mind, of course. Professor Long's argument is connected with the problem of guilt in O'Neill's work, however, and has relevance to the present study: "Nemesis, primarily the eventual punishment of the guilty, begins as a process interrelated with the acts of individuals." Fate, on the other hand, depends strictly on factors supposed to be beyond the control or foreknowledge of the individual."[25]

Because he worked in the western tradition of dramatic tragedy, O'Neill accepted as a given the place for guilt in the makeup of his characters. No guilt, no tragedy. (To Paul Ricoeur "guiltiness *is* the burden of sin."[26] Or, as I have said with less authority, guilt may itself be sin's punishment.) Such insistence strikes many moderns as irrelevant and old fashioned. Indeed, to many dramatists and their audiences, the inclusion of guilt as a precondition to purgation will seem an anachronism born of nothing other than a desire to keep company with the classicists. Yet O'Neill held to his vision. And, although he knew better than many that the old gods no longer spoke with authority to contemporary men and women, he continued to believe in the inspiration of the Greek tragedians. To him, tragedy is tragedy. It is a form, the classic form, whose individual components include sin, guilt, and punishment. Thomas E. Porter spoke to this concept some years ago.

When we look at tragedy from a distance, the pattern emerges: stripped to its essential framework, *the tragic action is a movement from guilt through suffering to purgation and insight*. The way in which this pattern is filled out differs considerably from age to age and culture to culture and even play-wright to playwright, but its outlines persist in Western drama. Whether the play is Aeschylus's *Oresteia* or *Oedipus* or *Hamlet* or *Death of a Salesman,* the structure is a progress from guilt to purgation. . . . Each dramatization of the conventional tragic pattern finally makes a statement through the specific experience of the individual play about the relationship of the guilty individual to his society."[27]

The modern problem was how to dramatize these dynamics without sacrificing credibility. O'Neill, who kept trying, never realized his aim perfectly. He could not, for he was trapped in a world where no institution can claim broad allegiance *(faith)* in its vision of sin, purgation, punishment, and redemption. This was precisely Krutch's point. The modern temper is incompatible with faith. The Greeks believed in the authority of their religion, what we now call mythology. Ever fewer contemporaries believe that priests are agents of salvation or that their liturgy is anything more than meaningless ritual. O'Neill's was a nearly paragon instance of the modern artist's dilemma: the desire but not the confidence to invest his moral vision with the authority of religion. Because drama was about good and evil, sin and redemption, he meant to be serious about eschatological things, just as the Greeks had been. So also did Shakespeare's colleagues. But the contemporary playwright has not that assurance: "The transcendent sphere that can reconcile dichotomies is not available to the space-and-time-bound American dramatist."[28]

It will not do to insist that O'Neill perfectly integrated his vision with the requirements of classical tragedy. He did not. In this he is linked to his melancholy soulmates (Nietzsche et al.), who accepted the death of God but who tried, nevertheless, to invest life with dignity. They insist, against hope, that life is tragic. Even so, the American remained true to his ideal. He retained a sensibility, born of his Catholic background but inspired by a Greek model, a sensibility that kept him alive to the value of suffering. Knowing from experience the depths of sorrow, he recognized the difference between fidelity to truth and a cheap pathos. To Eugene O'Neill it therefore followed that "the one eternal tragedy of Man [was] . . . the only subject worth writing about."[29] He was not tempted by any variety of modernism that lacked discipline or failed to esteem suffering. He could not take seriously any philosophy that denied that life is tragic. In this insistence he rejects one common assumption of our time: that guilt is insignificant or just a manifestation of sickness.

Is it possible, or even reasonable, to speak of tragic figures who feel no guilt? A society that lacks a concept of sin will find it difficult to take seriously the question of individual culpability. In this state of things, the idea of dramatic tragedy itself becomes difficult. O'Neill felt, apparently, that the very style of our times degrades and cripples our capacity to receive tragedy.

Literature offers many powerful examples of guilt-driven figures: Hawthorne's Dimmesdale, whose gesture of hand-over-heart gives full evidence of his interior sorrow; Coleridge's "grey-beard loon," the mariner, in his obsessiveness to confess; Raskolnikov, gaunt and silent, as Sonia recites St. John's account of Lazarus coming from the grave. Perhaps William Kennedy's Francis Phelan should be included in this unusual pantheon. Francis, having confessed to fellow bums his infidelity and cowardice, breathes on the diminishing embers of his spirituality: "In the deepest part of himself that could draw an unutterable conclusion, he told himself: My guilt is all that I have left. If I lost it, I have stood for nothing, done nothing, been nothing."[30]

Guilt: what is it? Is guilt itself a manifestation of sickness or an index of sickness? And if it is the latter, is that not good? Guilt encourages confession.

> Language is the light of the emotions. Through confession the consciousness of fault is brought into the light of speech. . . .
> . . . "Guilt," in the precise sense of a feeling of the unworthiness at the core of one's personal being, is only the advanced point of a radically individualized and interiorized experience. This feeling of guilt points to a more fundamental experience, the experience of "sin," which includes *all* men and indicates the *real* situation of man before God, whether man knows it or not.[31]

O'Neill disliked a time that has lost a sense of gravity almost in direct proportion to its loss of attention span. Once audiences had been trained, almost like athletes, to go the distance of tragedy. But the critics themselves complained about the length of *The Iceman Cometh.* Dudley Nichols recalled O'Neill's reaction.

> I use the phrase which Gene used in telling me, years ago, why he was reluctant to have the play produced even the first time. He said we have been conditioned by radio, TV, the movies, advertising, capsule news and a nervous brevity in everything we do, to a point where we have lost the power of sustained attention, which full-bodied works of art demand.
> Unless something moves and jerks, we soon turn away from it. If it doesn't chatter or talk like a machine gun, we don't listen for long. [Walter] Winchell knows this perfectly—he adopted a style which can hold anyone's attention for fifteen minutes and make what he says sound important no matter how trivial it may be. Winchell is a master of the modern style. He is its arch-creator. Joshua Logan catches this style in the theatre; he makes things happen for the eye all the time, no matter whether the play is saying anything or not. Now, a trivial play can be all movement, but a great play cannot. . . .
> "The truth is, about *The Iceman Cometh,* all kinds of things are happening all the time, but you have to listen and watch, and you hear repetition because that is the way O'Neill planned it, so that you cannot miss his meaning, and the emotions generated by his drama.[32]

It has only gotten worse in a world where sound bytes and "factoids" are taken for truth.[33] What of mystery, and silence? Who can hear the silence for the din? Thoreau observed a century before Walter Winchell came onto the scene: " . . . all *news,* as it is called, is gossip. . . . " St. Paul said that in childhood he spoke as a child; when he became a man, he put away children's things. We are in peril of being bored numb by noise and drivel, made childish by the juvenile narcissism of advertising.

Perhaps O'Neill's treatment of sin, guilt, and punishment derives from the Irishness he inherited and the ambience he experienced in the home of his parents.[34] Whatever, his approach is less theological than it is psychological. In his universe sin is still represented, as it had been in the catechism, as a violation of oneself or another. I am not thinking here of specific sins that are charged against various characters in his plays: Abbie and Eben in *Desire Under the Elms,* Abraham Bentley in *The Rope,* Rev. Hutchins Light in *Dynamo,* or even the fault of his sons named by James Tyrone: "Ingratitude, the vilest weed that grows" (*LDJ,* 32). Rather I have in mind one person's violation of another which, because he recognizes the evil of his deed, causes the perpetrator to feel guilt. Quite often these sins are offenses against charity, a disregard for another's sensibilities. One may, like Hickey in *The Iceman Cometh,* be unable to sustain the recognition of his sin. Then denial takes over. In that case the insight may, in fact, be more the audience's than the character's. But the point has been made.

Seldom would O'Neill's view of fate and the tragedy of human experience satisfy the orthodox Catholic theologian. That is, the resolutions to his characters' conflicts would almost never be acceptable in terms of Catholic morality—as it was taught in his lifetime, at any rate. (An exception may be *Days Without End,* examined at length in chapter 6.) Nor had O'Neill an obligation to satisfy the teachings of any intellectual system, theological or other. His allegiances were to his audience and to truth, as he saw it. But it seems clear that his Catholic training profoundly influenced his view of character.

He found in his own background a logic for motivating character and for resolving dramatic conflict. Often his resolution is little more than an ending of the action, but arresting in its definitiveness. The sin-and-redemption theme surfaces chiefly in failures of relationships, whether "God and man" or familial relationships. These failures are marked by offenses that devalue a character's sense of self-worth. Whatever injures one's sense of integration with being or with others constitutes a diminishment of self or other. Whatever violates the integrity of relationship constitutes sin, whether its cause be anger, envy, pride, or spite. The individual can, of course, devalue herself.

In part 2 we will examine selected plays with respect to the following criteria: *the dynamics of relationship; the manner of its violation (sin); guilt; a sense of the propriety of expiation (whether or not atonement actually takes place); and redemption.*

What did O'Neill mean by *redemption?* To come directly to the point, we can only guess. And yet, we read O'Neill both in terms of what he has revealed through his plays and by what he has said in other places: correspondence, interviews, and reminiscences offered by acquaintances. He did not imply anything about afterlife. Redemption, then, has to do with possibilities in the here-and-now. No specific act need be set in motion. What is required is a disposition of the heart, a renewal or recovery of the heart's state before a rupture in relationship had occurred. The capacity to reestablish an earlier condition, then, must be activated. Whether this bonding actually takes place within the play is not the critical test. Whether both or several parties once connected be thus moved is not truly crucial. But one party must be so disposed. When that happens, "redemption takes place."

For a time in the twenties O'Neill was regarded as both a realist and a naturalist. Neither he nor his critics seemed to know quite what that meant, but it had something to do with his brutally honest depiction of rude types: Brutus Jones, Yank Smith, Eben Cabot, and Abbie Putnam. But O'Neill saw himself as something more than a realist, as a "confirmed mystic." Once again, Professor Cady's definition proves helpful: "[Sensibility] connotes tact, a feeling for life, a way of taking events and making experience, a ground for life-style and at last for morality."[35]

Eugene O'Neill, it seems, honored in Catholicism its willingness to see life as a tragic condition, a view that accommodates the concept of sin. To him an appropriate sense of guilt might be the sign of one's humanity, as it were, one's saving grace. If religion seemed to confirm this truth, so much the better. Whatever, to be in the presence of tragedy constituted the highest moment that women and men could know, for then humans did not deny their fate but embraced it. In his mind that experience alone offered, as it did for the Greeks, a way to human redemption.

"What a Modern Tragedy Would Have to Be"

To paraphrase O'Neill's well-known statement to George Pierce Baker, "I want to be a tragedian or nothing." To be plain, it was only his endless talking about it that proved so vexing. Can we imagine Shakespeare's touting his own tragic intentions, he who was equally at home in comedy and love lyrics and who created Henry's galvanizing exhortations at Agincourt? Can we conjure an O'Neill who rendered Cyrano's brilliant wit and passionate confessions? We should be taxed to do so. "An artist or nothing!" Well, he meant it, whatever is said of the results. And the results were often impressive. Only the crank will deny the power of O'Neill's stunningly muted endings, Shakespearean in their power to crush us. Something more than self-intoxication drove him. The truth is that few dramatists have been more deeply moved by the classical forms than was Eugene O'Neill. " . . . [T]ragedy, I think, has the meaning the Greeks gave it. . . . It roused them to deeper spiritual understandings and released them from the petty greeds of everyday existence. When they saw a tragedy on the stage they felt their own hopeless hopes ennobled in art."[36]

Egil Tornqvist says that O'Neill's view of life and tragedy was in nearly all its shades identical to Nietzsche's.[37] To both men Greek tragedy was art's highest achievement. Of course, a great deal of attention has been paid to this Nietzsche-O'Neill parallel. Other useful commentaries have been supplied by Doris Alexander, Leonard Chabrowe, and Cyrus Day. But it is Tornqvist who makes a quite helpful distinction between O'Neill's "theory of tragedy" (never really articulated) and his "tragic vision."[38]

"O'Neill is almost alone among modern dramatic writers," said Krutch, "in possessing what appears to be an instinctive perception of what a modern tragedy would have to be."[39] Tragedy meant many things to the playwright: "the force behind life," the knowledge that we are exiles, the need to connect but the inability to do so. O'Neill is something like Santayana's hero, who faces a similar plight: "[Oliver Alden] ought to have been a saint. But here comes the deepest tragedy of his lot: that he lived in a spiritual vacuum."[40] Whatever the unfairness of things, one must not sink to his knees in abject surrender, even as one knows that existence had no purpose ["the one eternal tragedy of Man in his glorious, self-destructive stuggle to make the Force express him"].[41] Other creatures share this fate, but only women and men live in the knowledge of it.

Krutch argued in "The Tragic Fallacy" that our age cannot "appreciate" Sophocles and Shakespeare because we cannot live by their beliefs and sensibilities: " . . . the idea of nobility is inseparable from the idea of tragedy, which cannot exist without it."[42] But he paid O'Neill the high compliment of placing him, as it were provisionally, in the company of the high tragedians: "To find in the play [*Mourning Becomes Electra*] any lack at all one must compare it with the very greatest works of dramatic literature, but when one does compare it with *Hamlet* or *Macbeth,* one realizes that it does lack just one thing and that thing is language—words as thrilling as the action which accompanies them."[43]

Krutch must have seen in O'Neill's work an attitude that he found at least reminiscent of the classical form: " . . . tragedy is essentially an expression, not of despair, but of the triumph over despair and of confidence in the value of human life."[44] The modern formula for tragedy is one that, even when we defend it (Krutch did not), many of us find unsatisfactory: *the individual (victim) + innocence or good intentions vs. overwhelming forces (determinism) = tragedy.* This equation of modernist drama produced such worthy plays as

Winterset. In this approach guilt is left out or, if taken into account, is considered irrelevant.[45] O'Neill, on the other hand, seems to say that guilt must be accepted if one is to retain human dignity. Of course, tragedy is not algebra. If it were, O'Neill's view might be rendered in this shorthand: *Individual fault + guilt + Fate ("behind-life forces") = tragedy.* Nevertheless, this way of formulizing the human condition would come closer to the classical idea than most of what is called modern tragedy. Drama produced in the light of this equation will not become so quickly dated or trapped in the topical (*Awake and Sing!*). Such an approach makes valid certain assumptions I have introduced about the nature of O'Neill's moral imagination. He possessed three qualities of the pillar tragedians. He saw the human condition as universal; his vision was built on an idea of human nature; and he saw guilt as inevitable.

If, after appropriate consideration, we can infer an idea of guilt as it is revealed in Eugene O'Neill's dramatic practice, we will discover strong parallels to the terms as defined in post–Vatican II Catholic theology.

> The question of how guilt arises remains unanswered. Anxiety may well play a role, as S. Kierkegaard thought. However, anxiety is not enough to explain the phenomenon. Guilt is a cause rather than an effect of anxiety. Obviously, guilt is one of the ultimate basic traits of *human nature*. These traits, which are as mysterious as existence itself, explain and substantiate much, but they are no longer comprehensible by man himself as such.[46]

Apparently guilt carries salutary as well as destructive power. Sometimes, therefore, one ought to feel the emotion. How could there be any concept of tragedy (or sin) without an attendant idea of guilt? If guilt, in Catholic theology, is a compound of shame and confusion deriving from one's knowledge of her transgression,[47] some concept of guilt as salutary must be connected, *prima facie*, to a religious sensibility.

3 | Church Authority, Artistic Freedom, and the Search for God

From Anatole France to Theodore Dreiser the names of those who have given up faith for literature are many.

—George N. Shuster

A Note on the Climate of Opinion

THE CENTURIES HAVE brought forth an endless file of Catholic intellectuals and artists. In its dedication to the classical traditions the church became the world's greatest repository of art and thought: the ethereal chasteness of plain chant; the joy of illuminated manuscripts; the *Summa Theologica* itself; the Renaissance visions of Dante and Leonardo; Michaelangelo's triumph of the Sistine vault. Here were Yeats's "monument of unageing intellect." Yes, the church has also been guilty of unconscionable sins against intellectual freedom and social justice: the Inquisition, the murder of Joan of Arc and the jailing of Galileo, the embarrassment of the *Index Librorum Prohibitorum,* the hand-in-glove coziness with wealth and power. Even so, this magnificent system taught the value of silence, contemplation, and waiting. Centuries were for building cathedrals and cases for sainthood: "*Festina lente.* Make haste slowly." It seems a given, then: if ever an institution had cause and credentials to enter collegially in the modernist debate and not simply to condemn it, it was the church of Rome.

Yet, faced with the exigencies of expansion in the United States, and impelled, like other institutions, by a heady philosophy of enterprise, the American Catholic church was called upon to grow with the times. In many ways it did. In certain areas it shed its Roman habits of painstaking deliberation and procrastination. To meet its own needs, this ecclesiastical monolith adapted to and imitated the prevailing American philosophy of action.

In the nineteenth century the church was necessarily preoccupied with establishing on this continent a culture of Catholicism for thousands, eventually millions, of immigrants. The displaced were arriving in waves, scattered by such crises as the Irish potato famines of the 1840s or the general and ongoing devaluation of the person amid the mixed blessings of industrial "progress." The hierarchy, beset with an ever-expanding laity, felt constrained to address

53

the pressing concerns of parish-building and to find personnel to educate the first-generation immigrants, both in faith and in the skills for living in the young democracy. The story of James O'Neill, of Buffalo and Cincinnati by way of Kilkenny, is an astonishing account of rags-to-riches, yet it is for that very reason not typical. In keeping with formulaic Algerism, it blends a combination of givens (at once predictable and unlikely): opportunity, luck, and pluck.

In the fever of building, national values and priorities were inevitably ensconced. If the work of subduing nature was back-breaking, the rewards were immense. Between 1850–1950 a very cult of enterprise came to be named: "the American way." One shrewd observer saw a worrisome division forming between the poles of action and contemplation: "The one is the sphere of the American man; the other, at least predominantly, of the American woman. The one is all aggressive enterprise; the other is all genteel tradition."[1] The American Catholic church did not remain immune to the fever. As Msgr. John Tracy Ellis later observed, when an attitude of anti-intellectualism was virtually institutionalized, an indifference to if not contempt for the life of the mind began to characterize the spirit of things, even from the earliest days.[2]

Perhaps the hierarchy simply could not attend to all its priorities. If it could have, the Catholic church might have met more confidently the challenge of modernism in its American strain. American prelates and priests of the nineteenth century, however, were hardly in a position to foresee such crises. They placed a higher priority on the (apparently) more pressing needs of parish management and building schools; of increasing the number of priests and nuns; of making the effort to fit in with all other Americans. But the costs of neglecting the commitment to higher intellectual tasks proved to be very high. It is not surprising, therefore, that American response to the movement called "modernism," condemned as a heresy by Pope Pius X, was at once similar to and different from that in Europe. (For further background on the modernist crisis, especially its implications for Catholic intellectuals and artists, see my appendix, "The Immigrant Church Press and the Catholic Writer, 1920–1950.")

> . . . the presence of so widespread a prejudice among the great majority of the population prompts the minority to withdraw into itself and to assume the attitude of defenders of a besieged fortress. That this situation had such an effect on many Catholics, there is no doubt. Even so brave and talented a man as John Carroll, the first American Catholic bishop, revealed the timidity engendered among the Catholics of his day by hatred of their Church when he was compelled to go into print in 1784 to refute a subtle attack on Catholic doctrine from the first American apostate priest. As Carroll remarked, "I could not forget . . . that the habits of thinking, the prejudices, perhaps even the passions of many of my readers, would be set against all the arguments I could offer. . . . " More damaging than its direct effect on the

intellectual shortcomings of American Catholics, has probably been the fostering by this historic bias of an overeagerness in Catholic circles for apologetics rather than pure scholarship.[3]

Sinister clouds darkened the horizon of the early American church.

What I hope to describe in the next few pages of this chapter is a climate of opinion that Eugene O'Neill and other "Catholic" writers inherited. Here we enter an unhappy chamber where the artist, that one born into a tradition of faith, found little that promised support for his vision. O'Neill was but one writer to feel these chill winds of doctrine at his back.

> Instead of being a patron of the creative imagination, the church that quashed modernism became its critic and censor, rejecting the artistic impulses and works of great writers, driving them into rueful and brooding exile. Eugene O'Neill, whose works are a profound and painful exploration of Catholic culture, may be the most distinguished of American Catholic writers who had to live at a distance from it in order to write at all. What O'Neill did, however, is what today's Catholic novelists can do without abandoning their church.[4]

Catholic writers were in a difficult position. For, if they were charged with abandoning the faith, as many surely had (Farrell, Fitzgerald, O'Neill, and so on), they might have felt that their American church had all but abandoned them. As it is true in other institutions, politics in the church generally produced tension. In this case we have a classic example. It has to do with the very integrity of the artist: Should art serve the propaganda needs of the organization, or should it be permitted to serve its own ends? Should an artist be forced into the role of institutional loyalist and even the defender of the "party line"? To accept such a function, many will argue, is to denature the enterprise.[5] What is certain, however, is that the general suspicion fostered by the American Catholic church created a climate unpropitious to the free expression of opinion. The effect was to put the laity at odds with their own artists. "Because Catholics remained closed to the remarkable power of contemporary literature, they not only lost touch with the American mainstream but even with their own Catholic heritage."[6] William Halsey cites the case of O'Neill as that of a representative "Catholic" writer rejected by priest and parish.

> Eugene O'Neill represented the rarely acknowledged underside of American Catholic Irish optimism. It was not surprising, then, to find Catholics irritated by O'Neill's fatalism. During the 1920s Catholics were universally repulsed by the playwright's theme of bewilderment expressed in *The Hairy Ape, Desire Under the Elms, Dynamo,* and *The Great God Brown.* They found O'Neill's art absorbed in the grotesque and lacking the necessary quality of "good" art: the concern for "uplift." His fascination with personal suffering led critics to reject what they considered his obsession with the abnormal and brutal. As a poet and philosopher O'Neill was a failure

according to R. Danna Skinner [*sic*], dramatic critic of *The Commonweal,* because his intelligence was submerged by emotion and "raw feelings."[7]

To the extent that they could, writers tried to support each other. Eugene O'Neill, for example, put himself on the record with regard to James T. Farrell's *Studs Lonigan* trilogy (1935). He allowed himself to be quoted in support of Farrell, when the American Library Association withdrew *Lonigan* "from their list of American works to be exported to England in the interest of British-American amity." And he sympathized with the novelist in a letter and offered praise for the classic of naturalism: " . . . I have great admiration for STUDS LONIGAN. It is a splendid piece of work."[8] The following day he wrote to James Henle, Farrell's agent at Vanguard Press, permitting his name and remarks to be used in the novelist's defense.

Eugene Kennedy understands the difficult plight of writers confronted with this kind of defensiveness, a state of mind clearly born of fear and insecurity. But they did not get much help from the literary critics of the Catholic press. Later some observers (Halsey, Kennedy, Reher, and others) realized the damage that had been done.

> Thus, the church's long suspicion and oversimplified condemnation of the theories of thinkers such as Charles Darwin and Sigmund Freud, its muscular readiness to restrict the indiscriminate reading of books [*Index Librorum Prohibitorum*], the viewing of movies [the Legion of Decency],[9] or attendance at any college where a philosophical system other than Thomism was presented. . . . It is small wonder that artists who explored themes that seemed even slightly to challenge the institution or its view of itself—to explore the tortured depths of a certain strain of Irish family life as Eugene O'Neill and James T. Farrell did—were hardly welcome or comfortable within its boundaries.[10]

O'Neill and the Catholic Press

The earliest Catholic criticism of O'Neill's taste and literary allegiances came not from any official church agency but from his own family. From the day Eugene, at age fifteen, refused to attend Sunday Mass with his father, the boy's fidelity to Irish Catholic ideals was held suspect. No doubt much of this O'Neill family history is reflected accurately in *Long Day's Journey into Night*. To his sons, Edmund and Jamie, the elder Tyrone complains, "There's little choice between the philosophy you [Jamie] learned from Broadway loafers, and the one Edmund got from his books. They're both rotten to the core. You've both flouted the faith you were born and brought up in—the one true faith of the Catholic Church—and your denial has brought nothing but self-destruction" (*LDJ*, 77).

Of course, the public was not aware of that part of such familial tensions

until after Eugene's death in 1953. But, once he had become a Broadway lumi-
nary, it did not take Catholic journals of opinion long to pillory him and his
"stunt[s]," as Elizabeth Jordan termed the innovations in *Strange Interlude.*
James F. Kearney, S.J., found him straying from "normalcy." The chief criticisms leveled against O'Neill, however, were the same as those brought against
most "Ibsenites" (Kearney) and pessimists, whether scientists, philosophers, or
artists: Darwin, Freud; Nietzsche, Whitehead; Joyce, Lawrence, Stein, Sinclair
Lewis, Frost, Eliot, Faulkner, Dreiser, *ad infinitum*—many of the 1900–1930s
authors most revered today.

But for lapsed Catholic writers the criticism was more frequent and stri-
dent. Michael Earls, S.J., of Boston College, recalled the happier days of the
"wholesome nineties." The godlessness of modernism and the ascendancy of
scientific materialism, as they were perceived, were now found everywhere to
be an insult to moral authority and a threat to faith and hope. Authors who
abetted these trends were taken to task, especially those whose training and
tradition had prepared them to resist precisely that philosophy they seemed
committed to advance.

Overall O'Neill's work was met with disapproval, often rancor, by the
Catholic press, especially in the 1920s and 1930s. For nearly two decades
thereafter, he received almost no attention from the critics, Catholic or secular,
owing in large measure to the fact that he had effectively withdrawn from the
American theater through the Second World War. By the time of the O'Neill
"revival" in the mid-1950s, however, the spirit of Catholic journalism (prod-
ded, it may be, by thinkers like John Tracy Ellis) was itself undergoing fundamental changes in the direction of openness, if not of liberalism.

Of course, the "O'Neill case" was hardly equal in importance to that, say,
of Galileo. The Catholic church never officially censured the American playwright. In the first place, to make such a gesture would have been to accord
O'Neill more attention than he "deserved." In the second place, such condemnation would have appeared ridiculously antediluvian in twentieth-century
America. But in her diocesan weeklies and journals of opinion (*America, The
Catholic Mind,* and *Thought* [Jesuit magazines], *Sign* [Passionist Fathers], *The
Catholic World* [Paulist Fathers], and so on) O'Neill's plays were attacked
early and often. His view was typically characterized as immoral, ungodly,
vulgar, and morbid.[11]

As early as 1924 *America,* giving short shrift to the published text, observed that "in *All God's Chillun Got Wings,* Mr. O'Neill is true to himself in
choosing a most disagreeable theme and aggravating its unpleasantness." Even
so, like most Catholic journals, *America* acknowledged O'Neill's rank as "our
foremost American playwright."[12]

Perhaps the most qualified Catholic commentator was Richard Dana Skinner, from 1924–1934 drama critic for *Commonweal.* This magazine was, and

remains, a lay publication, never directly subject to ecclesiastical review. Skinner gave the best informed, most professional commentary of critics writing for Catholic journals in those years. He strove to give O'Neill a fair hearing,[13] finding him somewhat perplexing but immensely talented. Skinner's reviews, until the production of *Days Without End,* are generally mixed. In time he became a defender and eventually wrote a book-length study of O'Neill. Even in his early reviews, however, Skinner recognized something special in O'Neill. In the main, he tried to be objective. Few Catholic journalists were. His first in a long series of *Commonweal* essays was an attempt to characterize "The Moods of O'Neill" (10 December 1924). In this he was among the first American critics to remark on what came to be perceived as an enduring trait: "O'Neill can not disentangle himself from events. In this lies his power and his weakness."

> Dramatically the four episodes of *S. S. Glencairn* are unimportant. They show a definite interpretive ability, the power to convey to you and me a mood or the inner tragedy of a situation, but they utterly lack creative genius as applied to the theatre. That is, they do not by plot, arrangement, dialogue, or even by characterization pass beyond the trite and obvious. There is no suspense, no alternation of mood. . . . There is no moment in which the brute is raised above himself, or the finer man faces catastrophe. At times there is a sentimentality which is almost maudlin. Yet withal, O'Neill makes you feel the mood of the sea as he himself has felt it. The drama, such as it is, is the drama which you yourself, as spectator, supply the powerful insistent awesome brooding of the sea itself. It is drama suggested, not created.[14]

Skinner's review of *The Great God Brown* gives one of the fairest assessments of that brilliant but confusing work. After remarking on the play's challenge to general understanding, the critic gives the dramatist credit for making a major contribution: "His courage and vision . . . are not yet matched by ability to use the new medium [masks]. . . . The new play has high moments of rich spiritual insight, of abiding faith, and understanding of the mystic vale of tears." He continues:

> O'Neill allows himself to complicate the action of the play—the entrances and exits—to such an extent, that the exchange of masks becomes a technical bewilderment for the audience, no matter how clear its intention and meaning may remain.
>
> The greatest achievement of this play, however, lies in a discovery which O'Neill has made—or partly made—and which most of the critics have ignored. He has begun to fathom the meaning of earthly suffering. Probably *no poet of the theatre in recent times has been more intensely aware of suffering than O'Neill.* It has been his veritable obsession. Evil and its resulting catastrophe have been the central theme of most of his plays—evil in manifold forms, as pride, as sensuality, as cowardice, as avarice. But he has never seen beyond catastrophe to a possible resurrection. . . . Now there is an

astonishing change. He tells us in this new play that from the tears of earth is born the eternal laughter of Heaven—that resurrection lies beyond death—that man should keep himself forever as a pilgrim on this earth—(using Thomas à Kempis as his text)—and that God is.

. . . .

There is still confusion in his thought, for O'Neill feels more acutely than he thinks. But he has definitely come forth from the great shadow which fell forbiddingly over his recent work. He is approaching that ecstatic moment when tragedy transmutes itself, through song, into spiritual comedy.[15]

No other critic comes to mind, Catholic or not, who at that time employed so many religio-poetical idioms as did Skinner in assessing O'Neill: *spiritual insight, abiding faith, vale of tears, meaning of suffering, evil and its resulting catastrophe, resurrection, spiritual comedy.* It is not difficult to see why he called his book about O'Neill *A Poet's Quest* (1935). In terms of Christian sophistication, Skinner added something to the debate about O'Neill in the twenties and thirties.

Critics and friends of *America,* the Jesuit magazine established in 1915, seldom picked up O'Neill's frequency during his lifetime. To them he was, in the words of James F. Kearney, S.J., "a sad example among modern playwrights of the man with a lost ideal." That is, he was a typical spokesman for defeatist pessimism who thereby betrayed his Catholic mission. Kearney hardly equivocated in depicting O'Neill as an apostate.

The literary artist influenced by Rousseau and the evolutionists no longer looks to supernatural greatness—the saints, the Virgin, Christ—for his models, but to the Hairy Ape instead or to a type even lower and more degraded. Mark well, he is still swayed by ideals, but they are not what they were before; and the tendency towards them is now rather downward than upward, to earth instead of to heaven, to a sordid, brutal nature. It is to this that Eugene O'Neill has come. . . . O'Neill, in being "true to his vision," paints mankind in its lowest levels, in the stoke-hole, in the bar-room, among savage wildernesses. Christ made His strongest appeal to a similar type, to the poor and the downfallen and the sinner. . . . But O'Neill with the rest of the ultra-realists, because their eyes are riveted on earth and cannot gaze heavenward, would insist on depicting the Thief in his thieveries, the Magdalene in her sins, the Prodigal devouring his substance or quarreling over husks with the swine.[16]

One of O'Neill's most caustic and constant critics was Elizabeth Jordan, herself a novelist and playwright (thirty-nine books), and drama reviewer for *America* from 1922–1945. Seldom able to muster enthusiasm for his ideas, Jordan occasionally managed to honor O'Neill's craftsmanship. She condemned his taste and felt obliged to scold him for the godlessness of his themes and characters. To Jordan, *Strange Interlude* could fairly be described as a "stunt,"

the asides as *gaucheries* and "novelties." She thought "his play would be infinitely clearer and in every way better without them." Perhaps, but judging by
her typical reviews, one might have had reason to wonder if there was anything
worth improving.

> As to the play itself, it is laid in O'Neill's world, not in ours. . . . He looks
> at humanity with jaundiced, red-rimmed, astigmatic eyes. He shows us an
> abnormal young woman, an abnormal old woman, an abnormal friend,
> an abnormal scientist; he hurls them all into an abnormal situation; and he
> asks us to accept them simply and recognizingly as parts of a familiar exist-
> ence . . . Let us give thanks that at least we are not living on Eugene O'Neill's
> black-starred planet.[17]

Unlike Skinner but in agreement with Kearney, Jordan found O'Neill to be
without vision. She echoed the earlier *America* critic who had written that
"O'Neill is true to himself in choosing a most disagreeable theme. . . . " A few
years later, she enclosed a letter to Francis X. Talbot, S.J., editor of *America*,
with her review of *Mourning Becomes Electra:* "I hope you will agree with
what I have said about it. It's a strange season this, in which all good things
are so bad!"[18]

Miss Jordan was more at home with the "normal," apparently, than with
attempts at irony: " . . . I am giving [*Strange Interlude*] all the dramatic space
this month, and while I am about it I may as well explain the title, as revealed
in one of the profound 'thoughts' of the heroine."

Jordan's counterpart at *The Catholic World* was another veteran O'Neill
chronicler, Euphemia Van Rensselaer Wyatt. She too found weaknesses in the
work of the American-Irishman, calling one of her earliest reviews (of *Desire
Under the Elms*) "Eugene O'Neill on Plymouth Rock." Nevertheless, Wyatt
always saw him as a serious writer who never lost sight of his high goals. She
tried to be fair, and she gave O'Neill credit for integrity. She attended productions of his plays from the early twenties through a Fordham staging of *Lazarus Laughed* in 1948, which she felt revealed the "complete ineptitude and
bathos" of the play. In 1934, supposing like many others that *Days Without
End* signaled O'Neill's return to Catholicism, she took considerable care. "One
may like or dislike his plays but they can never be dismissed as trivial. We have
had confidence in his present confession of faith because in all the shifting
standards of a disturbed social order, he kept intact his sense of right and
wrong. He has written of sinners but he has never condoned their sinning. He
has painted sin in glaring pigments but he has never glossed it with humor."[19]
When few reviewers gave full-throated approval to O'Neill's return to Broadway in October 1946, Ms. Van Rensselaer Wyatt may have proved the long-
term value of her credentials. "The value of faith, even if only in a pipe dream,
is now set forth in grim fashion by Eugene O'Neill in *The Iceman Cometh*, a

play without parallel in drama. . . . [I]t bears the mark of a great playwright and, strangely enough, a poet. Only a poet could have probed those outcast, pitiful souls. As always, with O'Neill, evil has no palliation."[20] The playwright might have wished for such evenhanded criticism from his "Catholic" peer, Mary McCarthy, who saw the play in terms precisely opposed to Ms. Wyatt's.

It should be recalled that the criticisms reviewed in this survey were written by persons who had accepted a rather specialized mission: to advance the causes of Catholic literature and intellectualism. (For a further discussion of this "literary situation," see the appendix.) Of course, the Catholic press had every right and reason to promote a Christian agenda. We would not expect a Marxist critic to write approvingly of what he viewed as attacks on Marxist theory. Thus the Catholic press found it especially difficult to maintain an even hand in its treatment of "apostate" or independent Catholic intellectuals. Yet George Shuster, himself a talented and courageous Catholic layman, believed that such evenhandedness was the price the press must pay to insure its own credibility: "One great need . . . is a powerful and competent criticism exercised by men who blend the best endowments of humanism with the fervor of belief."[21] Rendering this service, of course, must sometimes have seemed impossible, given the implicit charge to defend a parochial intellectualism that permitted neither the approval nor even the relevance of the modernist challenge: "American Catholics will probably continue to devote the greater portion of their intellectual effort to apologetic[s]: first because that is so much needed [i.e., demanded], and secondly because they are in the habit of doing so."[22]

Not all critics were such creatures of habit, of course. The year following Jordan's retirement, Louis F. Doyle, S.J., who taught at St. Louis University, gave the playwright credit for artistic integrity and philosophical honesty in "Mr. O'Neill's Iceman." Fr. Doyle quotes with approval O'Neill's earlier developed view of tragedy:

> . . . to say that Mr. O'Neill has always been intellectually honest would be understatement. His intellectual integrity has been almost quixotic in a theatre not particularly noted for artistic honesty. He once said: "Sure I'll write about happiness if I can happen to meet up with that luxury, and find it sufficiently dramatic and in harmony with any deep rhythm of life. But happiness is a word. What does it mean? Exaltation; an intensified feeling of the significant worth of man's being and becoming? Well, if it means that—I know there is more of it in one real tragedy than in all the happy-ending plays ever written. It's merely present-day judgment to think of tragedy as unhappy." That is a perfectly sound statement.[23]

Fr. Doyle seems sad but not dismissive in his conclusion that O'Neill fell short of greatness, but not by much. Few Catholic critics had become this generous by 1946. More representative was the opinion, registered with astonishing moral certitude, in *Sign* magazine. "That illusions—or 'pipe dreams' as he calls them—are necessary in life is the basic argument of O'Neill's melancholy, materialistic probe. We certainly hope that he is not harboring one of his own in a belief that he has written a great play or contributed anything of value to a spiritually sick world."[24]

As noted, Richard Dana Skinner had tried to deal honestly with the legitimate questions of art. He kept focused on O'Neill but remained ambivalent. Skinner's difficulty was not so much the playwright's subject matter. For him, the question was whether O'Neill (who "feels more acutely than he thinks") was up to the intellectual challenge. Skinner was little encouraged by the evidence given in *Dynamo*. "He has become one of America's leading thinkers on the more profound questions of life. As a matter of fact, however, his thinking is of a very shallow order, frequently trite in the extreme and enormously over-influenced by his emotions."[25]

> The trouble with O'Neill of late has been his quite evident ambition to intellectualize his primitive poetic power. Instead of fusing the two faculties, he has unconsciously let one choke the other. This has never been more apparent nor more painful than in *Dynamo*.
> . . . he sets himself up as the analyst of a great world sickness of the day and proposes to dig at its roots with his intellect as well as his poetic intuition; and we can judge the fitness of his intellect for his self-appointed job only by the evidences he gives of clear thinking or the contrary.
> . . . [T]he play is not really about a world sickness, but about O'Neill's own sickness—a blind soul in an aching body which nevertheless cries out with the words and the power of a poet.[26]

Nationally the negative commentary and overall Catholic rejection had little impact on O'Neill's reputation. For, while the playwright's work had received a full measure of hostile secular criticism in the twenties and thirties, his stock had generally been rising. He had won Pulitzer prizes in 1920 (*Beyond the Horizon*), 1922 (*Anna Christie*), and 1927 (*Strange Interlude*). He had come to be respected internationally as a brilliant innovator for *The Emperor Jones* and *The Hairy Ape;* as a writer on the cutting edge of social issues for *All God's Chillun Got Wings;* as a *bona fide* tragedian in *Desire Under the Elms;* and as a Nietzschean coming to terms with the spiritual crisis of the times in *The Great God Brown, Lazarus Laughed, Strange Interlude* and *Dynamo*. At home and abroad, O'Neill was as great a presence in the theater as anyone on the contemporary scene. His being awarded the Nobel Prize for Literature in 1936 marked the international recognition of this high estate. Therefore, if his reception by Catholic critics in the U.S. was lukewarm and worse, they had little power to channel outside opinion against O'Neill. And their views had virtually no impact on many Catholics who were often not even aware of his presence.

> . . . if Eugene O'Neill cared little for Catholicism, it was equally true that the average Catholic paid little attention to O'Neill's plays. The typical Catholic was a blue-collar worker who didn't go to the theater. He had heroes like Gene Tunney, the heavyweight boxing champion, or Babe Ruth of the Yankees. Ruth was an unassimilated man, a crude, happy-go-lucky nonconformist who came out of a Xaverian Brothers industrial school in Baltimore. . . . He was a figure with which [*sic*] many Catholics could identify.
>
> There was still another sports hero during the 1920s who made Catholic hearts beat with pride, . . . Knute Rockne, and the teams he built at Notre Dame [an institution which] had a special meaning for rank-and-file Catholics who had never been to college themselves and who had a vague contempt for intellectual achievement.[27]

But O'Neill probably felt the chill of Catholic disregard. He would have taken pleasure in being honored. He achieved some of this, as we will see in chapter 6, with the productions of *Days Without End*. How strange is fortune. For that play he was accepted, in some cases almost ecstatically, by the Catholic press, while he was drubbed by secular critics. O'Neill was proud of his general reception in Ireland. No doubt he would have been warmed had the American (Irish) church seemed more inclined to celebrate his achievements. As William V. Shannon observed:

> O'Neill was . . . intensely proud that only Irish blood flowed in his veins, and he identified strongly with the American Irish. But like the great playwrights in Dublin, he felt his identification with the Irish so keenly that he took to heart their errors and failings, exposing and attacking them in his plays. Those who thought him anti-Irish did not comprehend that for an artist telling the truth is the highest act of love.[28]

Owing to the stunning success of *Mourning Becomes Electra* in 1931, many Catholic critics were probably forced, at least minimally, to reconsider their estimate of Eugene O'Neill. The phenomenon loomed too large to be ignored; because it was both huge and unconventional, the play demanded more than a conventional response. Here was a trilogy modeled on the lines of Greek tragedy and inspired by classical themes. Such an offering could hardly be dealt with by a mere rehashing of decade-old cavils. Skinner, still with reservations, allowed in his *Commonweal* column that "many of its passages are infused with the true greatness of the tragic spirit . . . and contain, by all odds, the finest dramatic writing of O'Neill's career."[29] The critic agreed that the play addresses a "classic tragic dilemma . . . [but it] is far removed from Greek objectivity." Even so, he granted, "There is no question that O'Neill is a true artist. . . . "[30]

From the distance of sixty years and more, it seems that the official Catholic assessment of O'Neill has had but limited influence. Aside from Richard Dana Skinner, little that was then registered has been carried forward. Perhaps that is in the nature of play criticism, typically registered with little time for sober reflection and dependent on the quality of dress rehearsals or first-night performances. Yet George Shuster's earlier point about the challenge of balancing "competent criticism" with the requirement for apologetics is cogent. Elizabeth Jordan's work seems especially to illustrate this principle. Again and again her criticisms of O'Neill seem unprofessional, sometimes even silly. Take the case of *Electra,* about which she had complained to Fr. Talbot. In her review Jordan extended a compliment with one hand and undercut it with the other: " . . . to what end must we follow these mad men and mad women into their various hells? Even the great art that is unmistakably present does not justify the appalling journey." Nor does the remainder of the essay strike one as the work of a serious commentator.

> The dead, the dying, the insane, the abnormal, filled the stage before us. All that O'Neill's imagination could conceive of as happening to one family (and what can his imagination not conceive?) was happening to the Mannons of New England. To a cheery start-off of two murders he had added two suicides and tossed in a heavy seasoning of vengeance, insanity, adultery and incest.[31]

That paragraph's opening sentence could just as easily be applied to *Hamlet.* In observing a little further along that " . . . his text might have been 'The wages of sin is death,' " Jordan may have been closer to the truth than she knew. An examination of that theme, in light of Catholic theology, might have inspired several columns.

It is true that O'Neill could not have expected, nor did he seek, approval as a "Catholic" writer. Dorothy Day might have given a more authoritative description of O'Neill's Catholic sensibility, however. She knew why we must "follow these mad men and mad women into their various hells." Hardly a sentimentalist, Day was never impressed by pretended virtue. She knew him. She had been with him and could speak with the authority of relationship.

Intellectualism might seem by definition to imply freedom to question. But for a time in Catholic America, where an authoritarian church had taken root (and, it should be noted, not against the will of the faithful), the prevailing climate of opinion proved unpropitious to Catholic writers. Because their work was usually met with suspicion and even outright hostility in the Catholic community, the writers began to make less and less effort to keep the conduits open. A Jesuit of our own time sees how tragic was this devastating loss, tragic to all concerned.

> Original sin, a God who "knows my most secret thoughts, words and actions," as the *Baltimore Catechism* has it, and the fleeting nature of this present life were themes repeated by Eugene O'Neill, wrestling with religious faith in his plays and with alternating doubt and belief in his life. However much or little religious ties affected their artistic imagination, no literary giant of the twenties managed to live peaceably within the Catholic community. For some it did not exist; for Farrell, Fitzgerald, and O'Neill at least, the ties were never quite broken. George Shuster pointed out in 1930 that artists of the twenties saw themselves as "makers of images." They did not find in the American representation of Catholicism, because it was not easily found there, a possibility of the freedom they felt must be theirs in interpreting world and humanity.[32]

O'Neill had his critics, a motley legion of them. If they were often hard on him, few were the commentators who questioned his integrity. But it probably mattered little in any event; he seemed to need the world's approval less than other writers. No doubt he would have appreciated Catholic support, had it been given for the honesty and dramatic quality of his work. He was unwilling to make concessions to obtain anyone's *imprimatur,* however. Here he was absolutely unyielding. To Bennett Cerf he wrote, concerning the divorce situation in *Days Without End:* "If . . . the Church wants to set the seal of approval on it, well that's up to them. But I don't give a damn whether they do or not."[33]

In time many, but by no means all, Catholic journalists would reevaluate O'Neill. They often chose to praise him rather than to bury him. But, generally speaking, this did not happen until after his death. Occasionally a commentator might place him in the pantheon with other immortals. This happened in 1956, when *Long Day's Journey into Night* was given its world premiere in Stockholm. "If our definitions of tragedy do not fit this work," wrote Stephen Whicher, "we should perhaps rethink our definitions."

> It may be that *Long Day's Journey Into Night* has succeeded in Sweden because this heartsick pessimism goes down easier here than it would in the United States. . . .
> Yet this may be *the* modern tragedy. In its passivity, its despair, its longing, its undramatic reduction of human life to meaningless suffering, and its agonized honesty, it strikes a keynote of our modern mood.[34]

This review established a new esteem among Catholic critics. Still, it was difficult for Mr. Whicher to withhold the habitual phrase of reservation: "Starting with a prejudice against O'Neill, . . . "

"The Substitute-God Search": Brief Remarks on Three Plays— *The Great God Brown, Lazarus Laughed, Strange Interlude*

Beginning in the mid-1920s and continuing for a decade, O'Neill broadcast one bulletin after another in response to the death-of-God crisis. The Catholic press failed to pick up his exact frequency. They were not alone. Everyone knew that O'Neill was doing important work, but few could say they always understood his message. He was searching for God-substitutes, something to console now bereft humanity in its unending trauma before the open grave. Almost every new play in these years was an attempt to answer the question of life's meaning without God.

In 1928 O'Neill wrote to George Jean Nathan about another play, *Dynamo*. "It is really the first play of a trilogy that will dig at the roots of the sickness of today . . . the death of the old God and the failure of Science and Materialism to give any satisfying new One for the surviving primitive religious instinct to find a meaning for life in, and to comfort its fears of death with."[35] In truth, he had been at this "digging" for several years. Between 1924 and 1929 O'Neill wrote a series of "big subject" plays, each proposing a substitute for the dead God. As one for whom the answers in the catechism no longer sufficed, O'Neill made his plays the stage on which other ideas were given a hearing. Again and again he raised the central question of human existence: Does life itself have meaning? Or is it merely a moment, an interlude, during which the individual soul awakens, comes alive to pleasure and pain, attempts to understand its plight, and finally loses awareness of itself in the act of dying? O'Neill was known to be extremely serious about his art. His preoccupation with human suffering had long since strengthened his reputation as America's arch tragedian. But something different, and not always beneficial, had entered his work: his plays had become very abstract and very long. A Yeats Noh play might carry the symbolic content through a single act. This was not possible, however, in a play of 420 roles (*Lazarus Laughed*), where nearly every character wears a mask. O'Neill had begun to focus less on the dynamics of character relationships and more on the importance of ideas. This emphasis sometimes yielded brave new achievements, but it sometimes played havoc with clarity. Certain critics wondered whether O'Neill himself always understood his own ideas.

In this subsection, I should like to make a brief examination of three plays from this period: *The Great God Brown, Lazarus Laughed,* and *Strange Interlude*. The sequence itself underlines the intensity of O'Neill's spiritual journey, of course. Further, each marks an important step by the playwright toward the work that came to be called his "Catholic play," *Days Without End,* 1934 (given chapter-length analysis further along).

Each of the works just named carries a heavy freight of ideas, so heavy that the usual focus on human motives is effectively diminished. All three plays are about God or some idea of God but not, strictly speaking, about "the relationship between man and God." This does not mean that the plays lack entertainment and intellectual merit. Indeed, all three have enjoyed far greater longevity than *Days Without End*. Moreover, all three demonstrate the playwright's willingness to risk failure in his attempts to break through the secret's mask. Thus, it was surely reasonable that, in his search for the "Force," O'Neill would invoke concepts such as Nietzsche's Eternal Recurrence and the Apollonian-Dionysian duality. Sometimes, however, the heavy freight of ideas caused these vehicles to ride unevenly.

Generally speaking, when an O'Neill play failed, it merely fell aside as inconsequential: e.g., *Welded, The First Man*. Whatever may be said of the success or failure of his search plays, this must be granted: they met the spiritual crisis of the times head-on. As he wrote to Krutch in connection with *Dynamo*, the first play in a projected trilogy that was never completed and was to have been called "Myth-Plays for the God-Forsaken": " . . . all [were to be] written around the general spiritual futility of the substitute-God search."[36] *The Great God Brown, Lazarus Laughed,* and *Strange Interlude* are by far the strongest of O'Neill's search plays of the 1920s, greater than both *Marco Millions* (1925) and *Dynamo* (1928). The playwright's quest to find a replacement for the old God was effectively closed out in 1933–1934 with the production of *Days Without End*. It was officially finished in 1946 with *The Iceman Cometh*.

Brown, Lazarus, and *Interlude* are all known for one or another startling quality. *Brown* makes fascinating use of masks to suggest psychological defenses; in its 420 masked roles *Lazarus* introduces collective types; *Interlude* is given in two parts and nine acts. But, because these plays do not deal primarily in human relationships, and therefore not in issues of guilt and forgiveness, they are not included for study in part 2.

The Great God Brown examines the question of how men and women might best live in harmony with the rhythms of nature. Any attempt to possess things or persons destroys this fundamental harmony; the very desire for possession tends to denature the person: one's relationship with the God of seasons and cycles, Nature herself, is sundered. In an effort to dramatize the concept, O'Neill took bold steps and achieved a high lyricism that he would seldom eclipse. As he wrote to Carlotta Monterey, "[I]t is my pet of all the published plays. There is so much of the secret me in it."[37]

Nearly always this play both fascinates and puzzles its viewers. A problem surfaces because the characters, in repeated masking and unmasking, reveal so many different components of their personalities at different moments in the play. In the most egregious example of this confusion, William A. Brown appropriates the mask of Dion Anthony, his lifelong friend, who has just died. In this (Freudian) act of *introjection,* Brown seeks to convince Margaret, now

Anthony's widow, that he is her husband. The audience, hard-pressed to follow the meaning of his gesture, is required to possess a degree of sophistication that taxes all realistic expectations.

We have already been introduced to the same three characters in the prologue on the evening of their high school graduation. Both young men love Margaret. She is madly attracted to Dion, whom she would make happy by suffocating him: "And I'll be Mrs. Dion—Dion's wife—and he'll be my Dion—my own Dion—my little boy—my baby!"[38] Margaret will domesticate this creative young man, who will throttle his own free spirit in order to enter into marriage with her. The play makes the point that most people are lethally conventional; they do not wish, and will not allow, others to be themselves. On this evening of graduation, however, no one has quite jelled yet. The self-conscious and unimaginative Billy Brown stands little chance in the competition for Margaret. Eventually, in a marriage that produces three sons, Margaret manages to achieve her goal: she smothers Dion Anthony.

Brown, "an uncreative creature of superficial preordained social grooves,"[39] a planner-builder of philistine "palaces" who sometimes employs Dion, true artist and architect, becomes immensely successful. Yet he remains forever envious of Dion's creative powers and his having won Margaret. She never appreciates the ravages Dion has suffered because of his self-betrayal in service to her. She too is "the eternal girl-woman, . . . properly oblivious to everything but the means to her end of maintaining the race."[40] Dion, in the end spiritually depleted and filled with self-hatred, dies in service to Brown (that is, to Mammon), the god of materialism and, as O'Neill sees it, of American success.

To Billy Brown, Margaret as she is would be any man's dream. Having drained Anthony, having used him as a quantitative resource, Brown imitates Dion's "lesser" and fallen self, thinking that will win Margaret. Thus, pleasing Margaret proves costly for both men. Dion Anthony, in his free response to Nature's rhythms, represents the pagan spirit of Dionysius. He succumbs to the "life-denying spirit of [Apollonian] Christianity. . . . " His spirit denatured, Dion has become "a Mephistopheles mocking himself in order to feel alive." Brown destroys himself when, upon Dion's death, he adopts Dion's mask (*persona*), which had been loved by Margaret. "When he steals Dion's mask of Mephistopheles he thinks he is gaining the power to live creatively, while in reality he is only stealing that creative power made self-destructive by complete frustration."[41]

It is all brilliant psychology, relatively new on the scene in the mid-1920s. As Kenneth Macgowan remarked in the original program note: "So far as I know O'Neill's play is the first in which masks have ever been used to dramatize changes and conflicts in character . . . or as a means of dramatizing a transfer of personality from one man to another." Yes, masks allow women and men to protect their vulnerabilities and to play parts that society accepts.

But masks also disfigure, for the habit of wearing them causes a spiritual-emotional bifurcation, a debilitating conflict within the self. The price of the masquerade is that we lose ourselves. Both Dion and Brown kill themselves in their attempts to be what they are not. But Margaret, who has always used a mask to fend off what she chooses not to feel, acts as a force to smother the artist in Dion. For she hates his Dionysian unpredictability, that is, the principle of spontaneity that animates him.

In order to function as men, both Anthony and Brown pay visits to the prostitute Cybel. But O'Neill's sex goddess, like all other characters in *Brown,* is a symbol. Her *"mask is the rouged and eye-blackened countenance of the hardened prostitute"* (III, 279). Since love is cheap, she is assigned the role of the harlot. Even so, because she does not cringe in abject self-effacement before her own natural impulses, she can give herself to the Anthonys and Browns: " . . . I'd like to run out naked into the street and love the whole mob to death like I was bringing you all a new brand of dope that'd make you forget everything that ever was for good" (286). Thus, the power of fecundity is represented more completely by this character than by Margaret, whose hatred of the artist's powers of creating undercuts the generosity of her own creativity. "Cybel," O'Neill insisted, "is an incarnation of Cybele, the Earth Mother doomed to segregation as a pariah in a world of unnatural laws, but patronized by her segregators, who are thus themselves the first victims of their laws."[42]

In the present context the point to be made is that human relationships in *The Great God Brown* cannot develop for two reasons, one dramaturgic, the other psychological. In a play where characters are assigned the function of symbols, there is little room for character development.[43] Further, since each character has learned to "play his part" in the social masquerade, he forgets (Cybel excepted) his natural responses in his learned constrictions. In *Brown* there are no true relationships, although they may exist in narrowly legal terms: child-parent, husband-wife, employer-employee. But, as Travis Bogard points out succinctly, " . . . neither Dion nor Brown finds any genuine human relationship to sustain him."[44] The social effect of these arrangements is to make one uncertain of his own true nature: "Why am I afraid of love, I who love love? . . . Why was I born without a skin, O God, that I must wear armor in order to touch or to be touched?" (264-265). The odd thing is that no one can commit a sin, for sin requires an act of faith. If there is not sin, there can be no redemption of one person by another through acceptance or forgiveness. More important to O'Neill was the idea he wished to advance in this play, a message Cybel is assigned to deliver:

Always spring comes again bearing life! Always again! Always, always forever again!—Spring again!—life again!—summer and fall and death and peace again! (*With agonized sorrow*)—but always, always, love and conception and birth and pain again—spring bearing the intolerable chalice of life again!—(*Then with agonized exultance*)—bearing the glorious, blazing crown of life again! (*She stands like an idol of Earth, her eyes staring out over the world.*) [322–323]

This is faithful Nietzsche, the doctrine of eternal recurrence.

In the play Dionysus, in his name and nature, is defeated by "St. Anthony" (the Christian version of the Apollonian). In *The Birth of Tragedy* Nietzsche made the distinction between two spirits or forces in Greek tragedy. These he called the Apollonian and the Dionysian. The first is the soul's inclination toward order and restraint; it distrusts whatever is unruly or bacchanalian in human nature. In *Ritual and Pathos: The Theater of O'Neill* (1976) Leonard Chabrowe has described very well how Apollo is associated with the sun and therefore with light and reason; how Dionysus is associated with the earth and moon and therefore with the mysteries of nature and night (see especially pp. 3–14). Today, having lost its original Hellenic inspiration, the Apollonian might be seen as akin to Irving Babbitt's and Paul Elmer More's civilizing "inner check."

Nietzsche's description of these powers should not be looked upon as a simple opposition of good and bad, however. He saw that both the Apollonian and the Dionysian are factors in the human equation and that the ancient tragedians sought to integrate them. Furthermore, he recognized that the Dionysian spirit, left unchecked, posed great danger. The Apollonian in his nature reassures man that, through reason, he can achieve at least some understanding of the violence and flux that besiege life. Even so, the rhythms of Dionysus pulse within each person, just as they do in nature itself. Thus, the Greeks brought both the Apollonian and the Dionysian elements of life onto the stage in their great tragedies; and they saw that in the end the Dionysian spirit, even though creative, forever threatened the order men and women attempt to achieve in life. O'Neill associated this Dionysian element with "the creative pagan acceptance of life."[45] The artist had put great faith in the message of his play. Indeed, he confided in a letter to Carlotta Monterey, whom he would marry in 1929, "Yes, one might very well sum up the meaning of *Brown* as my search for God in this life."[46]

One aspect of *Lazarus Laughed* seems quite curious in view of O'Neill's search for an acceptable answer to the modern human dilemma. In his ongoing denial of Christian dogma, he chooses here a clear example of the New Testament promise of resurrection. Jesus' miracle is taken as a given, or at least a starting point, in the story. Thereupon are imposed the teachings of Nietzsche. Perhaps, however, this is no more problematic than to appropriate the *Orestia* myth and attempt to explain it in terms of twentieth-century psychology, as happens in *Mourning Becomes Electra*.

At any rate, O'Neill knew the church was not likely to place its *imprimatur* on *Lazarus Laughed*. Thus he was annoyed with the response of the Catholic hierarchy and said so in a letter to his confidant and producer, Kenneth Macgowan. "The decision of the Catholics, I knew all along, having been one myself. Skinner [*Commonweal* drama critic, Richard Dana Skinner] must be a dull boy—or a bad Catholic—to imagine, after he'd read it, that they'd fall. If they are not stupid, it should hit them as a flat denial of all their fundamental dogmas. So after all—!"[47]

He spoke with the authority of experience. The church would not endorse Nietzsche, whose ideas were even more in the forefront of O'Neill's play this time than they were in *The Great God Brown*. For *Thus Spake Zarathustra* is the fountain from which *Lazarus Laughed* flows. Chief among "their fundamental [Catholic] dogmas," as O'Neill well knew, was the lesson of Ash Wednesday: "Remember, O man, that thou art dust, and unto dust thou shalt return." As both tradition and Catholic doctrine asserted, Christ himself died and was raised from the dead. But through Lazarus (Zarathustra) O'Neill proclaims the death of the old God and the ascendance of a new gospel: *There is no death.* Hence, there is no need of redemption.

The story of Lazarus is told in chapter eleven of St. John's Gospel. Jesus had been the close friend of Lazarus and his sisters, Mary and Martha. When their brother lay mortally ill, the sisters sent for Jesus. In a few days he came, but by then Lazarus had succumbed. In one of the great biblical narratives, John tells the story of Jesus' raising Lazarus from the dead. It is important to recall here that O'Neill is dealing with the account of a miracle, at least as Christians read John's story. Thus Martha, shocked when Jesus commands that the stone be removed from the opening of Lazarus's grave, exclaims: " . . . by this time he stinketh: for he hath been dead four days" (11:39). Jesus first tests Martha's faith and then that of the entire Jewish community. What had Lazarus seen? What had been the experience of death?

O'Neill takes up the story at this point and superimposes on it the philosophy of *Zarathustra*. Confirmed in his vision, Lazarus laughs, a sign of his triumph over death (or, perhaps, over his fear of death). His joy is infectious. First his Jewish neighbors embrace his message, although they quickly divide along the lines of tradition: the elders see their authority threatened by the new teachings. For a time Lazarus stays near his home in Bethany. Eventually he leaves to carry his message of joy to various culture capitals: Athens, Rome, and to Caesar's villa at Capri. Again and again his words at first intoxicate his listeners. Inevitably, however, most cannot sustain a capacity for the good news. First they fall into doubt and then into internecine conflict and then despair. *Men forget.* Even Caligula, a monster of self-indulgence, a sadistic and infantile Narcissus who fears his own death above all possible events, is for a time converted by the incandescence of Lazarus's faith in life. Death is only fear, says O'Neill's Zarathustra, the individual's petty fear in the face of his own extinction.

> Men pass! Like rain into the sea! The sea remains! Man remains! Man slowly arises from the past of the race of men that was his tomb of death! For Man death is not! Man, Son of God's Laughter, *is!* . . . *Is,* Caligula! Believe in the laughing god within you! (I, 359–360)

Women and men need no god other than themselves: Man is God, whose faith is the triumph of life over death. More important than the individual's life is the continuation of the collective life: Man.

The characters, both types and individuals, must wear masks to show the collective prejudices of racial and ethnic groups (their fears growing partly out of their fears of each other). In highly individuated characters like Miriam, the wife of Lazarus, the mask shows life changes, the friction of experience that molds our bodies and psyches. Thus Miriam, devoted but trained in fear and lacking her husband's vision, has lived always in the shadow of death. After his raising, her mask shows her progressive aging as she moves toward the moment of her own death. Lazarus, on the other hand, wears no mask, since the play begins after the miracle and he no longer suffers the ravages of fear that all other mortals do. He no longer needs defensive armor. Indeed, the further he moves, in time, from the miracle but still toward his own inevitable death, the younger he looks. Margaret Ranald makes a very acute point in this regard: "Death is simply the fear between one life and the next. In such a theology there is no room for a punitive or judgmental god, and as a result, one can easily see that this play is really a distinctly subversive piece of work, despite the aspects of Christianity that surround it."[48]

Indeed, one might wonder if any missionary had ever outpreached this O'Neill. For he placed his artistic credibility in the ideas that he came to promulgate in these years. In *Lazarus Laughed* O'Neill took up Nietzsche's philosophy of eternal recurrence: life lives, the cycle continues. He put the idea with admirable cogency in a letter to Arthur Hobson Quinn in May of 1927.

> The fear of death is the root of all evil, the cause of all man's blundering unhappiness. Lazarus knows there is no death, there is only change. He is reborn without that fear. Therefore, he is the first and only man who is able to laugh affirmatively. His laughter is a triumphant Yes to life in its entirety and its eternity. *His laughter affirms God,* it is too noble to desire personal immortality. . . . His laughter is the direct expression of joy in the Dionysian sense, the joy of a celebrant who is at the same time a sacrifice in the eternal process of change and growth and transmutation which is life of which his

life is an insignificant manifestation, soon to be reabsorbed. And life itself is the Self-affirmative joyous laughter of God.[49]

It is a nice question whether an idea alone can provide comfort. Barrett Clark was not inclined to think so. "There is no reason why O'Neill should not try to portray characters in the throes of mental and spiritual torture, but the moment he tries to solve the riddle of the universe he is lost."[50]

Lazarus Laughed, virtually unstageable with its hundreds of roles, is nevertheless a play O'Neill had every right to take pride in. It is a stunning work of the poetic imagination, clear in conception, and executed skillfully on the page. But it has its limitations as a work that throws light on the experience, even the religious experience, of possible viewers. As the playwright himself wrote to Macgowan, "It has no plot of any sort as one knows plot."[51] Well and good, but there is no reason to ponder the meaning of relationships in a work without plot.

Strange Interlude is a marathon play. To pretend satisfactory coverage here would be to invite ridicule. Yet a brief discussion, tailored to the objective of this subsection, allows us to complete this review of plays that culminated in *Days Without End*.

It might appear that *Strange Interlude* offers many opportunities to study character relationships. After all, in its nine acts the play covers a span of twenty-five years (1919–1944). Nina Leeds, heroine and absolutely dominant force, speaks of the satellites who revolve around her as "my men." She means particularly her somewhat fussy and mother-dominated friend, the novelist Charles Marsden; her husband Sam Evans; and her lover, the neurologist, Dr. Edmund Darrell. Strictly speaking her men are six, for Nina might also include her late *fiancé*, Gordon Shaw, World War I air ace shot down over France before the consummation of their bliss; Henry Leeds, her father, who has died by the opening of act 2; and her son, Gordon, who pledges his fealty to the beautiful Madeline Arnold at the end of the play. But generally, the men are her subjects to command, quite willing subjects. Thus, it might appear that the chances for significant relationships abound.

Nina Leeds, twenty years old in the opening scene, quickly catapults into a figure larger than life and is so perceived by the audience. "As she enters the main action of the play she has already begun to take on the appearance and characteristics of woman—with a capital W—to symbolize the Earth Spirit; she is a close relation of Cybel in *The Great God Brown;* she is mother, wife, mistress, adultress, materialist, idealist."[52] Therefore, relationships of a conventional sort simply cannot develop, let alone flourish. It is not so much that Nina seeks to possess each man, although she does seek that; it is more that she is so entirely epic that neither singly nor together can they match her power or will. Nina Leeds is herself God, a Force that shapes life.

Here is a character different from all others O'Neill had created, including Cybel. She occasionally sees "my men" with some degree of affection, even compassion. But the very pronoun "my" implies her possessiveness. She manipulates when necessary, but her inclination is more to absorb and thereby to reshape them to her own purposes. This power on her part colors them with her definition, and they fulfill themselves in fulfilling her needs. For example, virtually without worldly experience but precocious even at twenty, she is already casting Marsden for a part in the far-distant future, for situations she cannot yet even imagine. He cannot see himself as a worthy rival, even to the memory of the lost Gordon Shaw. Nina thinks: "Charlie doggy . . . faithful . . . fetch and carry . . . bark softly in books at the deep night . . . " (I, 14). Later, when she learns that her husband Sam carries the defective genes of his line and that she will have to abort the fetus she carries, Nina enlists the sober physician Ned Darrell to be the father of a healthy child. She speaks to Darrell without admitting to a personal relationship, invoking aloud neither his familiar name nor the diminutive. Her thinking is unnervingly clinical: "This doctor is nothing to me but a healthy male . . . when he was Ned he once kissed me . . . but I cared nothing about him." Her reasoning carries forward with an invincible logic: "I must have my baby! I must take my happiness! . . . Not Ned's child! . . . Not Sam's child! . . . mine! . . . I am a mother . . . God is a Mother . . . " (85, 86, 87, 109, 92). If this is not an example of using another person to fulfill one's own ends, it is hard to imagine what that might be. Nina absorbs men and shapes the life within her in her own image. Nina is God the Creator.

None of this can promote possibilities for a union, of course, any union in which one partner is equal to the other. All wait on her, in every sense of the word. (Marsden will wait for a quarter century, to fill at last the sexless role as her avuncular companion.) Professor Bogard makes precisely the correct assessment, seeing the men as less than persons: "The men, to put the matter bluntly, are not interesting either as types or as more fully realized human characters."[53] They are little more than pieces to be moved about on her board. Nina is the largest and most formidable of O'Neill's life-force creations, a God-Mother wholly self-sustaining, self-involved.

The Great God Brown and *Lazarus Laughed* were mask plays, the masks suggesting a facade behind which to hide or a *persona* that projects an acceptable social role. In *Strange Interlude* O'Neill reintroduced the aside. This device, which had been effectively dropped from dramatic practice since Elizabethan times, permitted a character to disguise her feelings from another character but to reveal her true motivation to the audience. This prop worked for and against effect: *for*, because it revived an ancient theatrical convention and put it in the service of contemporary psychological theory; *against,* because O'Neill overdid it and thereby lessened its effectiveness. Nevertheless, the use of the aside marked another risk the playwright was willing to incur. It would be joined with masks in the production of *Days Without End* a few years later.

But in the "big-subject" plays, human relationships do not form the vital center of conflict and resolution. Rather, these plays dramatize O'Neill's symbols of the life force that will replace the God who has been lost. In *The Great God Brown* one looks for transcendence of pain, or at any rate release from it, in the eternal recurrence of cycles that go on beyond the infinitesimal duration of the single human life. In *Lazarus Laughed* or *Strange Interlude* the forces of nature, or even the Superman or Woman, function as the ultimate force or reality.

The Great God Brown, Lazarus Laughed, and *Strange Interlude* all ride powerful currents of abstraction. In writing these plays, O'Neill made important contributions to the modern theater. As always, his willingness to see his projects through to the end stands as a model of artistic integrity. And one other trait keeps all the idea plays identifiably O'Neillian: each requires of its heroes some commitment of faith, usually faith in some force not visible. That force might be the eternal beneficence of Nature that Cybel sings: "Always spring comes again bearing life" (III, 322). It might be Lazarus's doctrine that there is no death, but only life. Of course, all women and men will encounter tragedy in the end. For, just as the spirit of Dionysus fails in the demise of Dion Anthony; and just as the Hebrews, Greeks, and Romans forget and lose their belief in the message of Lazarus, the tragedy of life is that faith must die. Eugene O'Neill knew this truth from experience. Yet, we might say, he kept faith with faith. As he had written to Sr. Mary Leo, " . . . my thwarted search must have its meaning and use, don't you think, for whatever God may be?"[54]

PART TWO

Catholic Sensibility and Thematic Development

Eugene O'Neill's life in art was more than a dedication to play-writing. Like all such consuming quests, his became an attempt to find God and to know man.

—Travis Bogard

An Introductory Note

I HAVE SAID that Eugene O'Neill retained a Catholic sensibility. This is not the same as saying that, after long years away from the church, he returned to Catholicism. I am speaking of a sensibility, a cultural imprint on memory. After childhood he seems never again to have taken comfort in the teachings of the church. Nor, after his heroic experiments of the 1920s, did he ever again find hope in a mere idea of God. Yet in his development as a tragic writer, O'Neill came to understand what many religions have taught and what would be reaffirmed in Vatican II: one cannot injure another without disfiguring himself. This is what Martin Buber teaches in *I and Thou*. But we know that a never-violated relationship is not possible in our lives. We have not the time, the generosity, or the discipline to keep from hurting each other, and ourselves.

In the chapters that follow I focus on relationships in O'Neill's plays. Characters move toward and away from one another in good will or with an intention to hurt. When pain has been inflicted deliberately, we may say that *sin* has entered the exchange, for that word implies culpability. Out of regard for the dignity of his characters, O'Neill was willing to say that sins are committed and punished in his plays.

Only in relationship is forgiveness needed, and possible. In *A Moon for the Misbegotten* Josie Hogan and Jim Tyrone choose to separate in love at the close of the play. She is by far the stronger force. Indeed, some see reminders of Cybel or Nina Leeds in Josie. It is true that in her largeness of body and spirit she calls Cybel to mind. But, as we will see in chapter 7, Josie has developed according to a different logic, what may be even more natural than Cybel's Earth Mother qualities. Josie possesses a capacity to redeem through forgiveness. It was not necessary to posit mythic powers in her.

In *The Iceman Cometh* the desperate residents of a flophouse support each other's pipe dreams in part because that strategy insures protection of their own dreams. A visiting salesman, in his breezy camaraderie, calls them "brothers and sisters." His words convey more than he knows. In fact, these men and women exist in relationships where, occasionally, one risks his own well-being out of compassion for another. Taking such risks may be the closest we can come nowadays to the heroic gesture. Yet these are risks of love (*caritas*). If I am correct, we may find in some O'Neill plays a humanity that rescues his work from the wasteland of meaningless howls.

4 | Plays: Early Period (1916–1923)

Ile

HERE IS A tragedy in the small. In *Ile*, created in 1917, the playwright gives his first demonstration of a powerful moral imagination. We can see the talent that will be fully vindicated in such plays as *Desire Under the Elms* and *Mourning Becomes Electra*. In this early sea play, in the confinements of one act, O'Neill gives the first signs that he can ply his proclaimed craft. *Ile* develops a significant theme; within its definition, it develops a credible plot; it creates genuine tension; and it presents a convincing background and atmosphere. Much of the work's plausibility derives from the skillfully suggested antecedent action.

The whaler *Atlantic Queen,* on a search for oil, is sailing under the command of Captain David Keeney. Against his better judgment he has given in to the wishes of Annie, his wife, to accompany him on the long sea voyage. As the scene opens the ship has been icebound for a year. Keeney, a hard man, refuses to turn the ship south toward warmer waters, even though the crew's pledge to serve two years is up on this very day. Instead he awaits the thawing of the northern ice, where he intends to pursue the whale and fill his ship with whale "ile." He fears having to return to Homeport empty-handed before his peers. If he is sometimes compared to the obdurate Ahab, Keeney is also different from Melville's captain in one critical respect: he is vulnerable to his wife's pleas for compassion. Indeed this relationship, with its hints of early bliss, conveys credibility, a significant achievement in a work of such brevity. The dominating character, of course, is Keeney, a man of iron will but who had succumbed to his wife's entreaties. (His having brought on board an organ wherewith she might amuse herself suggests a further degree of generosity.) Now, as she stands at the border of insanity, he is torn between his compassion for her and his pride; he wishes to be vindicated as a professional whaler.

Keeney is confronted by a second crisis. Will his second mate, Slocum, stand firm with him against an incipient mutiny? Although the tension is generated in a very short time, it enlists our curiosity. Like Starbuck on the *Pequod,* the mate cautions the captain about pushing the crew beyond endurance. Slocum remains loyal to his chief, however, and the crew back down in the face of this dual resolve. The play thus manages a splendid fusion of dynamics: weather, tension between crew and Keeney, and tension between Keeney and his wife; and the captain's inner struggle as he wrestles with his own pride. Annie, having witnessed the crisis and by now close to hysteria, gives a pitiable account of her loneliness and obtains her husband's momentary pledge to take her home: "I'll do it, Annie—for your sake—if you say it's needful for ye."[1] Then, in a deft stroke, O'Neill turns attention to the natural world:

> MATE. (*excitedly*) The ice is breakin' up to no'th'ard, sir. There's a clear passage through the floe, and clear water beyond, the lookout says. KEENEY *straightens himself like a man coming out of a trance.* MRS. KEENEY *looks at the MATE with terrified eyes.*) . . .
> KEENEY. (*his voice suddenly grim with determination*) Then get her ready and we'll drive her through.
> MATE. Aye, aye, sir. (I, 550)

Keeney tries to defend his logic and justify his decision, in the face of Annie's abject protestation: "Woman, you ain't adoin' right when you meddle in men's business and weaken 'em. You can't know my feelin's. I got to prove a man to be a good husband for ye to take pride in. I got to git the ile, I tell ye" (550).

His words are simultaneously brave and cruel. Keeney is wrong, even if (in *his* way) O'Neill is in sympathy with him. Margaret Ranald contends that *Ile* is really "a paradigm of the artist, to whom dedication to his calling is all-important."[2] This is a perfectly valid reading, if we have made certain assumptions. In the present study, however, we are mining a different lode. The focus on relationship compels a harsh reading of David Keeney's moment in the crucible. To judge severely but fairly, *Ile* is a paradigm not of artistic integrity but of betrayal. Like many a tragic figure, Keeney behaves, paradoxically, in a manner both admirable and ignoble. One thinks of Macbeth, as he buckled on his armor, who could not take time to mourn his wife's suicide. In a similar way, Keeney's fate is ironic because, in one view, it is heroic. Yet his pride has become a wedge that separates him from that person he loves most dearly. Keeney is no monster. Rather, he is a man, at once intimidating and noble, but not virtuous. That, indeed, is what both fascinates and frightens us. For, in confronting tragic characters, we cannot simply write them off as ghouls. Further problem: because *Ile* is merely a sketch, we hesitate to speak with full authority. Even so, we feel a need to close the case. David Keeney strikes us as a supremely gifted man, but also as being deeply flawed.

Given the luxury of aesthetic distance that O'Neill himself did not possess in 1917, we may see in Annie Keeney a certain foreshadowing of Mary Tyrone.[3] She has fallen in love with an idol: "I used to dream of sailing on the great, wide, glorious ocean. I wanted to be by your side in the danger and vigorous life of it all. I wanted to see you the hero they make you out to be in Homeport. . . . I guess I was dreaming about the old Vikings in the storybooks and I thought you were one of them" (545–546). Her break with sanity seems inevitable. As the curtain falls, Annie's mad playing at the organ recalls to us the frail Mary Tyrone's broken rendering of Chopin. Thus the ending will not be taken as ridiculous melodrama but as a coherent and logical closing down of the action.

The theme is focused on a lethal pride that makes the self the center of reality. In Keeney's baleful judgments, the crew is left to be damned and marital integrity to be sacrificed. We are paralyzed before such arrogance, even as we are constrained to admire its absolute unwillingness to bend. Keeney is made on the nineteenth-century romantic model. Here is a kind of majestic madness, reminiscent of Ahab shouting down Starbuck: "Talk to me not of blasphemy, man; I'd strike the sun if it insulted me." We know Keeney's sin is a form of egomania which, when mixed with bravery, causes us to tremble. Within the limits of givens, O'Neill's characters behave according to the logic of their motivation. The conclusion is appropriate and plausible. Because there is no fully developed denouement in *Ile*, there can be no redemption. At most a need for expiation is implied.

The play is a successful exercise, the sort that O'Neill had mastered by 1920 and that gave him the confidence to launch into full-blown dramas like *Beyond the Horizon*. He would make many a false step in the decade to come, some of them clumsy. But with him the American theater would also take giant steps forward. His apprenticeship in one-acts had honed O'Neill's talents. After *Ile*, he had earned the right to be called dramatist.

Beyond the Horizon

Why should a play that begins in hope open at sunset, a clear reversal of traditional symbolism? And why should a play that closes with the hero's death end at dawn? These seeming incongruities merely emphasize the oddity of this particular entry in the catalog of American drama. The "reviewers to a man," says Travis Bogard, complained of the play's structure. It should have been pruned and cut back. Indeed, the running time of the first performances was nearly four hours. Even so, the critics gave *Beyond the Horizon* overall glowing reviews, and audiences supported it in consecutive showings at the Morosco, the Criterion, and the Little Theatre through a total of 111 performances. Moreover, this vehicle that blends naturalistic philosophy with poetry was awarded the Pulitzer Prize, O'Neill's first of four. "The play seemed a work of a new and vital imagination, and its success was unquestionably valid. Cer-

tainly the play is the first major work of the O'Neill canon. It is fully charac-
teristic. It is also a clearly 'American' play, and thus an important 'original.' "[4]

After *Beyond the Horizon,* O'Neill would often retell a story of brothers,
sometimes literal siblings, sometimes representatives of a divided personality
(*Desire Under the Elms, The Great God Brown, Days Without End, Long
Day's Journey into Night*). That it was strongly influenced by Irish dramatists
(St. John Ervine in *John Ferguson* and T. C. Murray in *Birthright*) seems unde-
niable, but that interesting story cannot be taken up in these pages.

In one of those twists of family destiny that forever fascinate writers,
Robert and Andrew Mayo exchange life plans. Therewith they blight their
own and others' relationships and fortunes. Robert, who has wished always to
travel "beyond the horizon" to discover the source of dreams, has about him
"the touch of the poet." He is a man of the book. His hardier brother, Andrew,
"a son of the soil," good-naturedly scoffs at Robert's wanderlust. James Mayo,
their father, can spare the poet, who is of little help to him anyway. But he
prizes Andrew, a natural farmer. Andrew and Robert both love their childhood
friend, Ruth, but each assumes that she and Andrew will marry. When Robert
confesses his love to her, Ruth responds, "I don't love Andy. I don't. . . . Whatever—put such a fool notion—into your head?" (III, 91) This dissuades the
dreamer from embarking on a three-year sea voyage. He announces to his family that he has decided against leaving because he and Ruth love each other.
After a fitful coming to terms, Andrew announces that he will take Robert's
berth aboard ship. In each case the decision conflicts with the young man's
nature and proclivities.

The long-term effects are to poison all relationships. Ruth and Robert in
marriage will grow to loathe one another: she, essentially prosaic and practi-
cal; he, having sacrificed his dream to undertake what he is ill fitted to do,
farming. The marriage turns out to be a disastrous union. A child, Mary, becomes a further burden to Ruth, who must also care for a whining and bedridden mother. Robert destroys both the farm and his own health by giving up
his dream of finding whatever beauty there is beyond the horizon. To his
brother he had said, "You're wedded to the soil. You're as much a product of
it as an ear of corn is, or a tree. Father is the same. This farm is his life-work,
and he's happy in knowing that another Mayo, inspired by the same love, will
take up the work where he leaves off. I can understand your attitude, and Pa's;
and I think it's wonderful and sincere. But I—well, I'm not made that way"
(84). Andrew, having disappointed his father who curses him, betrays his vocation and becomes a speculator in land instead of its preserver. Each one loses
him/herself. The theme is ancient: the artist (in each of us) can be preserved
only by keeping faith in his own visions. This is as true for the son of the soil
as it is for the poet. Neither man can thereafter have compassion for Ruth, who

has, without conscious intent but for her own selfish interests, diverted the brothers from their true careers.

Andrew returns years later, having lost through greed most of the money he had made speculating in grains. The child has died; James Mayo has died an embittered man; Ruth has grown into a gnarled and sullen robot, and Robert, his health broken, lies at the gateway to death. Rimmed in by the black hills, forever denied his desire to see the greater world, Robert weakens visibly. He has lost his beloved mother, who had given him comfort; and he has lost his daughter Mary, who had been his single domestic happiness. Now, apparently, he seeks fulfillment only in what lies beyond death.

Each man, Andrew and Robert, has sinned against himself and against his brother. Although they had recognized their differences, each had respected and even felt affection for the other's values and temperament. In the beginning Andrew, who joshed Robert about his reading and impracticality, had his brother's best interests at heart. "You want to go—that's all there is to it; and I wouldn't have you miss this chance for the world" (84). And Robert had appreciated his brother's and father's love of the soil. Their fraternal bond is to be severely tested, of course. For, in violating his own nature, each man sins as well against the other. In the end their mutual love is redeemed, even if it can never be restored as it had been. It is part of O'Neill's skill to establish the logic for this dynamic near the end of act 1. Andrew has been deeply bruised by Robert's winning of Ruth but seeks to avoid bitterness.

> ROBERT. (*in a frenzy of rebellion*) Why did this have to happen to us? It's damnable! (*He looks about him wildly, as if his vengeance were seeking the responsible fate*). . . . Andy! Oh, I wish I could tell you half I feel of how fine you are!
> ANDREW. (*interrupting him quickly*) Shut up! Let's go to bed. I've got to be up long before sun-up. You too, if you're going to drive us down. . . . (*He slaps his brother on the back. ROBERT does not move. . . . ANDREW bends over and blows out the lamp. His voice comes from the darkness*) Don't sit there mourning, Rob. It'll all come out in the wash. Come and get some sleep. Everything'll turn out all right in the end. (110–111)

The punishment for failure to live one's own destiny seems clear enough. In a sense Robert's sin is that he gives away his harmony with life. If this behavior does not constitute an offense against the Decalogue, it seems nevertheless to stunt his natural generosity and openness of spirit. Although he had never been robust (he was, in fact, a sickly child), he had been prepared to go on a search for beauty. In a misguided step, he yields to an impulse to marry Ruth. She too makes the mistake of confessing love to him. Later he tells Andrew that he never loved Ruth. She in her turn, growing to despise his incompetence and "weakness," becomes spiteful like her querulous mother. In choosing to work the land, a task for which he is not suited, Robert destroys his health and purpose in life.

But Andrew's violation is greater, in Robert's view. Andrew has denatured himself: "You—a farmer—to gamble in a wheat pit with scraps of paper. There's a spiritual significance in that picture, Andy. . . . I'm a failure, and Ruth's another—but we can both justly lay some of the blame for our stumbling on God [fate?]. But you're the deepest-dyed failure of the three, Andy. You've spent eight years running away from yourself. Do you see what I mean? You used to be a creator when you loved the farm. You and life were in harmonious partnership" (161).

Robert, who possesses by far the greatest insight among the three, knows that he and Ruth have suffered justly. And he sees that Andrew cannot find peace until he too accepts his guilt. Even as he is dying, he is concerned for the welfare of the two who are closest to him.

> ROBERT. I want you to promise me to do one thing, Andy, after—
> ANDREW. I'll promise anything, as God is my Judge!
> ROBERT. Remember, Andy, Ruth has suffered double her share. (*His voice faltering with weakness*) Only through contact with suffering, Andy, will you—awaken. Listen. You must marry Ruth—afterwards. (162)

Both Ruth and Andrew at first reject the idea as absurd. They argue when Ruth confesses that she had told Robert, on Andrew's earlier visit, that she had loved him and not Rob. Andrew points out how cruel that was.

In a final scene, very short, Robert has left his deathbed and crawled out to the highway, where the play opened. The farm appears in great disrepair, all life having shriveled. Robert moves to the top of a bluff to see better the sun rising over the horizon. He tells Ruth and Andrew, who have come after him, that they should not mourn him; at last he will be "free to wander on and on—eternally! I've won to my trip—the right of release—beyond the horizon! Oh, you ought to be glad—glad—for my sake! . . . Andy! Remember Ruth— . . . Ruth has suffered—remember, Andy—only through sacrifice—the secret beyond there—" (168). He dies. Andrew curses Ruth who, for once, complains justly: " . . . he knew how I'd suffered too." Andrew sees the truth of this, and he forgives both of them: "Forgive me, Ruth—for his sake—and I'll remember. . . . I—you—we've both made a mess of things! We must try to help each other" (168).

*   *   *

From his earliest years as a playwright, O'Neill was alive to the mystery of human suffering. In all his plays he ponders its meaning. Like Dostoevski, he wonders, does it mean anything. Can suffering have a value, for assuredly much of it seems stupidly degrading, pointless, and dispiriting? It should be stated forthrightly that, as O'Neill gradually achieved insight into the mystery, he struggled early to express his understanding. *Beyond the Horizon* cannot be counted a technical achievement. Its arrangement of scenes seems noticeably arbitrary and mechanical: two scenes in each of three acts, one inside and one outside the farmhouse. Even so, the play shows an advancement in the symbolism he had established in the one-acts and would perfect by the end of his career. This is the symbolism of light and dark, of day and night. In *Beyond* this presence suggests the compatability of the artist's vision with his long-formed sensibility. I mean that his striving to express experiential knowledge appears less awkward. What he learned is that human error can be uplifted by suffering. Put another way, sin can be forgiven and the value of human life redeemed. And Eugene O'Neill, who found it hard to live in community, always recognized the necessity of relationship.⁵ If we injure others, we have probably committed the offense within the context of relationship. It is in the same crucible that we learn to forgive others, and ourselves.

The play comes full circle. The end is in the beginning, on the country road (the poet's "road not taken"). The difference is that now it is an autumn dawn, not a spring sunset. "It isn't the end. It's a free beginning—the start of my voyage!" (168).

All God's Chillun Got Wings

This play marks an important advance in both the craftsmanship and the intellectual content of O'Neill's work. His understanding of human psychology, already evident in *The Emperor Jones* (1920) and *The Hairy Ape* (1922), had deepened. In the earlier plays he had shown considerable sophistication in the use of Jungian theories, but in them he had focused on the single and isolated personality. With *All God's Chillun Got Wings* O'Neill moved into the complexities of a difficult human relationship. The story is traced from its inception in the characters' childhood through the stages of their adult (and often pathological) conflict. One party injures the other deliberately. The effect of such behavior (*sin*) is damage to the integrity of their marital relationship.

Because O'Neill put his sin-and-redemption comment on the record (in 1946), we can be certain that he was in earnest. Given his understanding of these terms, moreover, and given his Catholic grounding, we can infer that he was saying something about the mystery of human relations. No play of his reveals this sense of mystery more than does *All God's Chillun Got Wings*. In this respect, and perhaps in others, the play stands as an important document.

Two children from opposite sides of the street are found holding hands. She is white, he black: Ella Downey and Jim "Crow" Harris. They hold hands both as a sign of natural affection and as a pledge of mutual protection. Other children, because the fever of prejudice rages in them, have taunted the little friends. Later Ella will continue to love Jim, but she will also terrify him, and be herself terrified: " . . . the husband and wife are deeply committed to one another and yet are divided by a profound sense of alienation which prevents their happiness."[6] On this street (it might be called Division Street) no satisfactory antitoxin for the malaise has been discovered. The sickness is general throughout the neighborhood, which has itself become an incubator of the virus. The culture itself is infected.

Jim and Ella carry this virus, of course, but have not yet known its full power to disfigure their souls. Thus they are still beautiful children, but no longer innocent. In a "neighborhood" where black is formally divided from white, innocence is no longer possible, not even for an eight-year-old. In this world a germ is planted early in the chambers of the heart, the seed of America's most pernicious and lethal malady: racism. One of the effects of this sickness is the learned habit of seeing the world as divided: "reality" is we/they. In the neighborhood are introduced the lessons of intolerance. Because hatred and mistrust are inevitable products of the we/they view of things, the first traces of interracial tissue-ties are poisoned before a strong bond can develop. The disease is highly communicable. Any relationship can be subverted: friendship, family, and marriage.

Indeed, *All God's Chillun Got Wings* demonstrates how the conjugal union itself can be corrupted by suspicion, envy, even paranoia. A general debility may be studied as a social condition: alcoholism, for example. Yet all *isms* are in the end abstractions. One cannot attack an *ism* as one attacks a body. A human being is not an abstraction, nor is a relationship. Each is a dynamic presence in the social organism. The environment (the house) may be contaminated. But only an individual person can sin or be punished for sin. Just so, only the individual penitent can be redeemed.

The first of two acts presents a sort of fast-forward overview of the social organism. In this part of *All God's Chillun* we see how quickly the soul can be disfigured. For then we see what a struggle it is for love and self-respect to thrive in a climate of fear and intimidation. In effect, one is taught to feel shame for his worthier impulses.

In scene 1 we discover a community where blacks and whites are visibly separated. Strains of music drift into the street. The whites seem to be imprisoned in their "gilded cages"; the negro songs are less restrained, the people *"frankly participants in the spirit of Spring"* (I, 301). The children are permitted to play together in a sort of no-man's land of the street, but they too have already been conditioned to know that whites feel superior. Jim, who has a crush on Ella, accepts this "truth," but she cannot yet see it. By scene 2, nine years later, a sense of differences has become internalized. The psychological divisions created by these turf-identities have now become pronounced. Jim "Crow" is alternately condescended to and despised for seeking, through education, to become "white." Ella, who seems to have accepted "reality," joins in the public shaming of Jim and makes it known that she is the girl of the bully pugilist, Mickey. Even blacks hate Jim's academic ambitions.

> JOE. Listen to me, nigger: I got a heap to whisper in yo' ear! Who is you, anyhow? Who does you think you is . . . ?
> JIM. (*dully*) I'm your friend, Joe.
> JOE. No, you isn't! I ain't no fren' o' yourn! I don't even know who you is! What's all dis schoolin' you doin'? What's all dis dressin' up and graduatin' and sayin' you gwine study to be a lawyer? What's all dis fakin' an' pretendin' and swellin' out grand an' talkin' soft and perlite? What's all dis denyin' you's a nigger—an wid de white boys listenin' to you say it! Is you aimin' to buy white wid yo' ol' man's dough like Mickey say? (311)

In scene 3 another five years have passed. Predictably, Mickey has taken from Ella what he wanted. She has had a child, been deserted, fallen into prostitution to survive, and suffered the death of the child. She is approached by Shorty, Mickey's messenger, who offers her money so "Yuh won't make no trouble." Ella sees now that her single friend has been Jim, "the only white man in the world. Kind and white" (314). These two recognize their mutual needs and pledge to save each other.

Jim Harris follows the straight and narrow. He does not find it difficult to play by the rules; indeed, he prefers to do that. Jim hopes to succeed and thereby, in the approved way, to earn his highest possible place in society. As his dreams take on new dimensions, the image of lawyer becomes an obsession, becomes his idealized conception of himself. He lacks nothing in endowment—neither intelligence nor integrity, but he suffers a debilitating lack of self-esteem. To vindicate and fulfill his need to serve, Jim will place himself in a kind of bondage to Ella Downey. He tells her he is ready "to become your slave!—yes, be your slave—your black slave that adores you as sacred!" (*He has sunk to his knees. In a frenzy of self-abnegation, as he says the last words he beats his head on the flagstones*) [318]. Jim has given Ella a kind of power that, when the virus breaks out in her, will further demean him.

Scene 4, the shortest in the play, shows Jim and Ella emerging from the church, married. Neither side of the street has approved of this union. *The doors slam behind them like wooden lips of an idol that has spat them out. JIM is dressed in black, ELLA in white. . . . They stand in the sunlight, shrinking and confused* (319–320). It is worth noting that the church, shown and symbolized in the background, constitutes almost no force in the play. One cannot say confidently what precisely O'Neill intended. But we get the impression that religion provides no balm to soften human conflicts. Religion constitutes no ameliorating factor in race relations. It offers no civilizing influence, nor does it effectively instruct the faithful in how to treat one another with respect. The Christian law of love seems altogether irrelevant in the lives of "all God's chillun."

Following their wedding, Jim and Ella depart for France. Accepted with neither hostility nor fanfare, the couple experience a relative peace for a time. O'Neill makes here an implicit judgment on American racism, of course. But act 2 of *All God's Chillun* does not constitute a tract on race relations. Rather, in Jim's and Ella's marriage, the play examines the strain the culture places on partners in a love relationship. The scars from their premarital experiences are still massively present, of course. The effect of an intensely personal act 2, then, is to bring an important psychological and philosophical question to the surface: Raised helter-skelter, as they have been, can a marital partner be considered responsible for her acts of betrayal, or is the virus too powerful to be resisted? Is personal sin plausible in the modern order: and redemption?

* * *

When Jim and Ella return fom abroad, they are greeted in their new flat by Jim's mother and his sister, Hattie. The young husband and wife are quite tentative, since they have returned to reclaim a place in *their* world. Ella is especially unnerved and defensive, filled as she is with shame. Had she married an "inferior" man only because she had no alternative? Did the white world still claim her loyalty? Jim for his part must once again prepare to take the bar examination to prove himself, even in the face of black disapproval.

Jim's mother, who wishes to be kind, is nevertheless uncomfortable in the role of mother-in-law and uncertain how to treat Ella. Hattie, a "new" woman, educated and assertive, demands her rightful place in an unjust world. In Hattie, O'Neill has created a strong minor character, a black feminist in advance of a type to become quite familiar in the 1960s. Proud of her African heritage and confident in her intellectual liberation, Hattie will have little tolerance for Jim's willingness to serve an uppity white girl who offers nothing in achievement or credentials. A clash is inevitable. In the flat Hattie has placed a Congo mask, her wedding gift, which she describes as "a work of Art by a real artist—as real in his way as your Michael Angelo" (328). Jim, aware of his sister's capacity to intimidate, is prepared to send Hattie away. Ella, on the other hand, is desperate to assert her racial superiority. She calls the mask ugly and stupid. Furthermore, she declares, "Jim's not going to take anymore examinations. I won't let him" (329). This boldness simultaneously infuriates Hattie, discourages her mother, and perplexes Jim. When mother and sister depart, however, and Ella no longer feels threatened, she can allow Jim to become her "equal" again. She can even encourage him but remind him subtly of who and what he is.

> Don't cry, please! You don't suppose I really meant that about the examina-
> tions, do you . . . ? I want you to take the examinations! I want you to pass!
> I want you to be a lawyer! I want you to be the best lawyer in the country!
> I want you to show 'em—all the dirty sneaking, gossiping liars that talk be-
> hind our backs—what a man I married. I want the whole world to know
> you're the whitest of the white (329).

Ella, who shows every symptom of infection, is now a carrier of the cultural sickness. To what extent is she responsible for her acts? O'Neill has taken
pains to describe the origins, symptoms, and effects of the disease. The difficulties of human relationship as presented in act 2 are by far more complex than
those of act 1. In the first instance O'Neill has dramatized the sociological dynamics of racism, a necessary background but by definition a generalized statement. In act 2 we observe the psychological and spiritual devastation visited
upon a union weighed down under familiar cultural *impedimenta*. Given Jim's
and Ella's acute sensibilities, we see more clearly the implications of O'Neill's
examination of relationship. The pressures of the world press upon the individual. The demands for social conformity play a powerful role in shaping
the marriage. Such forces undeniably affect the dynamics of relationship, but
O'Neill does not permit the sharpness of his point to be blunted. His artist's
allegiance is to the mystery of the person and therefore of the relationship into
which the person is drawn. Nothing, then, is at last simple; nothing can be
explained by mere generalization. In one sense sin is socially engendered: *The
sins of one generation are visited upon the next.* One possible effect of this
phenomenon is the manifestation of guilt in the collective soul. This concept,
of course, has permitted our introducing in the first place the metaphor of cultural virus and disease in the body politic. And no doubt a great truth under-
girds this idea. But, if the person can be thus reduced to helpless victimhood,
we might question the value of dramatizing any such episode.

All God's Chillun offers a striking vindication of O'Neill's remark so often
cited in this study. Individual susceptibility to the virus may be a form of social
conditioning. Yet in the end sin is personal. One makes deliberate moves, even
in her weakened state. Is this really so different, in effect, from the concept
of *original sin?*[7] Perhaps one's commitment to a particular theological explanation—Calvinist, Catholic, whatever—is not the point. In the tradition of
Christian literature, from Dante to Bunyan, from Milton to Hawthorne, the
idea of sin's appeal is represented in the doctrine of original sin. If the *dramatis
personae* are to be drawn with fidelity to (fallen) human nature, if character is
to retain the mystery of personhood, the artist who creates must possess moral

imagination. In some of his plays, one may argue, O'Neill's figures are closer to puppets than persons. A character who is no more than an idea is a mere abstraction. But Jim and Ella are spiritually and psychologically "right," which is to say convincing.

Ella becomes quite ill, alternately depressed and panicked. As Hattie tells Jim, "The doctor said Ella's liable to be sick like this a very long time. . . . She'd get better so much sooner if you'd send her away to some nice sanitarium—" (333–334). When the mask begins to appear larger and the room smaller, we see the power the mask has taken on and the sense of entrapment that Ella feels. This distortion will be credited to expressionistic technique, but the effect intended is psychological realism. Ella must conquer African power, represented by Hattie, the mask, and by Jim too (even if he has offered to be her slave). Thus, by calling Jim "Nigger" and stabbing the mask, she "defeats" black power. Jim's power, however, such as it is, lodges in a real man. If he can conquer his fear of breaking the taboo by taking white power, he will have become Ella's equal, even her superior, in her world. He feels guilt for betraying his people, but his "failure" may actually stand to Jim's credit. For his allegiance is more to love than to symbolism. He truly loves Ella, who tries his devotion to the last measure by her self-indulgence and sickness.

The play's resolution touches on an ever-difficult problem for the playwright: the issue of determinism and freedom. Is anyone responsible for his own fate? In words that have now become famous, Mary Tyrone suggests that no one is to blame: "None of us can help the things life has done to us. They're done before you realize it, and once they're done they make you do other things until at last everything comes between you and what you'd like to be, and you've lost your true self forever" (*LDJ*, 61). Her words no more than Jim Harris's are necessarily O'Neill's. Even so, if Mary's view is insisted upon without qualification, no character can be a *bona fide* tragic figure. Like any other brokenhearted person in despair, Jim wants to place the blame for his defeat on forces outside himself: on God, if it must be that way. Near the end of the play, he achieves both his lowest and highest moments of manhood. Ella asks if the mail has brought news of his passing the bar examination. He grovels in self-mockery: "Good Lord, child, how come you can ever imagine such a crazy idea? Pass? Me? Jim Crow Harris? Nigger Jim Harris—become a full-fledged Member of the Bar! Why the mere notion of it is enough to kill you with laughing!" (339–340). Ella, pleased by this "good" news, elicits his homicidal wrath for the first and only time: "You devil! You white devil woman! (*In a terrible roar, raising his fists above her head*) You devil!" (340). Ella, recognizing for once the evil of her words, asks Jim if God will forgive her. "Maybe He can forgive what you've done to me; and maybe He can forgive what I've done to you; but I don't see how He's going to forgive—Himself" (341).

The power and clarity of O'Neill's endings, not always given due credit, are often quite stunning. And this play's resolution is quite affecting. Jim admits that people are to blame for some of their woes. But he also insists that certain causes of human failure derive from other sources: from God, if it must be put that way. Our lot is governed in part by forces the individual cannot control. As we have seen earlier, O'Neill put the matter as clearly as he could in his letter to Arthur Hobson Quinn: "Fate, God, our biological past creating our present, whatever one calls it—Mystery, certainly."[8] The answer then is to be found neither in mere naturalistic determinism nor in the sinful wilfullness of tragic characters ("None of us can help the things life has done to us"). But equally important is what we have done to ourselves and to each other. For that we have reason to feel guilt, to see that atonement is called for, and to seek our own and each other's better estate. Jim and Ella do this and, in so doing, gain a measure of tragic enhancement. Ella's mistreatment of Jim, whom she loves, cannot be assigned to her sickness alone. Yes, she is riddled with prejudice; yes, she assumes her culture's superiority in order to justify her "weakness" in allowing herself to be rescued by Jim. But she loves him, and he knows that. Moreover, Ella, even in her "madness," is capable of admitting her responsibility (guilt). After Jim has nearly injured her, he slumps in a chair, exhausted: "I'm tired," he says. "I haven't had much chance for sleep in so long—" Granted, Ella's response is somewhat giddy, but she says the appropriate words of contrition: "I know, Jim! That was my fault. I wouldn't let you sleep. I couldn't let you. I kept thinking if he sleeps good then he'll be sure to study good and then he'll pass—and the devil'll win. . . . Will God forgive me, Jim?" (341).

Who is to say what redemption means in a context such as this? Men and women who love each other injure each other. Even our indifference to those we are committed to cherish (let alone our abuse of them) constitutes a fault. In the traditions of the Old and New Testaments, the point is made many times: e.g., "Honor thy father and thy mother"; again, "Love each other as I have loved you." O'Neill, who spoke for neither tradition, had nevertheless been formed in a climate where these Judeo-Christian values were fostered. Their echoes reverberated in the chambers of his memory. Thus, while his commitment to the sin-and-redemption theme carries no doctrinal weight, it does suggest cultural ties.

Redemption, I suggested earlier, constitutes no more (and no less) than a disposition of the heart, a renewal or recovery of the heart's state before a rupture in relationship occurred. Jim, in the terrible recognition of impending tragedy, responds to her need. She confesses to him her fear that she will not live long. "Then I won't either," he says. "Somewhere yonder maybe—together—our luck'll change. But I wanted—here and now—before you—we—I wanted to prove to you—to myself—to become a full-fledged Member—so you could be proud— . . . *he is beyond tears*" (341).

In what vaults of the human heart are such words stored? Only a man with compassion still alive in him could have written with such authority. For such words, he knew, would very likely break some hearts, but not all. Only a brave man would chance being misunderstood by a foolish world. Whence derives such a soul?

5 | Plays: Middle Period (1924–1933)

Desire Under the Elms

IN THIS PLAY the question of relationship is difficult but very important. On the surface we discover connections that seem germane to the overall theme of this book: filial, sibling, and conjugal ties. But several of these can be defined as relationships only in narrow, legal, or technical terms; they suggest no dynamic interaction. The only bond between Ephraim Cabot and his older sons, Simeon and Peter, is mechanical: by providing them room and board, Cabot in turn receives their labor. If any feelings are exchanged between patriarch and offspring, they may be called contempt and indifference. None has any emotional investment in the other that would cause him to grieve upon losing the other's companionship. Functionally, then, their association is little more than that of boss to hired hand. When Simeon and Peter leave for the California gold fields, they are effectively forgotten: "Out of sight, out of mind." Dismissed at the end of part 1, their subsequent fate excites neither wonder nor curiosity of father or brother.

Ephraim and Eben can hardly be said to have a meaningful father-son bond. They share few values, except in their desire for the Cabot farm and, later, Abbie Putnam, Cabot's third wife. Eben, Ephraim's only child by his second wife, hates his father for "stealing" his mother's farm: "An' fur thanks he killed her" (I, 207). That is, he worked her to death. Eben believes that the land, in justice, belongs to him as his mother's only heir.

Relationship is possible if at least one party has some connection with the other that would cause him to feel personally diminished by the loss of the other. To put this another way, something of love or affection must have once existed, even if it is now virtually erased from memory. But neither man here sees any reason to value the other's personhood. Each sees certain animal powers or skills in the other, but little that is human and admirable. Cabot spits out his contempt: "Ye'll never be more'n half a man" (227). Interestingly, neither sees in the other the power and force of character that O'Neill sees in each. The playwright admired Ephraim's willingness to identify with and accept God's hardness and loneliness. Even if he could not approve the Puritan ethic Cabot espoused, he recognized in it a genuine virtue. Cabot speaks with the righteousness of earned authority as he looks back on his single journey west to gain land and wealth.

> We came t' broad medders, plains, whar the soil was black an' rich as gold. Nary a stone. Easy. Ye'd on'y to plow an' sow an' then set an' smoke yer pipe an' watch thin's grow. I could o' been a rich man—but somethin' in me fit me an' fit me—the voice o' God sayin': "This hain't wuth nothin' t' Me. Git ye back t' hum! . . . God's hard, not easy! God's in the stones! Build my church on a rock—out o' stones an' I'll be in them! That's what He meant t' Peter! (*He sighs heavily—a pause*) Stones. I picked 'em up an' piled 'em into walls. Ye kin read the years of my life in them walls, every day a hefted stone, climbin' over the hills up and down, fencin' in the fields that was mine, whar I'd made thin's grow out o' nothin'—like the will o' God, like the servant o' His hand. It wa'n't easy. It was hard an' He made me hard fur it. (237)

Eben, equally committed to his concept of justice, has set about to right the wrongs done to his mother, who he feels was swindled by Cabot: "I hold him t' jedgment" (207). To Abbie, whom he sees at first as his rival to inherit the farm, he protests, "I'm fightin' him—fightin' yew—fightin' fur Maw's rights t' her hum! . . . An' I'm onto ye. Ye hain't foolin' me a mite. Ye're aimin' t' swaller up everythin' an' make it your'n. Waal, you'll find I'm a heap sight bigger hunk nor yew kin chew!" (229). Obsessed as each man is, he is blind to the considerable formidability of the other. In effect, therefore, relationship is not possible, if no memory of something shared can be evoked in either. Tissue links cannot be reestablished, since neither believes any have ever existed.

Abbie's marriage to Ephraim is little more than a legal arrangement. She looks upon him as a means by which she will establish herself in his "hum" and will take possession of Cabot's "jim-dandy farm" when he dies. She feels no love for him, certainly not carnal desire. Indeed, his slightest intimate gesture or attempt at physical contact between them causes Abbie to feel disgust: "*She shrinks from his touch*" (252).

Yet each party in this odd *ménage à trois* stands as one of O'Neill's splendid creations. The three seem destined to suffer yet "command sympathy, not because they are victims of forces they cannot control, but because they are capable of choice and responsibility."[1] This says something of immense importance, for it places *Desire Under the Elms* in a fully legitimate context of tragedy. In modern drama Ephraim and Eben Cabot and Abbie Putnam take on a stature larger than life. In the sheer force of their self-assertion and in their willingness to implicate themselves in their own fate, they invite comparison to other great figures of dramatic tragedy. If their language is homespun and coarse in the country ways of pre–Civil War America, their speeches nevertheless ring true to the time and world in which they are placed. Cabot had sinned in his earlier years, when he foresook the hard life for an easy, almost slothful life of farming the fertile loam of the West. He accepted God's judgment and returned. But in his sin he had injured no man but himself. The sins of Abbie and Eben result in the destruction of their issue. The law's judgment on them will be harsh; God's judgment would be fierce. But their own judgment of themselves is most terrible, and wonderful, of all. In this dimension they vie with giant figures of classical drama. O'Neill gives us a portrait of partners in sin who work out their redemption and who, within a modern context, evoke echoes of classical tragedy. The relationship of tragic dimensions in this play is that between Abbie and Eben, and no others. " . . . [O'Neill] formed a story in a typical tragic pattern: his characters follow a course of sin and redemption in recognition of error and the assumption of responsibility."[2]

We are well into this play before any substantial relationship develops between Eben and Abbie. They recognize their strong attraction first in part 2, scene 2, and consummate it in the next scene. But the logic that explains these moments had been well established in the final scene (4) of part 1. In their first meeting each senses a threat from the other. Both want the farm, Eben's claim having been long grounded in familial blood and history. She first sees him, however, as part of the farm and therefore part of her implicit claim: "*Her eyes take him in penetratingly with a calculating appraisal of his strength as against hers. But under this her desire is dimly awakened by his youth and good looks*" (225). She strikes Eben as incredibly bold in confessing to him her aims: "Waal—what if I did need a hum? What else'd I marry an old man like him fur? . . . This be my farm—this be my hum—this be my kitchen! . . . " (226). She represents a formidable challenge to Eben's autonomy, an important factor in making her later appeal plausible: "(. . . *putting her hand on his arm—seductively*) Let's yew n' me be frens, Eben."

> EBEN. (*stupidly—as if hypnotized*) Ay-eh. (*Then furiously flinging off her arm*) No, ye durned old witch! I hate ye!" (227)

The stage is set for torrid love-making, brought on by the disorienting dizziness that inevitably attends high passion. But what begins in lust will end in love, with all the important implications that attend such a transformation.

Is Abbie an early Cybel, a vital feminine force who pledges allegiance neither to cause nor to God, but only to life itself? Her watchword to Dion is the declaration of her own *modus vivendi:* "Life's all right, if you let it alone" (III, 280). Interestingly, Cybel the harlot lusts for nothing; and she is owned by nothing or no one she takes pleasure in. She sees little value in competition. When Dion complains at his poor luck in cards, she reminds him that his desire is the kind that spoils *joie de-vivre:* "You keep getting closer, but [your luck] knows you still want to win—a little bit—and it's wise all I care about is playing" (285).

In certain ways Abbie Putnam is also a powerful feminine force, capable of sweeping Eben off his moorings. His primary desires have been to vindicate his mother's memory and to possess "her" farm. Now is activated a desire for this intruder's flesh. Abbie appears to be a force larger than life, stronger than either Ephraim or Eben. The story is more complex than a brief history of her elemental passions, however. Dion Anthony calls Cybel "Miss Earth," and we may wonder if such a name suits Abbie. It does, and it doesn't. To be sure, Abbie emits a white heat of sexual passion; in this she has the power of allurement. And, long dispossessed, she lusts to possess. In her moral nature, however, Abbie is very different from Cybel, who operates without regard to the standards of conventional morality and seems altogether uninhibited by assaults of conscience. The golden-hearted prostitute can hardly be understood in terms of typical capitalist motivation to own either a person or property. But *Desire Under the Elms* is in many respects a commentary on the American lust to possess. Because Abbie is capable of sin, her possibilities for analysis are infinitely more complex than Cybel's and, therewith, more interesting. Cybel is an amoral force. In the beginning Abbie is an immoral force; she ends by admitting her guilt and accepting punishment.

In responding to a letter of inquiry, O'Neill remarked on his intentions in this play. "*Desire*, briefly, is a tragedy of the possessive—the pitiful longing of man to build his own heaven here on earth by glutting his sense of power with ownership of land, people, money—but principally the land and other people's lives. It is the creative yearning of the uncreative spirit which never achieves anything but a monetary clutch of failing fingers on the equally temporal tangible."[3] Abbie, as we come to see, transcends her lusts and achieves tragic stature.

* * *

Perhaps all great drama, especially tragedy, must suggest the rapid but believable passage of time. This illusion, which requires the "suspension of disbelief," can be produced only by a master craftsman. Here the partners come together, as much in lust as in affection, conceive a child, endure the pregnancy, and suffer the infant's loss at an age of less than one month. We are moved from the summer (1850) through *late spring of the following year.* In tragedy all things natural, and unnatural, must convince of their own possibilities. A mother's suffocating her own baby surely constitutes an unnatural act. In Abbie we may be reminded of the daunting will of a Medea or Lady Macbeth. But we will believe only in what the storyteller makes credible in terms of the motivation of his characters. O'Neill set himself a high challenge in *Desire Under the Elms*.

In a riveting scene the build-up to sexual union is rendered with remarkable efficiency. "*The interior of the two bedrooms on the top floor is shown*" (235). In one room Cabot and Abbie sit on the edge of the bed. He introduces his desire for a son and thus of their having relations. She wishes to secure the farm but thinks of the act only in connection with Eben, whose presence she feels penetrating the wall that separates them. Their physical awareness of each other is virtually palpable. It is interesting that, although he continues speaking, Cabot feels nothing of the moment's passion. Indeed, feeling only a chill, he decides to repair to the barn: "It's cold in this house. . . . They's thin's pokin' about in the dark, in the corners." He says he will go to the barn, " . . . whar it's warm. . . . I kin talk t' the cows. They know. They know the farm an' me. They'll give me peace" (238). He leaves and Abbie enters Eben's room. After a moment of passionate embrace, Eben reverts to his earlier distrust and pushes her away. She, after a brief argument, pushes boldly for her desire. She tells him that she will wait for him in the parlor, a room sealed against entry since the day of his mother's funeral. Its penetration will have both adulterous and incestuous implications. Eben protests but "*stands swaying toward her helplessly.*"

> ABBIE. (*holding his eyes and putting all her will into her words as she backs out of the door*) I'll expect ye afore long, Eben. (240)

Thus is their desire for each other's flesh consummated: in the room where the ghost of his mother has, Eben feels, waited for release through love. Abbie attempts at first to play the dual role of mother and lover (foreshadowing a later Josie Hogan).

> EBEN. . . . She was kind. She was good.
> ABBIE. (*putting one arm over his shoulder. He does not seem to notice—passionately*) I'll be kind an' good t' ye!
> EBEN. Sometimes she use t' sing fur me.
> ABBIE. I'll sing fur ye!

But this chaste sympathy cannot be sustained.

> ABBIE. (*both her arms around him—with wild passion*) I'll sing fur ye! I'll die fur ye! (*In spite of her overwhelming desire for him, there is a sincere maternal love in her manner and voice—a horribly frank mixture of lust and mother love. . . . Then suddenly wild passion overcomes her. She kisses him lustfully again and again and he flings his arms about her and returns her kisses*) [242–243].

Yet even here, consumed by passion, Abbie makes clear her willingness to defy the moral law if that is required to win Eben's love: "Vengeance o' God on the hull o' us! What d' we give a durn? I love ye, Eben! God knows I love ye" (244).

Eben returns the sentiment. He sees that he has defeated Ephraim. Even though he recognizes the dual elements of his sin (adultery with Abbie and the violation of his mother's memory), Eben feels a sort of exhilaration. For a time he is even willing to call a truce with Ephraim: "Yew 'n' me is quits. Let's shake hands" (246). He gains neither affection nor respect from Cabot, however: "A born fool!" And Ephraim Cabot is a formidable and resourceful man. In another argument about who owns the farm, the old man shrewdly tells his son of Abbie's earlier agreement to have a son and of her desire to turn out Eben: "An' she says, I wants Eben cut off so's this farm'll be mine when ye die! (*With terrible gloating*) An' that's what happened, hain't it? An' the farm's her'n! An the dust o' the road—that's you'rn! Ha! Now who's hawin'? (255). These are all such prosaic and predictable events in family feuding that we are amazed at O'Neill's capacity to make the terrible derive from the natural. The anger Eben feels in his assumption that he has been duped is also plausible, for it is wholly in accord with his behavior since the opening of the play. When Eben, enraged, accuses Abbie of plotting to have her son "steal" from him, she utters a dark prophecy: "He won't steal! I'd kill him fust! I do love ye! I'll prove it t' ye . . . !" (258).

The sin is terrible, but tragedy examines such extremes of human error and capability. Furthermore, something is greater than the sin and crime that Abbie commits. What is noble can actually be more awful than what is evil. Here again we confront the mysteries possible in human nature. The veil of the temple was rent in the great sacrificial moment of the New Testament. The steady gait of the "Hound" who seeks to reclaim His "lover" terrifies the one in flight. Both her ownership of her deed and her willingness to accept punishment make fair the claims of Abbie's love. Eben's need to share and to acknowledge his part in driving her to infancticide impresses even the "jedgmental" Cabot: "Purty good—fur yew" (269).

Sin is punished. Ephraim himself, having faltered, knows that his God requires suffering. For he has injured his own sense of integration with being and thereby suffered, and knows he has suffered a kind of personal diminishment. He will miss Abbie and Eben, if in nothing more than their presence on the land. Having discovered that Eben has "stolen" his hidden money in buying off Simeon and Peter, he reflects: "I kin hear [God's] voice warnin' me agen t' be hard an' stay on my farm. I kin see his hand usin' Eben t' steal t' keep me from weakness. I kin feel I be in the palm o' His hand, His fingers guidin' me. (*A pause—then he mutters sadly*) It's a-goin' t' be lonesomer now than ever it war afore—an' I'm gittin' old, Lord—ripe on the bough. . . . (*Then stiffening*) Waal—what d'ye want? God's lonesome, hain't He? God's hard an' lonesome!" (268).

But the greater glory is Abbie's and, by the power of her example, Eben's.

More than once they have violated the integrity of relationship. (One hesitates to call it sacred.) On the first and conventional level, they have committed adultery and, in their own eyes, have thereby broken the law. Great violations of the natural law are the way of things in tragedy. But violation and punishment alone do not effect a satisfactory working out of things, especially in this time when (to Krutch, O'Neill, and so on) the ancient religious meanings of drama no longer obtain. The characters must be not only willing to suffer but also able still to see a human propriety in the law. The sheriff who comes for them is no representative of such a law.

Although we can find no valid theological meaning in the end of *Desire Under the Elms*, we find a logic that derives from an understanding that was formed by faith in a deity. Because O'Neill had been raised in a puritanical Irish Catholicism, he may have been inclined to follow the lines of this logic. The Cabots' moral sensibility has been formed by a New England Calvinism, which retained an Old Testament understanding of God. Ephraim has always admired this God, whom he saw as contemptuous of human self-pity. Even Abbie and Eben, once driven only by their individual selfishness, acknowledge the gravity of their sin and therewith accept their punishment as just. Their sensibilities are not, as it turns out, so different from Ephraim's. That is, they too have been formed by a strong religious tradition.

To O'Neill there remains firmly ensconced in the human consciousness a sense of an inevitable moral reciprocity in the nature of things. By embracing her guilt, Abbie comes to see the efficacy of suffering: "I got t' take my punishment—t' pay fur my sin" (266). In nearly contrapuntal tones, Eben joins in: "I got t' pay fur my part o' the sin! And I'd suffer wuss leavin' ye, goin' West, thinkin' o' ye day an' night, bein' out when yew was in—(*Lowering his voice*) 'r bein' alive when yew was dead. (*A pause*) I want t' share with ye, Abbie— prison 'r death 'r hell 'r anythin'!" (267). In these speeches we hear echoes of Greek tragedy, but we also recognize familiar Christian strains. Redemption is still understood in terms of an act of suffering accepted in good grace. Men and women save each other's humanity.

As they depart in the custody of the sheriff "*in attitudes strangely aloof and devout*" (269), the sun is shining. Their willingness to atone confirms their value as human beings. *Redemption takes place.*

Mourning Becomes Electra

By 1930 Eugene O'Neill had become a major figure in world drama, rivaled perhaps only by Shaw among contemporaries. He had established himself as a bold innovator, a playwright who was willing, indeed eager, to experiment with new forms and techniques. His plays had already been performed for a decade in world capitals: Stockholm and Berlin, Moscow and Paris, London and Dublin. O'Neill's celebrity was registered in the wide recognition of his very titles: *The Emperor Jones, The Hairy Ape, All God's Chillun Got Wings, Desire Under the Elms, The Great God Brown,* and *Strange Interlude.* But his greatest achievement would be mounted on Broadway in October of 1931 and quickly thereafter on stages across Europe.

In *Mourning Becomes Electra* O'Neill had attempted to imitate the Greeks he so admired. In both form (trilogy) and theme (a retelling of the House of Atreus myth), he hoped to restore the grandeur of classical dramatic art. Did he achieve his end? As in all things that touch O'Neill's reputation, the reviews are mixed. Robert Brustein has called the results "a tabloid version of the *Oresteia.*"[4] Krutch, on the other hand, declared that one must go to Shakespeare to find a worthy comparison. Despite the widely contrasting evaluations, however, the play's success has been generally acknowledged. Indeed, it seems clear that *Mourning Becomes Electra* gave Eugene O'Neill his place in the pantheon. "It did more than any other single play to win the Nobel Prize [in 1936]," he wrote to Theresa Helburn. "In every capital of Europe where it was done before the war it was an event. And it still goes on, despite the war, 13 years after your [Theatre Guild] production, and it will go on."[5]

Devoted as he was to his Greek mentors, however, O'Neill was not unwilling to rework their materials. In 1928 he entered this passage in his work diary: "Greek plot idea—give modern Electra figure in play tragic ending worthy of character. In Greek story she peters out into undramatic married banality. Such a character contained too much tragic fate within her soul to permit this—why should Furies have let Electra escape unpunished?"[6] He knew well that the art of tragedy demanded more than a psychological treatise offered in the form of a play. It required moral intelligence and imagination. If a modern version of the story were to be true to its Olympian model, it must honor the idea of fate. Does such a concept imply a belief in the supernatural? And must not tragedy take as valid the laws of sin and punishment? O'Neill says no to the first question, yes to the second.

The play's parallels to Greek legend have been frequently studied, of course: Berlin, Bogard, Brustein, Heilman, Krutch, Porter, and others. But let us supply a brief review and sketch these parallels once more. In the *Oresteia* Aeschylus brings the warrior-hero Agamemnon home from Troy only to be victimized by his wife's perfidy. In O'Neill's *Electra* Union general Ezra Mannon returns to his unfaithful wife Christine (Clytemnestra), who with the help of her lover, Adam Brant (Aegisthus), poisons Ezra. The Mannon children, Lavinia and Orin (Electra and Orestes) punish the adulteress by murdering Brant and thereby driving Christine to suicide. A year later, plunged into melancholy and guilt for his part in his mother's death, Orin takes his own life. Lavinia inflicts an even harsher sentence on herself. When she discovers that she too had loved Brant and had been envious of her mother's love for Adam and Orin, she consigns herself to lifelong immurement in the family mansion, "a temple of Hate and Death."

What had O'Neill hoped to accomplish in the modern *Electra?* In 1926 he had wondered whether it was "possible to get [a] modern psychological approximation of Greek sense of fate into such a play, which an intelligent audience of today, possessed of no belief in gods or supernatural retribution, could accept and be moved by."[7] To be sure, the playwright had found his paragon in the genius of Aeschylus. The discussion that follows, however, is grounded equally in the belief that O'Neill's understanding of guilt may be located in the spiritual insights of Catholicism. Since the modern story can introduce no ineluctable divine plan, we may well ask what shapes the destinies of these characters. They are driven both by the inherited history of their family and by their own inner dynamics, appetites, and complexes. To O'Neill these forces constitute an equivalent of fate, what Normand Berlin calls determinism.[8] The most powerful determining factor, however, seems to be guilt. Sin and punishment make up a part of the blueprint, but the characters are apparently denied the graces of redemption. I am saying that redemption does not take place in *Mourning Becomes Electra.* Yet O'Neill achieves in his trilogy a success of such stunning magnitude that his very "failure" deserves the highest credit. Perhaps the reader will tolerate a reminder of Krutch's observation: "O'Neill is almost alone among modern dramatic writers in possessing what appears to be an instinctive perception of what a modern tragedy would have to be."[9]

*   *   *

Mourning Becomes Electra is a modern analogue to the *Oresteia.* Its setting in the time of the American Civil War provides coherence, but the play focuses less on matters of American history than on perennial issues of familial discord and individual psychological calamities. O'Neill's Agamemnon has some classic proportions: Ezra Mannon is a patrician, a member of New England's Brahmin caste. Bound in duty to the nation and the commonweal, he has been immensely successful as ship builder and packet-line owner, lawyer, mayor, and judge. As Seth, family servant for decades, puts it, "He's able, Ezra is! Folks think he's cold-blooded and uppish, 'cause he's never got much to say to 'em. But that's only the Mannons' way. They've been top dog around here for near on two hundred years and don't let folks fergit it" (II, 7–8). His military service in the Mexican War has fitted him to serve under Union commander Ulysses S. Grant as a brigadier general. Competent if not brilliant, Mannon has by the war's end been described by Grant as "old stick" [stick-in-the-mud] for his tenacity and unwillingness to surrender his ground.

True to his type, Mannon is governed by an inner check, all spontaneity and outward signs of pleasure throttled by a killjoy spirit. Fixed on the things of death, he seems strangely animated by mortality, as all Mannons are. In the war, he says, reflecting on death seemed to liberate him: "Death was so common, it didn't mean anything. That freed me to think of life. Queer, isn't it? Death made me think of life. Before that life had only made me think of death" (53). Although he has been uncomfortable in the role of husband, he waxes nearly lyrical on his hope for improved relations with Christine.

> I can't get used to home yet. It's so lonely. I've got used to the feel of camps with thousands of men around me at night—a sense of protection, maybe? (*Suddenly uneasy again*) Don't keep your eyes shut like that! Don't be so still! (*Then, as she opens her eyes—with an explosive appeal*) God, I want to talk to you, Christine! I've got to explain some things—inside me—to my wife—try to, anyway! (*He sits down beside her*) Shut your eyes again! I can talk better. It has always been hard for me to talk—about feelings. I never could when you looked at me. Your eyes were always so—so full of silence! That is, since we've been married. Not before, when I was courting you. They used to speak then. They made me talk—because they answered.
> . . . I came home to surrender to you—what's inside me. I love you. I loved you then, and all the years between, and I love you now. (53, 55)

Christine, like her prototype Clytemnestra, is beautiful, willful, and daring. While Mannon was at the front, she has taken Adam Brant as her lover, with whom she now plots Ezra's murder. She can think of Mannon only in terms of his brutal lust on their wedding night. Forever after she connects Lavinia, conceived in that lust, with disgust for Ezra. On the other hand, Christine loves and pampers her second child Orin, whom she bore while Ezra was serving in Mexico. This child rekindled in Christine associations of sex with love and pleasure. Lavinia reveres her austere and authoritarian father; Orin adores his high-spirited mother who recalls to him Melville's islands in *Typee,* the lushness, fertility, and heat of a tropical paradise. (Indeed, all the Mannons have fantasies about the "Blessed Isles," which symbolize for them all freedom and love uncontaminated by lust.)

Adam Brant is actually a Mannon cousin, the son of Ezra's uncle David, disowned by his brother Abe for marrying "a lowly Canuck nurse girl" of dazzling beauty, Marie Brantôme. Thus, although Lavinia hates him both for his lowly origins and for his affair with Christine, she is unconsciously attracted to him who is, in features, so like her father and brother. When later Orin murders Brant, he stares at the corpse: "By God, he does look like Father" (115). Brant too, captain of a clipper *Flying Trades,* has love dreams of the "Blessed Isles," the place of ultimate escape and sinless passion. He had planned to take Christine there, after Ezra's funeral.

* * *

Mourning Becomes Electra presents seven major relationships: husband-wife, wife-lover, father-daughter, father-son, mother-daughter, mother-son, and sister-brother. On one level, then, the play appears exceptionally complex in the interlocking of the characters' fates. In this *Electra* presents the most complicated set of relationships in the O'Neill canon. Three of these ties are dissolved with Ezra's death of "natural causes" in *Homecoming*. Three others are ended in *The Hunted,* with Brant's murder and Christine's suicide. Of course, just as Ezra's spirit hovers over the remainder of the trilogy, so does Christine's influence the events of *The Haunted.* The surviving Mannons, Orin and Lavinia, are the "haunted" of the third play. After Orin's suicide in act 3, the great Electra figure closes the trilogy. (It is interesting to note that Seth, the main choral figure, has the last word, a technique that harkens back to Greek practice.)

Yet, even with its impressive classical parallels, a strange spiritual lethargy attends this play. The relationships in *Mourning Becomes Electra,* for all their legal and traditional legitimacy, lack the dynamic power that permits normal growth and development. Enveloped in a climate of hatred and suspicion, hostility and guilt, intimacy and healthy exchange are frustrated again and again. Guilt, deriving from habitual rejection of intimacy, *can* be helpful when it assists healing, reconciliation, and sympathy. Let us recall Thomas Porter's cogent remark noted in chapter 2: "When we look at tragedy from a distance, the pattern emerges; stripped to its essential framework, *the tragic action is a movement from guilt through suffering to purgation and insight.*"[10] This, Porter explains, characterizes the guilt-purgation dynamic in classic tragedy. In O'Neill's *Electra,* however, the atmosphere of death-in-life is so pervasive that health-inducing properties of love cannot develop. Guilt cripples when it registers contempt for one's very nature (the "sin" of being born, the "crime" of being human). Here is a by-product of narrow Calvinistic puritanism, which has been the spiritual nourishment of the Mannons. Everywhere in this play a character hates life, for he/she sees that life produces only paralysis, sickness, or feelings of disgust. Ezra can never take satisfaction from his sacrifices or performance because these have been inspired only by a rigid sense of duty. A generous response to person (wife, son, daughter) or to cause (the Union, the commonweal) derives from a principle of spontaneity or joy in serving. But the Brahmin, Ezra explains to Christine, has merely been conditioned to respond:

> That's always been the Mannons' way of thinking. They went to the white meeting-house on Sabbaths and meditated on death. Life was a dying. Being born was starting to die. Death was being born. (*Shaking his head with a*

dogged bewilderment) How in hell people ever got such notions! That white meeting-house. It stuck in my mind—clean-scrubbed and whitewashed—a temple of death! But in this war I've seen too many white walls splattered with blood that counted no more than dirty water. I've seen dead men scattered about, no more important than rubbish to be got rid of. That made the white meeting-house seem meaningless—making so much solemn fuss over death! (54)

Christine associates home and marriage with death. "I felt our tomb needed a little brightening," she says to Lavinia, as they await the General's return.

(*She nods scornfully toward the house*) Each time I come back after being away it appears more like a sepulchre! The "whited" one of the Bible—pagan temple front stuck like a mask on Puritan gray ugliness! It was just like old Abe Mannon to build such a monstrosity—as a temple for his hatred. (17)

She associates her conjugal relations with a lack of joy, something mechanical and obligatory: "Duty! How often I've heard that word in this house! Well, you can't say I didn't do mine all these years. But there comes an end" (45). Lavinia would deny herself the normal expectations of womanhood because "I've got my duty to Father" (45).

A war background is appropriate for this *Electra*, since conflict and death constitute the focus. But explicit connections to the Greek-Trojan War, or even the American Civil War, are not in the end crucial. To O'Neill the heart of the matter was the psychology of the family and, therefore, of men's and women's most intimate relationships. As he wrote to Robert Sisk:

Don't get the idea there is a lot of the Greek stuff in this. There isn't much as a matter of fact. I simply pinch their plot, as many a better playwright has done before me, and make of it a modern psychological drama, realistic and not realistic at the same time. I use the plot because it has greater possibilities of revealing *all* the deep hidden relationships in the family than any other—and because Electra is to me the most interesting of all women in drama. But I don't stick to the plot even. I only use some of its major incidents. The rest is my own.[11]

Death makes up the main moments and events in the trilogy: the countless deaths associated with the background of the war; Ezra's poisoning by Christine and Adam, Brant's murder by Orin and Lavinia; Christine's and Orin's suicides. "Death becomes the Mannons" (94), Orin has said. Lavinia, steeped in the constraints of her rearing and the perpetual ambience of gloom, remarks mordantly to Seth near the end of the play, "You understand, don't you? You've been with us Mannons so long! You know there's no rest in this house which Grandfather built as a temple of Hate and Death" (171). Her death-in-life punishment will be to survive in this crypt as the last of the Mannons; she will atone for her own sins by willingly enduring a fate worse than death: she will forever be reminded of every macabre nuance of Mannon history.

*   *   *

Several important questions remain, if we wish to follow the theme of this study. For example, how shall we explain the spiritual impotence of these exceptionally gifted characters? At bottom, what conditions work to preclude the joys and satisfactions, indeed all the normal expectations, that their talents can be expected to promote? Because this is a large question, I should like to ground the solution in a large assumption: For O'Neill, all that is worth talking about eventually comes back to the matter of "faith," faith in the importance of relationship. Denied the psychological comfort that belief provides yet knowing that we live now "without benefit of [the] supernatural," *Electra's* men and women are not prepared to enter full (we might call them mature) relationships. This is because, without faith in another person or cause, one stands naked, vulnerable, and paralyzed. In *Mourning Becomes Electra,* because blood or love partners approach each other spiritually impoverished, their relations tend to become morbid.

As modern readers we can hardly miss O'Neill's wasteland theme in this connection. His Civil War characters, still impressive in their own sheer power, will eventually peter out in such hollow souls as Mildred Douglas (*The Hairy Ape*) and Charles Marsden (*Strange Interlude*). In *Electra's* historical setting, they antedate Eliot's Prufrock and Gerontion and Fitzgerald's Daisy and Tom Buchanan. Every reference to the wasteland theme is a reminder of modern spiritual paralysis: Gerontion's "word within a word, unable to speak a word." Paul had said that the greatest virtue was love (*caritas*). Who will dissent? Yet, with trepidation, one wishes to suggest that an equivalent virtue is faith (*fides*). Perhaps these qualities are at last difficult to distinguish, anyhow: Love for another, faith in another. Is there a difference? Keeping faith may be no less difficult than practicing love. At any rate, those dynamic virtues necessary to mutual growth cannot fructify in the Mannon soul: nor can goodwill flourish, the goodwill that promotes a sense of security; nor can unqualified sympathy, which makes possible forgiveness. The point is that modern life has denied faith in its own value. This given, the individual lacks faith not only in self but also in any other to whom he might commit himself, for any reason, unconditionally.

A year before the idea for *Mourning Becomes Electra* had come to him, O'Neill had responded to a letter from his friend, Sr. Mary Leo (Tierney), O.P.

She had suggested that, to find material for his plays, he reread the *Lives of the Saints:*

> I write tragedy. . . . It is only those who are ignoble in themselves who cannot appreciate the nobility of tragedy. It is only by suffering in the suffering of others that *we can save ourselves,* is it not so? . . . I must confess to you that for the past twenty years almost, (although I was brought up a Catholic, naturally, and educated until thirteen in Catholic schools), I have had no Faith. Therefore, my interpretation of the lives of the Saints would be purely of their nobility as men and women, their essential characters as human beings, without bias either one way or another as to the truth of their doctrine. I'm afraid such a neutral attitude would be liable to be misinterpreted by Catholics in general, especially if they were aware that the author had once professed the same Faith as theirs. Such resentment would be only human on their part.[12]

*   *   *

The trilogy presents several issues that require attention at this point. Despite the Mannons' apparent ties to New England puritanism, for example, the dynamic power of religion hardly exists in the trilogy. Religion certainly has no life-giving force, its only representative being the shallow and petty Rev. Hills. Even more significant, the workings of guilt in individual psyches are almost entirely debilitating. In a world where faith is dead, of course, guilt will almost surely deepen the spiritual malaise. Purgation cannot be experienced. Most assuredly redemption, in any meaning of the term, will not take place. Therefore, in the apparent number of important relationships (seven in *Electra*), we *seem* to confront the greatest complexity in all of O'Neill's plays. But these relationships as such are not necessarily the most complex (unless we take "complex" only in a narrow psychological sense). To put this another way, the characters in themselves and in their relationships are not so complex as are the characters in *Long Day's Journey into Night*. The "four haunted Tyrones" are vastly more complicated human beings than the two survivors in *The Haunted*. Creations of genius, the Mannons nevertheless strike us in the end as abstractions. They are pseudo-mythic, while the later Tyrones are realistic. This is not the same as saying that the characters in *Electra* are zombies of no interest to us. Several of them are quite formidable — Christine, Mannon himself, and Lavinia. But the latter two are spiritually stunted, their potential for virtue benumbed, their capacity to love frozen. Nevertheless, let the record show the international high regard for *Mourning Becomes Electra*. The overall coherence of this modern classic is so impressive that most critics have acknowledged that it deserves a place in the catalog of world masterpieces. And because he held with such fidelity to his high intentions, with *Electra* O'Neill took a convincing step toward the Prize.

If we should have reservations about the trilogy, then, they have to do not with its greatness of scope. Nor in the end is it the credibility of the characters that denies them full tragic stature. Rather, what they are *not* given constitutes their limitations. Macbeth and his Lady are able to perpetrate monstrous deeds only because they can progressively anesthetize their consciences. But in their love for each other they compel our deep sympathy. We *believe* in the king's broken heart upon receiving the report of the queen's suicide. Why is it (for this seems to be the case) that no character in *Mourning Becomes Electra* elicits our deep sympathy? This response is even stranger if we hold, like Krutch, that O'Neill's trilogy comes as close to achieving the greatness of Greek and Shakespearean tragedy as anything produced in the last century. Then what is lacking? Many argue that the play's language is not equal to the play's august theme. Yet, even if we accept this judgment, we do not find it a fully adequate explanation. The full explanation, I will venture, can be found in the characters' lack of faith in their own relationships. We do not find in the Mannon relationships that gift of unconditional acceptance that betokens the grace of union. This gift Macbeth and his Lady do exchange, and we honor that exchange.

Because the Mannons are modeled on mythical figures, they tend perforce to seem larger than life. And, for all O'Neill's effort to keep them accessible to "an intelligent audience of today," the task proved impossible. Patterned on heroic figures but given motivations derived from Freudian theory, these characters slip too easily into abstraction and thereby lose something of plausibility. When the Greeks estimated their gods and demigods, they agreed that these heroes *were* larger than life and lived above the laws that governed mere mortal beings. Therefore, we find it difficult to see the Mannons (the very name suggests Man) as governed by the laws and customs that shape mass man. Indeed, encouraged to see themselves as "top dog," they could hardly fail to think of themselves as remote from the group. To possess economic, political, and social power over the community for decades (nay, for centuries) tends to elevate the family from the plateau of equality to the heights of dynasty. Both Mannon and Lavinia express grief for the slain President, as good citizens might be expected to do. Yet are we not taxed to believe that they can feel the same devotion for the man "of the people" as that conveyed by Seth, their servant of three score years? O'Neill set for himself a mighty task indeed, for his scheme requires a superimposition of Greek mythic history on the American democratic experiment then not yet one century old. Even granting the brahminism that obtained in this "New England small seaport, shipbuilding town," the audience is asked to suspend a considerable measure of disbelief.

O'Neill thought he could bring it off and keep "a lot of the Greek stuff" out. But neither audience nor reader can quite forget the basic allusion to a mythic world. In fact, before the curtain rises, the title itself reminds us that we are about to enter the House of Atreus.

*   *   *

The mystery of Greek drama resides in the world above cloud-capped Olympus, a zone shielded from the sight of mortals. A constant in classical tragedy, but a force absent from modern attempts, is the impact of religion on the lives of the characters. Do Shakespeare's tragic figures sense such a presence? Hear Macbeth:

> I go, and it is done; the bell invites me.
> Hear it not, Duncan, for it is a knell
> That summons thee to heaven or to hell.
>   (II, i, 62–64)

After his conference with the ruffians who will murder his friend, Macbeth recognizes the meaning of his sin:

> It is concluded. Banquo, thy soul's flight,
> If it find heaven, must find it out tonight.
>   (III, i, 142–143)

Again, listen to Hamlet's lament:

> O . . . that the Everlasting had not fix'd
> His canon 'gainst self-slaughter!
>   (I, ii, 131–132)

Santayana once wrote an essay on "The Absence of Religion in Shakespeare." If we bring together Shakespeare and O'Neill, for whatever reason, we will usually agree that the former is the greater. He is indeed the genius of the millennium. Even so, we might not agree that O'Neill is Shakespeare's inferior if judged by the intensity of his religious sensibility. The great burden for O'Neill, however, or for any other modern, is that faith is seldom an operant factor in modern drama, except in morality plays like *Murder in the Cathedral* or *A Man for All Seasons*. In *Winterset,* even Anderson's pious rabbi Esdras doubts the efficacy of his "wisdom." If these be fair observations, they tell us much about men's present understanding of their earthly plight. Krutch was correct: faith does not move modern women and men.

For all its nineteenth-century Puritan background, therefore, *Mourning Becomes Electra* hardly touches upon the power of the New England church. The clergyman who calls on the Mannons, First Congregationalist Everett

Hills, D.D., is merely a lightweight gossip worthy of dissection by Sinclair Lewis or H. L. Mencken. When such men represent the depth and charity of religion, we are compelled to see the churchman as a fool.

As O'Neill describes the Mannons' world, men and women have available to them no rites of confession, sacramental or secular. They can neither be forgiven nor effectively forgive. The play is not so much about guilt as it is about what to do with guilt. Without recognized rituals of absolution, men find it difficult to throw off their burdens of shame. If Hawthorne's Salemites fanned the fires of public confession into lurid voyeurism (e.g., "Young Goodman Brown"), in *Electra* the need to unburden is blocked. The culture might produce heroes like Mannon and Lavinia, but it could not invest them with faith in the value of their sacrifices. "They went to the white meeting house on Sabbaths and meditated on death" (54). The drama critic for *The Catholic World*, Euphemia Van Rensselaer Wyatt, felt the author had failed in his bid to vie with Aeschylus. But she "always had faith in the outcome of O'Neill because he has recognized unflinchingly the difference between right and wrong and never failed to see that s-i-n spells sin." She gained, moreover, a high stylistic eloquence in her estimation of the play's atmosphere of doom:

> The green front door with its knocker becomes as ominous as the great brass portals of the *Agamemnon*. The doorway in the Mannon drawing room frames with sepulchral dignity the black robed figure of Lavinia. And how full of foreboding is the straight and stern young Lavinia of Miss Alice Brady! For once she has a part worthy of her force. Her quiet dominance is as magnificent in its way as the gliding grace of Nazimova as Christine with her lies, her passion and despair.[13]

Heroes possess virtues not possessed by their lesser counterparts, of course, at least not possessed in the same degree. Ezra and Vinnie are at once the play's most distinguished personages and the least accommodating and flexible. They alone have the power to meet the challenges of tragedy without whimpering. The General, who sees his limitations, can acknowledge the *rigor mortis* that has stiffened the Mannon soul. Even so, he musters sufficient resources of character in his attempt to connect via the approved rubric of marital exchange. But a successful confession requires a compassionate listener. Unfortunately, Christine refuses to listen sympathetically to Ezra's conciliatory words; she dismisses his gesture as a *gaucherie*.

> MANNON. Something keeps me sitting numb in my own heart—like a statue of a dead man in a town square. (*Suddenly he reaches over and takes her hand*) I want to find what that wall is marriage put between us! You've got to help me smash it down! We have twenty good years still before us! I've been thinking of what we could do to get back to each other. I've a notion if we'd leave the children and go off on a voyage together—to the other side of the world—find some island where we could be alone for a while. You'll find I

have changed, Christine. I'm sick of death! I want life! Maybe you could love me now! (*In a note of final desperate pleading*) I've got to make you love me!

CHRISTINE. (*pulls her hand away from him and springs to her feet wildly*) For God's sake, stop talking. I don't know what you're saying. Leave me alone! (55–56)

That O'Neill understood the sacred character, and the power, of intimate exchange is demonstrated elsewhere in his work, perhaps most convincingly in *A Moon for the Misbegotten* and *Long Day's Journey into Night*. If he had gained his appreciation of tragedy from the Greeks, his sensibilities had already been shaped by his Catholic training. This combination of resources made possible his peculiar sensitivity to the mystery of human relationship. Characters in his plays who can listen to another (Anna Christopherson, Jim Harris, Larry Slade, Josie Hogan, the elder James Tyrone, and others) are capable of generosity and love. Perhaps O'Neill gained this knowledge more from experience than he did from reading, more from his religious sensibility than from Aristotle and Nietzsche. Such a knowledge of deep human needs suggests that his Christian sensibility was never cancelled: his sensitivity to the presence of guilt, the need to confess, the hunger for redemption. This presence, it is important to repeat, is not the same thing as belief. As he had written to Sr. Leo, "I have . . . no Faith." But it suggests that an experience of faith, even though it was lost, was kept alive in his memory and enhanced his insight.

Brant and Christine are driven more by hatred than by love. Indeed, their own love, although they desire a return to pagan innocence, conveys the scent of lust. Orin, whose maturity has been retarded by his mother's pampering, develops little capacity to fulfill another's needs. All three of these characters seem to be arrested in a state of adolescent selfishness.[14] Travis Bogard includes father and daughter in this state: " . . . Lavinia, Christine, Orin, Ezra and Adam are placed in a crucible. They are concerned with nothing but themselves, and even that concern is limited to the psycho-sexual problems which they all fatally share."[15] This characterization may be too harsh with respect to Ezra and Lavinia. If they are not activated by love, at least they are capable of devotion to a person or cause outside themselves. In neither father nor daughter do we discover many lovely qualities, but each demonstrates a willingness to serve—something. Like Ezra, Lavinia is committed to duty. Like him, she has an almost soldierly carriage: "*Her movements are stiff and she carries herself with a wooden, square-shouldered, military bearing*" (10). These two characters are complex in the sense of being high-strung and obsessive. They seldom respond to life with joy or with anything that permits a lowering of defenses. Unwilling to expose their vulnerabilities, they must live by mechanical response to all situations, challenges, and crises. Put it another way: in the end they rely on training and appreciate a like response in others. More than once Lavinia commands her soldier brother, as she has been ordered by her father: "Go in the house! (*As he hesitates—more sharply*) Do you hear me? March!" (122). They find indecorous whatever is spontaneous or inspired by joy. Thus, Mannon and his daughter do not strike us as likely to behave conventionally in normal relationships, not because they are selfish but because they are too inhibited and intense.

"I write tragedy." Such an assertion commands attention. And nowhere had O'Neill set out to vindicate his claim more than he did in his *Mourning Becomes Electra*. After six drafts and several seasons in hell, he felt he had achieved his aim: " . . . there is a feeling of fate in it, or I am a fool—a psychological modern approximation of the fate in the Greek tragedies on this theme—attained without benefit of [the] supernatural."[16] But a few months before the opening, he wrote a strange *apologia* to Brooks Atkinson, who had apparently suggested some observations on the script. He seemed to deny his clear debt to the Greeks, including the first great commentator on tragedy.

> As for Aristotle's "purging," I think it is about time we purged his purging out of modern criticism, candidly speaking! What modern audience was ever purged by pity and terror by witnessing a Greek tragedy or what modern mind by reading one? It can't be done! We are too far away, we are in a world of different values! . . . Greek criticism is as remote from us as the art it criticizes. What we need is a definition of Modern and not Classical Tragedy by which to guide our judgments. If we had Gods or a God, if we had a Faith, if we had some healing subterfuge with which to conquer Death, then the Aristotelian criterion might apply in part to our Tragedy. But our tragedy is just that we have only ourselves, that there is nothing to be purged into except a belief in the guts of man, good or evil, who faces unflinchingly the black mystery of his own soul.[17]

He may have believed this in part, but the tone tends to be defensive. O'Neill did not find Greek tragedy "remote" from the modern period. Just the opposite: he had protested that "the Greek dream in tragedy is the noblest ever." Perhaps, if one or the other had thought of it, Sophocles or Aeschylus might have said, "In all my plays sin is punished and redemption takes place." They very well could have, and O'Neill knew that.

If there were any doubt about who is the tragic figure, the question is answered in the very title. Was it presumptuous to set about "finishing" what the Greeks had left undone? St. John Ervine thought so (see his three-part essay in the *London Observer*, March 1932). Yet O'Neill put the questions that it now seems obvious ought to have been posed long ago. "—[W]hy should Furies have let Electra escape unpunished? Why did the chain of fated crime and retribution ignore her mother's murderess?—a weakness in what remains to us of Greek tragedy that there is no play about Electra's life after the murder of Clytemnestra."[18] "Escape unpunished"? Why should anyone have been punished? The idea implies some offense—what was to the Greek *hubris*, to the

Judeo-Christian *sin*. If we say that Oedipus should have been punished, we need not be called self-righteous moralists. It was, after all, Oedipus who called himself guilty and demanded to be judged (punished) according to the very edict that he had promulgated. Thus, in this part of his story, O'Neill accepted the model and logic Sophocles had supplied: Lavinia Mannon imposes punishment upon herself. O'Neill demonstrates that sort of boldness and brilliance that mark the genius.

Lavinia may remind us of Antigone in the implacability of her resolve. Berlin notes this comparison but with an emphasis different from that suggested here.[19] Lavinia has that remoteness often associated with great figures. No one else in the play rivals her in sheer formidability. Except in her temporary emancipation in act 2, suggested by the green of her gown, she dresses characteristically in black and so binds her hair and figure that we see in her the very model of restraint. Literally, she is held in. Her response to life is governed by the principle of inner check. Such a character may be intimidating. In this, Lavinia can be compared fairly with Antigone, who also possessed a severity uncharacteristic of young adulthood.

Lavinia demands of life not fairness (the rule of children's games) but justice, the demand of an entirely judgmental individual. Let two instances be cited. After the murder of Brant, she addresses the stricken Christine: "He paid the just penalty for his crime. You know it was justice. It was the only way true justice could be done" (122). After Orin's suicide and after she comes to see that she cannot have a life with Peter Niles, who is good-hearted but lacking altogether in depth of character, she consigns herself to living death: immurement in the Mannon "sepulchre": "I've got to punish myself! Living alone here with the dead is a worse act of justice than death or prison! I'll never go out or see anyone! I'll have the shutters nailed closed so no sunlight can ever get in. I'll live alone with the dead, and keep their secrets, and let them hound me, until the curse is paid out and the last Mannon is let die!" (178).

She is superb, but her greatness is not seamless. In act 2 of *The Haunted* Orin reminds her of her fate. "Were you hoping you could escape retribution? You can't! Confess and atone to the full extent of the law! That's the only way to wash the guilt of our mother's blood from our souls" (152). She does not respond directly. Why? Lavinia cannot care about the common law (more's the pity), for her vision is majestic but inhumanly severe. It is true that she demands justice with a singlemindedness of purpose that is fairly chilling. For she does not exclude herself from her vision's judgmental sweep. "I'm not going the way Mother and Orin went. That's escaping punishment. And there's no one left to punish me. I'm the last Mannon. I've got to punish myself!" (178). Such austerity of will matches the Olympian coldness of any goddess or hero we can call to mind.

Lavinia's father had chided her for a display of tearful joy when he returned from the war: "Come! I thought I'd taught you never to cry. . . . Tears are queer tokens of happiness!" (47). And Orin reminds her when, in a moment of weakness, she breaks down, "The damned don't cry" (156). We can hear irony in Orin's words. Sometimes, perhaps, women and men should cry; they should give the appropriate signs of remorse. Thus is precluded the redemption of Lavinia.

O'Neill did not see it this way, of course. "I flatter myself I have given my Yankee Electra an end tragically worthy of herself! The end, to me, is the finest and most inevitable thing of the trilogy. She rises to a height there and justifies my faith in her! She is broken and not broken! By her way of yielding to her Mannon fate she overcomes it. She *is* tragic!"[20] One is tempted to agree, for she is magnificent. And in *Mourning Becomes Electra* O'Neill was justified in feeling that he had brought something truly classical onto the modern stage. Moreover, one ought to be modest in these matters. It is O'Neill's work, after all, that gives us something worthy of study in the first place. Nor will any criticism in this book affect at all the stature of his achievement. But the critic too is bound to follow his own thesis and make judgments according to its logic.

The redemption of Lavinia cannot take place for a reason that is at once simple and profound. Redemption can occur only in the context of relationship. In neither *The Homecoming* nor in *The Hunted* does Lavinia experience what might be called viable relationships. Her father, no matter their mutual affection, had not encouraged her to grow in all the talents and healthy inclinations that were natural to her as a woman. If she had felt love for Adam Brant, it was unconscious. When she asks Peter Niles to kiss her passionately, deeper inclinations are revealed to her: "Want me! Take me, Adam! . . . Adam? Why did I call you Adam? I never even heard that name before—outside of the Bible! (*Then suddenly with a hopeless, dead finality*) Always the dead between!" (177). Certainly after Orin's suicide in act 3 of *The Haunted* no blood or love connections are left to her. As we have said, Peter Niles has never been her worthy match.

Redemption requires a renewal or recovery of the heart's state before a rupture in relationship had occurred. There is no one now to bless her heroism or to whom she can confess whatever guilt she feels. The opportunity to reestablish an earlier condition, even those limited situations she has known, can no longer be exploited. No bonding has occurred except the bond that she feels with the dead. Thomas Porter makes the point with admirable precision: "[Death] is the epiphany that concludes the action, the vision to which the plot progresses. If Greek tragedy included the death of the hero, it also provided a means of encompassing the idea of death in a framework of death-and-rebirth. O'Neill's modifications, however, result in a hopeless reiteration that death is final, absolutely conclusive, the end."[21]

O'Neill could never have expected that his play would be judged by a re-mark he was to make fifteen years later. (One sometimes feels he is making more out of the playwright's comment than it warrants.) In this connection criticism often seems a little specious, perhaps even petty. Even so, he did make a sweeping observation when he said something that included *all my plays*. One can hardly think that O'Neill would not have included the trilogy as most prominent among them. Let us give him the last word on this noble play, there-fore, and concede that in the deepest sense he did achieve his end.[22]

> Title—*Mourning Becomes Electra*—that is, in old sense of word—it befits—it becomes Electra to mourn—it is her fate, also, in the usual sense (made ironical here), mourning (black) is becoming to her—it is the only color that becomes her destiny—.[23]

Ah, Wilderness!

> . . . my purpose was to write a play true to the spirit of the American large small-town at the turn of the century. Its quality depended upon atmosphere, sentiment, an exact evocation of the mood of a dead past. To me the America which was (and is) the real America found its unique expression in such middle-class families as the Millers among whom so many of my own gen-eration passed from adolescence into manhood.[24]

Had his name been Norman Rockwell, the playwright could not have touched more deeply into the average American sentiment. His words elevate the sanctity of village green and Home-Sweet-Home. But they don't remind us much of the O'Neill who created Brutus Jones and the "hairy ape," Nina Leeds and Lavinia Mannon, Larry Slade and Jamie Tyrone. Indeed, his stand-ard characterization of the national idyll was made up of equal parts acid and anger. Consider this remark in 1946, reminiscent of his early anarchist sympa-thies: "This American Dream stuff gives me a pain. Telling the world about our American Dream! I don't know what they mean. If it exists, as we tell the whole world, why don't we make it work in one small hamlet in the United States?"[25] We may be forgiven, then, if we are somewhat unsure when O'Neill speaks in softer tones about American life. Since his work typically summons us to the brink, we wonder if we ourselves have not been made the target of his cynicism. Or it may be that in *Ah, Wilderness!* we discover a blend of Celtic-American magic.

*   *   *

Whatever else, here is a play about relationships that work. If we discover in it only "venial" sins, all the dynamics, and dangers, of functioning relation-ships lie under the placid surface. The Millers, unlike the Mannons and the

Tyrones, have not become ensnared in conflicts that cripple ordinary family intercourse. Yet, if they are in this sense typical, we should resist the impulse to idealize them. We should resist, that is, an impulse to turn the play into a valentine. *Ah, Wilderness!* brings together a rare combination of family fare and literary muscle. The miracle of the Millers derives in part from O'Neill's capacity to imagine a happy family life by drawing on his own experience with unhappiness. He was able to provide verisimilitude by inversion: that is, to turn the negative of the family portrait into the positive. And in part it has to do with making the image accessible without straining to communicate a message. The medium strikes the audience as normal. The surest sign of all this was George M. Cohan's willingness to star in the Broadway premiere.[26] It ran for nearly 300 performances, outdrawing all earlier O'Neill productions except *Strange Interlude* (with its marathon run of 426 performances). In fact, he did have a marvelous good time. For once the business of creation was not agony. The play came to him in a dream: he even supplies the day (11 August 1932). In writing to Eugene, Jr., O'Neill observed, " . . . [I]t's new ground for me. . . . But what a pleasure I got out of writing it! It was such a change from the involved and modern and tragic hidden undertones of life I usually go after. It's about the last play they would ever suspect me of writing."[27]

Ah, Wilderness! works for various reasons. We should not exclude O'Neill's thorough knowledge of the old theatre,—his father's theater, which Eugene claimed to hate. He had absorbed its stock-in-trade of melodrama and popular comedy. In that carpenter shop he had mastered the stereotypes of character and situation. For instance:

A. the lovable drunk, who wrings merriment from every moment and even exploits his own weakness for a laugh. Sid Davis's total predictability thereby makes him all the more appealing;

B. the fussy and somewhat befuddled mother, who frets over her son's behavior but is unwilling to have the father chastise him too severely. She seems to say, "Punish him, but don't hurt his feelings";

C. the wise but gentle father, who still recalls the pleasant effects of moonlight on young love;

D. the maiden aunt, who is disappointed in love but remains affectionate and generous. She is satisfied, she says, to be close to the children of her brother's union;

E. the young and awkward lovers, who pretend sophistication but confirm at every step our reassuring assumption that they are God's sweetness visited upon the world again, their very souls models of innocence.

Wilderness! shows us the possible satisfactions and health of family life. It does this, however, without straining under the weight of Pollyannism. The characters are not perfect, any more than the characters in O'Neill's tragedies are evil. The strain of enforced company cannot be avoided in familial life, what Jacques Maritain once called "the cuffs and kisses" that are the hurt and the balm of one's early years. If life is never without pain—physical, psychological, and spiritual, this truth need not depress us. Somewhere Frost called tension "the necessary principle of life." In the family organism, individual members cannot escape conflict. Sibling rivalry, even marital discord, appear to be inevitable but also natural givens. When relationships are not blocked by pathological illnesses, however, the healing that nature encourages takes place. Richard Miller, for example, must endure episodes of normal stress. Such experience often induces frustration and anger, confusion and self-doubt. Even so, he has available to him the deeper treasures of relationship, trust, and tolerance.

We wonder, then: Is this play radically different from the rest of O'Neill's work? Or, despite its upbeat character, does it possess the "sterner stuff" that is the hallmark of his plays? The answers are yes *and* no. Of course, there is no other entry in the collected works whose surface compares with the sparkle of *Wilderness!*. Put it this way: the fabric of anything created by Eugene O'Neill will inevitably reveal his stitching. A comedy it may be, but not one bereft of the "tragic hidden undertones . . . I usually go after." O'Neill could not abandon himself. Because he was a serious dramatist, he inevitably brought heavy equipment to his work.

An O'Neill comedy was itself an anomaly. For that reason alone it seems an unlikely candidate for discussion here. Upbeat, tripping the light fantastic down the sunny side of the street (hardly the *via dolorosa*), it suggests nothing about "the Catholic sensibility." Why include it in this study? I am quick to grant that none in the audience will be reminded of the sin-and-redemption theme, even if such content is implicit. Yet in the greatest comedies (this is one), tragedy *is* implied. *Ah, Wilderness!* treats the dynamics of relationship (the family). Great comedy is serious.

O'Neill gave us two plays about his own young manhood, each centered in the family. One stands as this century's consummate American tragedy, the other as "a comedy of recollection." Their most fundamental difference is that *Long Day's Journey into Night* presents the family as the world in itself, as the metaphor for all human relations and interactions. In *Wilderness!*, however, the family is placed in the larger context of the community. Thus, since the plays' givens are in this sense unlike, each offers a different view of reality. *Long Day's Journey* presents a symbolic world eventually shut down in fog and darkness. In it dates and place names hardly matter. The past is the present. But the comedy gives us a world in which every seam is welded with rivets of Connecticut topicality in July 1906. Its statement is truer to life, then, in socio-political terms than is its darker counterpart.[28] O'Neill places his hero in an authentic turn-of-the century world, standing on the bedrock of geographical-historical data. Real names, places, and institutions give us a sense that we know this world: Waterbury and New Haven; Yale, Harvard, and Princeton; the sitting U.S. President, Theodore Roosevelt, and the mogul J. Pierpont Morgan—against whom Richard, the young iconoclast, rails. The Millers' Buick, perhaps a status symbol, was probably more toy than necessity. Thus, when Nat suggests a "drive around town and out to the lighthouse," we do not fret that there could not have been many miles of paved road.

As Richard Miller seeks to liberate himself from family and middle-class values, his future has both tragic and comic possibilities. We know that in *Long Day's Journey* O'Neill surveys the same ground where stalked the demons that would later deform his spirit: endless conflict with his father, the morphine enslavement of his beloved mother, ambivalence toward his brilliant but self-destructive brother, his own sense of not belonging, and his loss of faith. But when the sophomoric Richard utters a version of *fin de siècle* pessimism, his pose does not fool us. He declaims with Byronic contempt, "Life is a joke . . . everything comes out wrong in the end" (II, 215). We know, in part because of the play's tone, that as he moves into new territory, he will not stray far.

Richard raises a few eyebrows but little hell. His racy literary tastes mildly offend his mother's sensibilities, but he is surprised to discover that his maiden aunt quotes easily from the love lyrics of Omar Khayyam. He censures the rapacity of the ogre Morgan as worthy of the guillotine, only to find that his father is also acquainted with Carlyle's "French Revolution." Richard causes the near apoplexy of David McComber, father of his sweetheart, Muriel, by introducing her to "dissolute" and "blasphemous" influences. The elder McComber confronts Nat with Richard's verses, found by his wife "in one of Muriel's bureau drawers hidden under the underwear" (201). Miller detects his neighbor's low-voltage prurience and defends his son's honor and natural high spirits.

> Why, you damned old fool! Can't you see Richard's only a fool kid who's just at the stage when he's out to rebel against all authority, and so he grabs at everything radical to read and wants to pass it on to his elders and his girl and boy friends to show off what a young hellion he is! Why, at heart you'd find Richard is just as innocent and as big a kid as Muriel is! (202)

Richard likes to think of himself as worldly and experienced. In fact, he is unable to hold the sloe-gin fizz he consumes in Pleasant Beach House (albeit one laced with "dynamite"). And he is paralyzed when the prostitute invites him into her business chambers. Richard may for a time have convinced himself that he feels alienation (*angst,* it would come to be called) in a purposeless universe. But his affectations convince no one, since he has not convinced himself. O'Neill will bring him back home a bit unsteady but unscathed by tragedy.

What Richard does is healthy enough. He tests limits, the limits of what is permissible within the familial and social orders. He knows then that there are agents who will enforce the rules. He has a sense, that is, of how far he can stray into the wilderness and still maintain his bearings. The claim for independence makes the Fourth of July implications obvious, but it is worth recalling that rebels frighten even themselves sometimes. And what Richard wants most is the order and goodness established by his parents, at least he wants to know that he can retreat into that. Nat and Essie, confident in the present, possess a guarded certainty of the future, precisely that certainty that their own less secure children need. Richard especially does not suffer the additional strain of parental warfare added to his own life-division at seventeen. Is it any wonder that Eugene O'Neill saw in this home and family something he wished might have been the background of his own youth?

If called upon to name them, what authors would we suppose appealed to the neophyte rebel of 1906? The answer is easy: those Eugene O'Neill was reading in that year (the summer before he left for Princeton). Richard admires the writers both for their ideas and for their shock value upon his elders. He flaunts names that suggest his Fourth of July independence. But Nat Miller is more amused than outraged at his son's catalog of heroes: Ernest Dowson, Ibsen, Shaw, Swinburne, Wilde, and, of course, Edward FitzGerald, whose translation of the *Rubaiyat* he quotes. The moment of confrontation turns to humor.

Ah, Wilderness! evokes the very texture of a time and place now gone but recoverable through popular history. The Millers represent both the strengths and the weaknesses of their world. They represent what is normal. (We may wish to recall, of course, that "normal" carries positive implications: "standard, functioning, or occurring in a natural way.") Their friends and neighbors are also normal people: most go to work or perform domestic offices; the happy few go to college. All live in a country with a named President. They are *bourgeois,* as O'Neill shows with unsparing fidelity: the parlor is *"furnished with scrupulous medium-priced tastelessness of the period. . . . The walls are papered white with a cheerful, ugly blue design"* (185). Even so, in this setting a boy who strays into an uncertain zone, his own wilderness, can return.

Thus, we meet in *Ah, Wilderness!* the citizens of any "large small town" in the United States. As O'Neill wrote to Philip Moeller, "It could be laid in the Middle or Far West with hardly the change of a word. There are no colloquialisms in it, I think, that aren't general American small town."[29] Something else is noticeable: even in *Our Town* the nationality groups are identified. But here issues of ethnicity simply do not surface. O'Neill, whose background was Irish-Catholic, performed an alchemy familiar to great storytellers: he was able to universalize his art by projecting its truth beyond his own milieu. He found a way to translate his vision into an American vernacular.

* * *

Explicit religious content is no more a factor here than in a Booth Tarkington novel about adolescence. Yet the play treats values and conflicts that religion talks about, especially American religion: home, family, the innocence of youth, elders as the repository of homely truth. With the exception of the Bible, of course, the sources of this wisdom go unnamed. There is a certain American constituency in which the fright power of religion is felt but tends to be softened. In this social group, which is one pattern of Protestant life, the subject of religion hardly enters daily conversation. Discussion of doctrinal matters is left to preacher and Sunday school teacher. The names of Savior or saint come seldom to the lips, except perhaps in reference to something in Chaucer or Milton. People may speak of the Golden Rule, but they become uncomfortable if asked to voice an opinion on a theological issue. To insist on such conversation is considered somehow invasive and not in good taste. Most in the congregation attend Sunday services, yet this activity connects only vaguely with their workaday world and social life. One doesn't wear one's religion on one's sleeve. The oracular dicta of the fireside poets, Emerson, and other sages might be invoked in occasional moments, such as the high school commencement, but Ben Franklin probably makes more sense to the average man. Better to leave some things in the meadows of mellowness. Let piety remain a private matter.

Such are the mores of the Miller family, whose values are firm and quite admirable, beyond question. In biblical language, such people are called the salt of the earth. If their values come ultimately from American religious tradition and practice, the sources of belief seldom come to the surface of consciousness. The religious zeal of earlier days has abated by July 4, 1906, the day of the play's setting.

O'Neill's "intelligent modern audience" might identify the theorists behind his "big-subject" plays: Nietzsche, Jung, Freud, Strindberg. The "philosophy" behind *Ah, Wilderness!* seems to be folk wisdom, however. It goes like this: the people in the play make mistakes, but the audience knows that everyone falls, often tragically. We hurt each other, sometimes cruelly. How do we learn forgiveness? We learn by being forgiven. The sixteen-year history of Sid's and Lily's broken engagement at once amuses us and scalds our hearts. At bottom, the story tells of Lily's inexhaustible capacity to forgive the chronic drunk and clown, Sid Davis. (One is surely reminded in Sid of Jamie O'Neill, whose levity no doubt masked a pitiable insecurity.) Those who forgive have themselves been forgiven and have, therefore, known the pain of guilt. The family redeems itself. What is true in *Our Town* is true in O'Neill's comedy: with quiet reassurance, men and women redeem each other.

In many O'Neill plays relationships are charged with hostility, the tissues of love scarred by ongoing internecine insults. Individuals suffer in part because their familial and conjugal relationships, which might be supportive and grace-giving, cannot be developed. Nor does *Wilderness!* dismiss this sorrow out of hand. It certainly does not deny the pain that life inflicts.[30] The play achieves something quite rare in comedy: it expands our expectations and builds the comedy with the steel of drama.

Here all the tragic possibilities, though present, are muted. Thus O'Neill describes the alcoholic failure, Sid, not as one in the fraternity of drunks in *The Iceman Cometh* but as *"short and fat, bald-headed, with the Puckish face of Peck's Bad Boy who has never grown up"* (188). Behind his merry manner and incessant silliness, however, Sid is still in love with Lily, who turned down his proposal of marriage some sixteen years earlier. Unspoken but evident is his human failure. He reminds all of his own (and their) lost opportunities—the most recent, his being fired from yet another job. How the story of Sid and Lily might have served as the stuff for another kind of play, the actors must always keep in mind. Indeed, sensitive directing and acting will carry us some distance behind the comedy's smiling facade. (Doris Alexander offers a rewarding account of O'Neill's ill-fated romance with Beatrice Ashe, whom he loved in New London and who no doubt influenced his rendering of several characters in various plays. In *Ah, Wilderness!* she is incarnated, says Alexander, in three separate characters: Mildred Miller, Richard's sister; Lily Miller, his aunt; and Muriel McComber, with whom he falls in love. The tragedy of the Lily-Sid relationship is given one of the finest treatments in all O'Neill criticism.)[31]

Put another way, there surfaces in this cheery family circle the spectre of debilitating alcoholism and the threat of deadly cynicism. All this is viewed with kindly tolerance, yes. But we should understand that tolerance signifies no condescension. Because the possibilities for deep injury at every moment threaten, the family situation is real. *Wilderness!* creates an unusual appeal, neither mordant nor saccharine. If we think about it, such is the mature tolerance that provides the greatest support for the insecurity of youth.

But it will not do merely to say that children wish to test authority, that adolescents fall into love too soon, and that parents worry about their children's judgment. We could make similar observations about Romeo and Juliet. Adolescence is that time when one undergoes baffling stress and pain, unwanted but apparently necessary shapers of personal identity. To enter this zone is to move into one's own wilderness, sometimes a frightening experience. We cannot always find our way back home when we have finished experimenting for the day, or week, or year. But in this developmental stage we find it more natural than in any other to test roles. Thus, like many another seventeen-year-old, Richard Miller is divided, *"alternately plain simple boy and posey actor solemnly playing a role"* (193). He is fitting himself out in the costume of social rebel. Such a type is contemptuous of the mere freedom achieved by the democratic masses; he finds their patriotism, as measured by his own high mindedness, an embarrassment. Richard is so divided, but not in the dramatic context of other O'Neill romantic heroes (which is to say, of Eugene O'Neill himself).[32] The difference is that Richard feels the quite natural emotional strain but not the metaphysical ambiguities that can devastate young adulthood. His good fortune derives in part, no doubt, from his parents, who are secure in their own roles and love for each other.

* * *

In addition to the sub-theme of the Lily-Sid tragedy, three specific relationships ought to be highlighted by a few excerpts of dialogue. Nat and Essie Miller are first of all husband and wife. This relationship supersedes but also strengthens their other relationships—as parents, brother and sister, and in-laws. Their marriage is comfortable but not casual. They respect one another. In this they stand as models *par excellence* for their four children. Their mutual trust makes it possible for them to confide in and kid each other but also to disagree without releasing the poison of acrimony. Their offspring, sensing all of this, do not suffer the uncertainty and stress that can chill the domestic atmosphere. Thus, when Richard comes home tipsy from a night of "carousing," Essie agrees with Nat that the lad should be punished. She knows, however, that neither of them wants to perform this duty.

> MRS. MILLER. And that's just what it's your duty to do—punish him good and hard! The idea of him daring—(*Then hastily*) But you be careful how you go about it, Nat. Remember he's like you inside—too sensitive for his own good. (265)

How different they are from David McComber, who confines his daughter to her home for one month for reading and hiding Richard's "dissolute and blasphemous" verses. McComber complains to Nat and Essie of their son's attempt "to corrupt the morals of my young daughter, Muriel" (201).

Miller has that kind of relationship with his son that many fathers envy but find difficult to establish. Nat is no fool, of course. He knows what trouble adolescent boys can get themselves into (and get their girlfriends into). After he raises these possibilities with Richard, the boy is only surprised that his father could have thought such things could have taken place. This contributes a strong moment to the play.

> MILLER. . . . I've got something else to talk to you about besides firecrackers.
> RICHARD. (*apprehensively*) What, Pa?

MILLER. (*suddenly puts both hands on his shoulders—quietly*) Look here, Son. I'm going to ask you a question, and I want an honest answer. I warn you beforehand if the answer is "yes" I'm going to punish you and punish you hard because you'll have done something no boy of mine ought to do. But you've never lied to me before, I know, and I don't believe even to save yourself punishment, you'd lie to me now, would you?

RICHARD. (*impressed—with dignity*) I won't lie, Pa.

MILLER. Have you been trying to have something to do with Muriel—something you shouldn't—you know what I mean.

RICHARD. (*stares at him for a moment, as if he couldn't comprehend—then, as he does, a look of shocked indignation comes over his face*) No! What do you think I am, Pa? I never would! She's not that kind! Why, I—I love her! I'm going to marry her—after I get out of college! She's said she would! We're engaged!

MILLER. (*with great relief*) All right. That's all I wanted to know. We won't talk any more about it. (*He gives him an approving pat on the back.*)

RICHARD. I don't see how you could think—Did that old idiot McComber say that about me? (206–207)

Benefitting from the example of his parents' relationship, Richard has been prepared to treat his sweetheart honorably: "I'm going to marry her." Because Nat and Essie know their own limitations and the disappointments that love can bring (e.g., Sid and Lily), they do not have unrealistic expectations for their children. Nat's question is a sign of love, not of little confidence.

Richard's courting of Muriel is both humorous and reassuring, for we see him as he is trying out an unfamiliar role. In attempting to demonstrate sophistication beyond her innocence, he tells of his meeting with Belle the prostitute in a "secret house of shame." This draws from Muriel precisely the response he does not want. She does not want him to be worldly in a way that will degrade his dawning manliness. Flustered and angry, Richard tells even more outrageous lies: about his drinking prowess and his beating up the bartender who insulted Belle's "honor."

MURIEL. And did you kiss her?

RICHARD. No, I didn't.

MURIEL. (*distractedly*) You did, too! You're lying and you know it. You did, too! (*Then tearfully*) And there I was right at that time lying in bed not able to sleep, wondering how I was ever going to see you again and crying my eyes out, while you—! (*She suddenly jumps to her feet in a tearful fury*) I hate you! I wish you were dead! I'm going home this minute! I never want to lay eyes on you again. And this time I mean it (284).

How quaint seems this exchange, how innocent. We cannot help reflecting on the transformation in etiquette and values that has taken place over the past ninety years. Today, at earlier and earlier ages, children are forced to respond to tyrannizing peer demands. Such episodes are fraught with risk, of course, simply because one's "models" lack the very resource that children require: judgment as the product of maturity. If the gang, in lieu of family, becomes the chief transmitter of mores and values, the vulnerable inductees must rely on the vision of the peer group. Lacking the habit of prudence and unprepared to take the long view, the child is encouraged to seize the moment of gratification. She must confront the awful weight of urgency! By its natural limitations, youth has not yet acquired an index by which to measure the relative good and evil of the choices available.

If not saddled with the demands of a spurious freedom, however, and if not asked to make adult exchanges without preparation, children can grow without such paralyzing anxiety. In time they will, of course, be drawn to the mysteries of intimacy. But will not the child, who is helped to be herself, move toward adulthood with greater equanimity? For she will be spared the mortifying sting of her natural dependency.

The Millers, sitting snugly before the hearth or sporting on the village green, have little connection with the life of the contemporary urban family, often ravaged from within and without. Thus, we wonder, is the play nothing more than an idealized portrait of Richard's (and Eugene's) adolescence? It is an idealization, to be sure, as O'Neill was quick to concede. This was his youth, he said, as he wished it had been. Still, a truth told in softer tones is not necessarily less valid. Because certain family and generational conflicts are timeless, moreover, the play's gentle wisdom may be more relevant than we suppose. In his happiest play, O'Neill described the model laboratory in which to build and repair relationships: the family. This is surely the gift one generation can pass on to the next.

*   *   *

Nat and Essie are prepared to bestow these blessings, since their relationship has been established on the solid ground of respect. Their fidelity derives from a friendship that cannot be pretended. Insincerity will surface in the moment of stress. Thus, parents who know but do not demean each other's limitations can live in the confidence of love. Moreover, they can rest assured that their call for filial obedience derives from a rightful authority. Thus blessed, the child, whose insecurity is as natural as it is real, can form the virtue of prudence. These authentic gifts of family ennoble the human need to imitate. And childhood, otherwise remembered for its humiliations, can be recalled with honor.

All the relationships in *Ah, Wilderness!* are structured on love, trust, and remembered experience. Richard learns that his own parents have had a romantic past, a discovery that seems to shock each new generation. If O'Neill has not created elsewhere many characters who feel deep trust in their fellows, here belief in each other's basic value lends a quiet dignity to the proceedings. In an observation made to Kenneth Macgowan, O'Neill remarked on the apparent truth about basic relationships the play carried to varied audiences: " . . . the damn thing moves young, middle-aged and old! It's astonishing. And a proof to me, at least, that emotionally we still deeply hanker after the old solidarity of the family unit."[33] Who would have expected this from Jamie's brother and fellow traveler? It has not been fashionable for some time now to say it, but let us risk the charge of sentimentalism. We all want to prove worthy of our ideals and to count for something greater than our money and our possessions. In the right story, rightly told, such an assertion might surprise us, but we accept it.

The very existence of this play tells us that Eugene O'Neill valued the principles of healthy relationship: trust and love. As a child he had felt abandoned and betrayed, both by his mother and the church. The scars were deep. He could not deny the darker side of reality. Yet, in an interesting way, *Ah, Wilderness!* verifies the power of the dark, which cannot be understood except in its relation to the light. Nor can there be much sense in saying that *life is a tragedy* unless we know, at least in theory, that tragedy has an opposite. The play is a comedy, but also something more.

Ah, Wilderness! is what it is, a wonderfully constructed play of the sort certain to win mass approval. It warms the heart, recalls the old days, and reminds those who have lived through such times of their own lost youth. The theme has to do with the cyclical nature of things. Spring is exciting and a little unpredictable; thus, we delight in the sportiveness of Richard and Muriel. But a further implication is that autumn and even winter are equally natural states that suggest mellowness and wisdom. The parents know the lesson that life teaches: youth must be lost. Indeed, existence itself perishes. But this play does not lament these sobering truths; rather, it comes to terms with them. All is thereby universalized. We may be reminded again of *Our Town* where, in one way, the characters are nobody; in another way, they are everybody.

Long Day's Journey into Night also begins in morning sunlight, but it closes down in fog and under the staggering weight of time. O'Neill's comedy, though, moves into the nimbus of a mid-summer's night. It works because the love, songs, and moonlight, their effects deftly muted, make up a natural part of the setting and season. O'Neill himself seemed a bit giddy before releasing the script to the Theater Guild. And, although he could not sustain the mellowness, he must for a moment have felt blessed. It was as if he wished to share that moment with his tragic fellows and say, "It's time for all those out in the wilderness to come home for the night."

6 | The "Catholic" Play: *Days Without End*

JOHN . . . *perhaps if we could again have faith in—*
LOVING . . . *No! We have passed beyond gods!*
There can be no going back!

BROADWAY REJECTED *Days Without End* quickly and finally. After a trial run in Boston's Plymouth Theatre (December 27–January 7), it moved to the Henry Miller Theatre in Manhattan on January 8. The play closed February 24, 1934, after the two-city run of fifty-seven performances. It has seldom been revived. Although *Days* was treated civilly in Boston (H. T. Parker in the *Transcript* and Elinor Hughes in the *Herald*), rave reviews were few except in Catholic circles. In New York, however, it took a drubbing: Percy Hammond in the *Herald Tribune* called it "lugubrious affectation," while Burns Mantle in the *News* labeled it "sophomoric" and "maudlin." Brooks Atkinson, perhaps the most influential play reviewer of the day, was doubtful about O'Neill's commitment and was unimpressed with the overall effort: "*Days Without End* smells of the lamp. It gives the impression of having been written in isolation. It is studious in a bookish sense. It is dry and airless, and it leads one to suspect that Mr. O'Neill's heart is not really in it."[1]

Conspicuous admirers were the leaders of the Catholic literary revival: Jesuits Francis X. Talbot, Daniel Lord, Michael Earls, and Gerald B. Donnelly; Rev. Joseph A. Daly in *The Catholic Mind* ("A Catholic Looks at Eugene O'Neill"); R. D. Skinner in *Commonweal*; and Martin J. Quigley. Even Elizabeth Jordan, O'Neill's perennial *bête noire*, waxed enthusiastic, although she could not suppress a degree of condescension: " . . . Eugene O'Neill has been for years a lost child in the wilderness of life."[2] But she called it "a great offering" and acknowledged that, "[as] a theologian O'Neill is sound and deeply impressive." Ms. Jordan found it more than she could manage, however, to eliminate altogether the smugness that characterized her criticism: "It is safe to predict . . . that the amount of theological talk in the play will be greatly exceeded by the amount of talk concerning it that will be heard around New York's luncheon and dinner tables this season. To be discussing their souls, and the relations of those souls to their Creator, will be a new and uplifting experience to our so-called intelligentia!"[3]

In order to appreciate the Catholic press's view of *Days,* it may be helpful to look at a single complete review. The following essay appeared in the Brooklyn *Tablet* (diocesan weekly). It examines both the play's "great merit" as well as what it saw as the universal unfairness of the secular press. The piece was written by Patrick F. Scanlan, managing editor of the *Tablet,* who gained wide recognition in an astonishing reign from 1917–1968.

From the Managing Editor's Desk

Few Catholics ever thought the day would come when it would be possible to warmly praise one of Eugene O'Neill's plays. But "Days Without End," which began its New York run under the auspices of the Theatre Guild in the Henry Miller Theatre last Monday, can be commended as a work of great merit, well produced, and leaving an impression which might be called tremendous.

Mr. O'Neill turns toward the truer, nobler and finer things of life in "Days Without End." He depicts the struggles of a soul in the throes of unbelief. A strange and moving performance[,] it is in truth a profession of faith. The story is of a man possessed of a demon—a devil of hate, destruction, blasphemy and paganism. The demon is a masked actor, a shadowy monster, who follows the man about to express the conflicts of the mind, the malevolent elements of his nature. The demon is always peering over the shoulder, urging the doing of harmful things, forever speaking bitterly and striving for the possession of the soul.

The leading character of the play is composing a book of his own life. As he outlines it to his wife and his uncle who is a priest, we first see him as a boy. There is related how he lost his religious faith following the death of his father and mother, despite prayers of anguish. Love as represented by Our Saviour died for him then and his soul was filled with blasphemous hatred. Then tormented, seeking a new faith, he found it in the love resulting from a happy marriage. But the devil struggled to break that love, to reconquer his soul. He possessed the man and caused him to violate his marriage.

The play then shows the outcome of this act. The cruelly deceived wife seeks her death because of the husband's sin. She falls seriously ill and he fighting the demon within him struggling winds up at the foot of the cross, renounces his sins and pledges himself to serve God. Meanwhile his wife's life has been saved.

The play may be fantastic, and it has one or two features that could have been omitted, but it is an impressive, gripping and thrilling production. It is an overwhelming attack on modern philosophy, particularly that represented by Bertrand Russell. The text is magnificent. The cast is exceptionally competent. The character of the priest will cause discussion, for to some it will appear too stiff and not sufficiently human, but he leaves a fine impression. The acting of the central character, Earle Larimore, and of Stanley Ridges, his devil, is masterly. The closing scene with the victory of good over evil, and love over hate, so beautifully and simply portrayed, is a spectacle never to be forgotten. There we find not only the explanation of the divine character of the Church, but of the human element so beautifully expressed by the non-Catholic novelist, James Oliver Curwood, in these lines: "I think the reason the Catholic Church is the only Church which is growing to any extent is because it is the only Church which is holding out its arms as a mother and giving a human being a breast on which to lay his head when he is in trouble."

"Days Without End" has given the public a different impression of Eugene O'Neill. And undoubtedly the reception of the play by the New York critics has contributed to his enlightenment. Most of these critics are pseudo-intellectuals who hide their ignorance under the misapprehension that faith is outmoded. For this reason the grotesque reviews appearing in many of Tuesday's papers were particularly asinine. The critics did not understand what it was all about, although the simplicity of the story could be appreciated by any Catholic high school student. Richard Lockridge, in *The Sun,* and Burns Mantle, in *The News,* gave respectful reviews, and our Brooklyn papers showed intelligent appreciation, but *The Times, World-Telegram, Post* and *Mirror* reviews were dreadful. Why must a playwright have to drive a swill wagon to get attention from these fellows? Perhaps because they understand the latter and not the former. And suppose they did understand it, how would they write? Probably worse, because anger at Christianity would supplant ignorance of it.

Robert Garland's two reviews in the *World-Telegram,* were insulting. He argued not so much against the teachings of the day, but against Christian truth. The minions of anti-Christ will attack this play. Its reception clearly shows what a battle Christian truth is in for in this city.

The comments of some of the audience during the first two nights betrayed an equal ignorance. They seemed to be members of the Guild. So obsessed with sex, smuttiness and vulgarity are some that they cannot appreciate the true, the beautiful and the noble. The play spoke a language which they did not understand. Aside from the attitude of the ultra-sophisticates the remarks of the superficial were both common and banal for, it seems, their idea of art is such that they consider Mae West America's sweetheart.

Mr. O'Neill has put on a good play, and it should have a good run. He showed his sincerity by seeking Catholic opinion on the religious parts and by refusing to pawn it as a film to the Hollywood butchers unless they guaranteed not to hack it. One thoughtful man coming away from the theatre on Tuesday evening said to his companion: "O'Neill betrayed a weakness." That weakness, perhaps, is that he belongs back in the bosom of the Church.[4]

In sheer judgmental self-assurance, Scanlan proved worthy of comparison with Ms. Jordan.

Among literary critics, *Days Without End* has elicited little support over the decades. Even O'Neill's inveterate defenders have dismissed the play as something of an embarrassment. Indeed the most damaging evaluations have been registered by dedicated O'Neillians. John Henry Raleigh called it "Dickensian in its wildly improbable happy ending . . . with the impossible Father Baird purring in the background."[5] Travis Bogard noted that it was "written without real craftsmanship or imagination [and was] thematically arbitrary, if not confused."[6] Louis Sheaffer wondered if any major playwright had "ever written a play so awkwardly contrived";[7] and Margaret Ranald called *Days* "dramatically . . . clumsy, with entrances and exits very obviously contrived, the exposition heavy-handed, and the epiphanic reintegration of John Loving ill-prepared and even trite."[8] Virginia Floyd, generally sympathetic to the author's religious turmoil, called it "the weakest and least successful play of O'Neill's mature period" and termed the ending "hopelessly contrived and outrageously dramatic. . . . As he did in *Welded,* O'Neill takes a simple domestic drama and attempts to make a profound philosophical commentary on spiritualized love, the sanctity of marriage, and, in *Days Without End,* the duality of man."[9]

It is revealing to examine the criticism of *Days* at the time of its premiere. Many observers, both negative and friendly, drew the wrong inferences about its meaning, at least those readings O'Neill claimed he had not intended. Yet, as we review the writing and production history of the play, we can hardly be surprised at the general misunderstanding. For nearly all interested parties saw in the script every sign that Eugene O'Neill had returned, or would, to the faith of his youth. He himself had first thought to call it a "Play about Catholic boyhood."[10] And not a few critics keyed on his description of *Days* as a "Modern Miracle Play." He tried to clear up any misunderstanding in a letter to Leon Mirlas: " . . . the simple fact is I chose Catholicism because it is the only Western religion which has the stature of real Faith, because it is the religion of the old miracle plays and the Faustian legend which were the sources of my theme—and last and most simply because it happens to be the religion of my early training and therefore the one I know most about."[11] The prints of his "early training" could not easily be erased from the play, moreover, a fact that provides further evidence of his mindset. The point is that *Days* seems to suggest an ancient theme: the wages of sin is death. Thus we cannot be surprised that a Jesuit priest, on viewing the play in Boston, saw it as "a morality play on pride." It was not "modern" but medieval, "the ancient Catholic concept in which pride is the primal and terrible sin, . . . the sin of Lucifer and the angels. . . . "[12] If, as O'Neill insisted, his play was "*not Catholic propaganda,*" Fr. Donnelly missed the point. To him and others *Days Without End* appeared a work whose clear intention was to reinforce the Catholic view of things. Perhaps the Donnelly response vindicates the axiom that we get from something what we bring to it. But an even more striking demonstration of this phenomenon can be seen in Daniel Lord's ecstatic letter to Martin Quigley, who had sent him a copy of O'Neill's script.

I am simply overwhelmed by the new O'Neill play. I read it aloud and I could hardly finish the thing.

Emotionally it is magnificent and I have never seen a finer technical job. As for the Catholicity, it is so thoroughly saturated with it that it leaves me completely astonished. I have never seen so fine a priest on the stage and I have never seen a play that was so satisfying, adequate and so completely convincing in its Catholic tone.[13]

If O'Neill did not wish to be considered a Catholic megaphone, he ought not to have written back to Quigley as he did: "I am very grateful to you for sending the quote from Fr. Lord's letter. As you can imagine, what he says about *Days Without End* is exceedingly gratifying to me. . . . Whether there is enough strength and conviction in the play to overcome the pseudo-intellectual pose of New York critics and subscriber audiences that religious faith is an outmoded subject is now the one question to be decided. I hope, ay [*sic*] least, it will run long enough to reach those it was written for, who have ears to hear."[14] Elizabeth Jordan would observe, approvingly, that "Mr. O'Neill has become a propagandist."[15]

*   *   *

It will not do to claim that *Days Without End* is a great work. It isn't. Even so, as drama the play earns some merit, a fact that few have been willing to concede. (The dramatist correctly predicted the barrage of boos and hisses that *Days* was certain to elicit from the New York "pseudo-sophisticates.") Our interest here, however, is less to estimate the play's value as a dramatic vehicle than to examine it as a striking illustration of O'Neill's Catholic sensibility.

Because this "miracle play" is O'Neill's most explicitly Catholic work, it commands extended examination in this study. It confronts certain issues of faith and doctrine: that is, the efficacy of prayer and the sin of adultery. If the theological emphases and "intransigency" of traditional Catholicism have become less rigid since Vatican II, we must judge O'Neill's personal struggle in view of church teachings and practice as he had experienced them and as they obtained in the 1930s. To put this another way, *Days Without End* draws our attention for the insights it affords us into O'Neill's own Catholic dilemma.

Days marks a telling moment in his spiritual odyssey. He had protested to friends (Macgowan, Cerf, and others) that he did not want *Days* to be seen as evidence of a personal recantation or any willingness "to return to the faith." No one can say what might have happened to the "apostate" had the play been acclaimed a success by the New York critics and audiences. But we must surely wonder what possibilities for reassessing his religious situation could have been opened to him had things gone differently. As it turned out, the experience proved devastating: he was humiliated and embittered; and he was unable thereafter to broach publicly the subject of his own possible return to Catholicism, although he was sometimes asked about it. By the time of his next Broadway production twelve years later (*The Iceman Cometh*), O'Neill would scotch any earlier suggestions of faith in his work. Thus, writing *Days* had required an act of courage, for he was all but certain that the critics, including his friend George Jean Nathan, would misinterpret its meaning.

He had wished it to be understood that the miracle play was but the second tier in a planned trilogy (to be called "Myth Plays for the God-forsaken"), of which *Dynamo* stood as the grounding. He had explained the project's importance in the now well-known letter to Nathan (mentioned in chapter 3 at note 35).

Days Without End continued his examination of the bifurcated soul begun in *Beyond the Horizon* (1920). By this time, having followed the trail through *The Great God Brown* (1925), *Lazarus Laughed* (1927), and *Dynamo* (1928), he had rather completely examined the problem of all alienated modernists, especially the artists. The characters in these plays are divided, on the one hand, by their mocking self-contempt; on the other, by their unending search for integrity. The chief sign of their malaise is the loss of faith, in some instances represented by the distorted lineaments of a mask. The mask had once conveyed an idea of power, especially as it was employed in Greco-pagan ritual. But how does the device function in the modern world, where faith has been denatured into boosterism? In the drama it might signify the individual's failure to preserve his identity.

> Symbolist or naturalist, the playwright has once again found ways to stylize his characters' features. He knows that the mask can suggest liberation; but he knows as well that, worn too long, it can erase a character's sense of self. Thus a befuddled Willy Loman, uncertain of his identity, may be forced to confess, "I still feel—kind of temporary about myself."[16]

Because *Days Without End*, the last of his mask plays, was very important to O'Neill, its commercial failure and the stinging critical reception rankled deeply. We cannot know what effect, if any, a positive reception of the play might have had on his later work; nor can one say that its failure explains why he mounted no more productions until 1946. But the unfavorable New York treatment, following on the heels of the smashing success of *Ah, Wilderness!* (starring the glad-hand trouper, George M. Cohan), can hardly have lessened O'Neill's contempt for Broadway-as-usual.

* * *

It is no part of the task at hand to defend or attack the doctrines of Roman Catholicism. But we have every reason to wonder if the writing of *Days With-*

out End offers evidence of O'Neill's desire to return to his days of faith. He was, it seems fair to say, understandably mistrustful of his own inclinations. This ambivalence is suggested by the mixed signals he gave about the play's content, signals certain to baffle interpreters of his work. Even Saxe Commins, O'Neill's close friend since the Provincetown days, saw evidence of the author's movement "backward," an inference that infuriated Carlotta Monterey (and, she said, her husband). She wrote to Commins, more than seven months prior to the Boston opening, to relay her own and O'Neill's distress and to disabuse him of his erroneous view:

> Gene and I nearly had a fit when we saw you had taken the end of the play quite from the wrong angle. It has *nothing* to do with *Christianity* or *prayer* that brings Elsa back—it is her *great & all consuming love for her husband!* Thro' her love she senses that her husband is in danger & that *love gives* her the strength *to come back* & live with him—We suppose *no one* will understand that tho—that you didn't.[17]

Many in the Catholic press, however, and audiences in Dublin, also fell quite easily into "misreading" the play's meaning. So, even if Commins shared nothing in religious background with the playwright, the Catholic critics did. Gerard B. Donnelly, S.J., discounted the review of many "who obviously failed to understand the play and who, I think, faintly resented it." Donnelly himself suffered no such bafflement or resentment:

> For I have seen a magnificently Catholic play—a play Catholic in its characters, its story, its mood, and its moral. With a Catholic priest in it—the noblest priest in the history of the modern theater. With Catholic prayers in it. With dialogue about the Faith, mortal sin, Confession, and the mercy of God. A play that defies all the Broadway traditions and dares to close with its hero kneeling in a Catholic church before a great carved crucifix. I happen to be a Jesuit, whose job it has often been to preach the Spiritual Exercises. I had never thought to find Loyola's Principle and Foundation talked of in the theater. Yet I have just seen a play that is nothing less than a deeply earnest sermon on the End of Man. . . . I have no idea how it has come about that our foremost American dramatist, hitherto known as pagan and naturalistic in his sympathies, has now turned his sympathies to the spiritual. But, incredible as it sounds, Eugene O'Neill has written a drama on the yearning of the human heart for God.[18]

Would not the pious Ella have been edified and James made proud by this tribute to the name of O'Neill? "Indeed," Donnelly continued, "the author has given his work an Ignatian title. . . . Without belief in God our life is without purpose, our days are without an end." O'Neill, if he read this review, must have experienced more mixed feelings. Like anyone else, he wished to be approved, and it must have caused him to preen a little to be placed in company of Ignatius of Loyola. But Donnelly's words, and those of others in the Catholic press, put him on the spot. Could he acknowledge the validity of his renunciation of "paganism"? He had insisted to Kenneth Macgowan that "it was only Jesuits and Catholic theologians who saw" his purpose.[19] Well?

One critic among Catholic intellectuals spoke with greater secular resonance: Richard Dana Skinner. As drama critic for *Commonweal*, he could comment with a somewhat more worldly sophistication than official church spokespersons, an authority that might carry further into the consciousness of the broad intellectual community. "*Days Without End* is the culmination in religious spirit, at least, of nearly every play he has written before, as inseparable from *Beyond the Horizon*, *The Great God Brown*, and *Mourning Becomes Electra* as Dante's ascent of the mount of Purgatory is inseparable from his passage through the Inferno."[20] More interesting, perhaps, are Skinner's private remarks to Michael Earls, S.J.

In 1935 Skinner would publish a study of the playwright, *Eugene O'Neill: A Poet's Quest*. He said he had maintained independence of critical judgment but benefited by cooperation from the "poet." His purpose was to study the plays "from the viewpoint of their inner continuity." O'Neill apparently appreciated the seriousness of Skinner's intentions but understandably did not approve *carte blanche* whatever might be suggested in a manuscript he was not to see before publication.

At any rate Skinner passed along certain information about O'Neill's spiritual struggle to Fr. Earls. "It may interest you to know that his wife is working very hard to bring about his definite return to the Catholic Church as she feels that that is his one salvation."[21] Perhaps this was true, but it does not sound much like the Carlotta most O'Neillians have come to know or the person who had expressed quite different feelings to Commins only a few months earlier. Skinner seems to have taken a rose-colored view of O'Neill's "problem."[22]

The playwright had placed some importance on the younger man's opinion. In 1926 he wondered to Macgowan, "Has Skinner read *L[azarus Laughed]?*"[23] As late as 1939 the two continued to correspond, exchanging information on matters familial as well as dramatic. The point is that Skinner clearly felt that he wrote to Michael Earls with authority about O'Neill's religious dilemma: " . . . let me beg you to storm heaven for the intentions of both of them [Eugene and Carlotta]. They still have a long and difficult road ahead."[24] A week later he responded to the priest about Philip Barry, who "has written the kind of Catholic play that is really good." (The work in question was *The Joyous Season*, which starred Lillian Gish as a nun and opened at the Belasco Theatre on 29 January 1934.) The New York critics would praise it, said Skinner,

> in order to justify their non-partisan position if for no other reason. The real truth of the matter, however, would be that the O'Neill play stirred their

resentment by calling adultery a sin, and making the surrender to Christ crucified a reality whereas Barry's play is, from what I have heard about it, more sentimental, and would do less to disturb the inner sensibilities of a group of amiable pagans.[25]

O'Neill might have felt deep ambivalence had he had the opportunity to read these words. He would most surely have been embarrassed by "the surrender to Christ crucified." On the other hand, he was quite emphatic in a number of ways about the lethal urbanity of the critics. In May of the same year he would write to Sophus Winther: "*Days Without End* challenged and insulted their superiority complexes . . . and they reacted like bigoted, priest-burning, Puritan atheists! Also my play treats adultery seriously—as a sin against love[26]—and how could the first-night intelligentsia of New York countenance that!"[27]

Whatever his deepest feelings in this connection, O'Neill took considerable pains, in writing and revising *Days,* not to seem too Catholic. He had at one point written the Father Baird part as that of a Protestant clergyman. Later, realizing he could speak with greater authority by creating a Catholic background, he wrote to Nathan: "I have been working like hell on it [*DWE*] . . . and have finished the change back to Catholicism and the priest-uncle. It certainly gives it its proper quality. I was a damned fool ever to change it to a vague Christianity."[28]

From his *Commonweal* platform Skinner broadcast his "conviction that in this play Mr. O'Neill has achieved a degree of spiritual as well as dramatic triumph which sets *Days Without End* above and apart from any [other] play he has written."[29] But the critic was aware that O'Neill would be made uncomfortable if *Days* were praised by prelate and pastor for defending (or seeming to defend) Catholic morality. Thus he cautioned Fr. Earls: "I would not refer directly, of course, to any of the matters I have told you about their personal religious feelings, but I do think it would be well 'in order' to say that you are constantly remembering his intentions and praying that he may find the peace and comfort he is seeking."[30]

* * *

The one constant in O'Neill criticism, friendly and unfriendly, has been that his plays are manifestly autobiographical. He would not have been believed if he had tried to deny this presence in his work and, except for *Days Without End,* he did not expend great energy on the question. Would a student of his plays draw a fair inference if she saw in *Days* evidence of the author's longing to return to the faith? The play did not imply, O'Neill insisted, "that I have gone back to Catholicism. I haven't. But I would be a liar if I didn't admit that, for the sake of my soul's peace, I have often wished I could."[31]

Because his plays typically deal with his own tragic and spiritually complex experiences, they defy easy unravelling. Certainly they defy the audience's instant understanding. Here was a divided soul, a man at war with his allegiances: to family and friends; lovers and children; church and theater. Sometimes he complicated things beyond any viewer's power to fathom. One thinks of the mask plays in this connection, brilliant as they may be. *Days Without End* is such a play, although only one character is masked. "*LOVING's face is a mask whose features reproduce exactly the features of JOHN's face—the death mask of JOHN who has died with a sneer of scornful mockery on his lips. And this mocking scorn is repeated in the expression of the eyes which stare bleakly from behind the mask*" (III, 493–94). This prop contributes to a dramatic portrait of a man's inner division: love and hate, compassion and coldness, humility and arrogance. One wonders if O'Neill had unconsciously recalled the characteristics of a sacrament as defined in the catechism: "*an outward sign of an inward condition.*"

The main plot line of the miracle play is the division of loyalties within one man (John Loving), one side contemptuous of "weakness" (faith), the other side generous of spirit and struggling to recover belief. In this characterization O'Neill pursues the bifurcation study undertaken in the Dionysus/St. Anthony division dramatized in *The Great God Brown*. (In such dynamics we may be reminded of a head-and-heart duality such as that created by Nathaniel Hawthorne: those characters who fear love for its power to make them vulnerable: Ethan Brand, Dr. Rappaccini, Aylmer.) The plot is complicated by John's betrayal of his wife Elsa in a brief liaison with her friend Lucy. But the complex John Loving is sketched in sharp contrast to the nearly cardboard characterizations of Elsa, Lucy Hillman, and Fr. Matthew Baird, the hero's uncle. In all of this we discover a fundamental problem, a matter that deserves some attention.

Elsa, age thirty-five and a survivor of an earlier ill-fated marriage, believes that she has now entered a "perfect" union, the "true sacrament" that she and John bestow upon each other. (Their stilted exchanges, reminiscent of the marital conversations in *Welded,* signal early trouble for audience-playwright rapport.) She remains innocent of the knowledge of John's affair with Lucy until she begins to reflect on the plot of his novel, for he insists on reading the scenario to her and Fr. Baird. On the one hand, she is supposed to be a mature woman, sophisticated about the world's deceits. On the other, she holds expectations of conjugal bliss that place her grasp of reality in doubt. It is this very innocence, however, which her close friend and husband's brief lover seeks, in envy, to puncture.

Fr. Baird (in physique and manner reminiscent of James O'Neill, Sr.) is a man of cheerful and generous nature, a model of the forgiving and tolerant priest. His wisdom is revealed, not in the power of rhetoric or logic, but in the simplicity of his faith. This man who has lived his virtue has come to "Jack" because of what happened "one night while I was praying for you in my church, as I have every day since I left you. [The priest had years earlier been appointed the younger man's guardian when John's parents died in a flu epidemic.] A strange feeling of fear took possession of me—a feeling you were unhappy, in some great spiritual danger. . . . [A]s I prayed, suddenly as if by some will outside me, my eyes were drawn to the Cross, to the face of Our Blessed Lord. And it was like a miracle. . . . That's the real reason I decided to take my vacation in the East, Jack" (507–508).

John had lost his parents at age fifteen. Once a pious believer, he thereafter became a cynic who gave up his faith and sought life's answers in one philosophy after another, from the classic Greeks through Buddhism to Nietzschean godlessness and Bolshevism. The parallels to O'Neill's own life are quite apparent to one who knows his biography. At the end of the school year in 1902, at about the same age as John Loving, Eugene would announce to his parents his unwillingness to return to De La Salle in Manhattan. Disheartened by his mother's continuing melancholy and distance from him, he was losing his faith.

> The inner struggle went on for months while his schoolmates and teachers found him polite and detached. He looked forward to Sundays, when the boarding students attended Mass at St. Patrick's Cathedral on Fifth Avenue; surrounded by the sacred images and symbols, the tall stained-glass windows and soaring pillars of the church named for the patron saint of the Irish, the boy felt in closer touch with God.
> Thirty years later O'Neill, freely revising his actual history, dramatized the essential points of his crisis in *Days Without End*, the story of an embattled Catholic apostate named John Loving.[32]

In the following year (1903) Eugene learned from his father and brother of Ella's morphine addiction. Thereafter, he would no longer attend Sunday Mass. He had given up Catholicism and become the apostate. But, like John Loving, he would discover that the claims of religion could not be easily dismissed. In Fr. Baird's recalling lines from "The Hound of Heaven," the echo of O'Neill's own spiritual struggle can be inferred:

> "Ah, fondest, blindest, weakest,
> I am He Whom thou seekest!
> Thou dravest love from thee, who dravest Me."[33]

The priest visits John's home that evening, where Elsa is recovering from the flu. John, encouraged by wife and uncle, sketches out the novel he has been writing, a barely disguised account of his affair with Lucy. His purpose in composing it seems to be twofold: it permits him to recapitulate his own behavior and thus to examine his own motives; and it provides a device for testing Elsa's capacity to forgive him.

> ELSA. You want me to put myself in the wife's place?
> JOHN. Yes. I want to see whether the man was a fool or not—in his fear.
> ELSA. No. She could never forgive him. (539)

Loving here, "*in a sinister, jeering tone*," insists that the appropriate denouement would call for the death of the wife "to make my romantic hero come finally to a rational conclusion about his life!" (539). We must remember that Loving, though his "life principle" is precisely the opposite of John's, can possess no more information than his other self. He cannot invent facts; one side of this divided personality can know only what the other knows. In that sense, John can fight him on equal terms. It is only in their motives that they differ.

Elsa withdraws for the evening and the men repair to the study. Fr. Baird asks what happens to the hero after the wife's death. John says that the hero returns to the church of his *boyhood,* where he kneels at the foot of the Cross and "feels he is forgiven" (545). Loving curses God, and the men discuss John's need for forgiveness until Elsa enters—disheveled, wet, and feverish. Nearly hysterical, she reveals that Lucy's tale of infidelity and John's "novel" of adultery have caused her to draw the inevitable inferences. Can she forgive his sin? "No! I can't forgive!" (550).

Then the play, in two brief scenes, is brought to an end. A week has passed. Elsa, bedridden and in a semi-coma, weakly utters a heart-breaking cry: "John! How could you? Our dream!" (554). John is near collapse. Among the men (Stillwell, a physician, is present) a battle is waged for the soul of John. The priest, believing less in polemics than in submissiveness to a higher power, prays: "Dear Jesus, grant me the grace to bring Jack back to Thee. Make him see that Thou alone hast the words of Eternal Life" (558).

Some power moves John Loving into the old church, where he falls prostrate before the crucifix.[34] In this final scene Loving, his arrogance diminishing, is defeated by John's faith and willing surrender. As he looks upon "*the face of the Crucified*," he speaks in trembling voice, "Ah! Thou hast heard me at last! . . . I can forgive myself—through Thee! I can believe!" (565). Since John has "*at last surrender[ed]*" ("Thou has conquered, Lord. Thou art—the End"), Francis Thompson's equation has been worked out as a divine paradox: God's conquering is impelled by the surrender of the one pursued. Both the stalker and the stalked are victorious: "Thou art the Way—the Truth—the Resurrection and the Life, and he that believeth in Thy Love, his love shall never die!" (566). Fr. Baird, entering the sanctuary, tells John of the miracle: "Elsa will live." *Tableau. Fade out*

Days Without End is seriously impaired by the sheer improbability of its dialogue and the unreality of its character motivation. These conditions affect both major ribbons of plot: the wife-husband coming to terms with the latter's adultery; and the Fr. Baird–John Loving discussions on questions of religious faith. The talk on these issues lacks plausibility. But why? After all, the problems are intrinsically compelling. O'Neill, moreover, knew from experience whereof he spoke. Furthermore, such problems beset an ever greater number of men and women today than when the play was first produced. The answer may lie in the very *personalism,* if we may call it that, that did not permit O'Neill to achieve sufficient distance from his characters and their problems. The stage itself becomes the field whereon his own battle for faith is fought out. It is as if the artist were standing on the very ground he sought to uncover.

Further, these conditions explain the presence of the play's swollen language. It adds little to say, as one type of critic unfailingly does, that O'Neill had no ear for the spoken word. That is, frankly, an invalid pronouncement. One need only think of his upbringing, his education, and the theater world in which he was trained (George Pierce Baker, the Provincetown Theatre, and his colleagues Kenneth Macgowan, Robert Edmond Jones, and George Jean Nathan). Yet it must be granted that the dialogue in *Days Without End,* as in *Welded* and *The First Man,* is stilted precisely because the "agonies" are so patently self-dramatizing. In his last plays, that self takes its rightful place in the wings: as the compassionate observer of brother (*A Moon for the Misbegotten*) and friends (*The Iceman Cometh*). The *personalist* agenda had been discarded. The craftsman could then take his materials from the workshop of memory (like Yeats's "circus animals") and therewith construct great edifices of modern tragedy. No longer would audience or reader be obliged to respond to such an exchange as this recapitulation of his personal spiritual turmoil.

> JOHN. . . . at school he learned of the God of Punishment, and he wondered. He couldn't reconcile Him with his parents' faith. So it didn't make much impression on him.
> LOVING. Then! But afterward he had good reason to—
> JOHN. But then he was too sure in his faith. He grew up as devout as his parents. He even dreamed of becoming a priest. He used to love to kneel in the church before the Cross. . . .
> LOVING. So the poor fool prayed and prayed and vowed his life to piety and good works! But he began to make a condition now . . . if his mother were spared to him! (510–511)

Students of O'Neill will require no interpretation of these lines.

Days Without End may have taught O'Neill a valuable lesson: the artist must never think only about himself. O'Neill's correspondence relating to the play shows first that he was thinking mainly about himself and second that he felt precious little confidence in either critic or spectator to respond to his meaning. "I never in my wildest dream," he wrote to Sophus Winther two months after its closing, "hoped it would be understood by the general public. And I foresaw all the time I was writing it the critical outburst against it in New York, altho' I didn't think they would be so cheaply wise-guy as they were. I thought it would run about six weeks. It lasted seven. So I was one to the good!"[35] None of this was worthy of him.

* * *

Whatever faults cripple its dramatic effectiveness, however, *Days Without End* is a play about faith. In it O'Neill shows, if not traditional Christian (Catholic) belief, something like a faith in faith. No one can now determine with certitude O'Neill's deepest intentions, but Professor Floyd shrewdly noted that the playwright several times recorded in his plans for the hero, "once a Catholic always a Catholic."[36] Even so, what does the assertion truly reveal about a personality like O'Neill's? What is a "Modern Miracle Play," as he described it to Macgowan?[37] What did O'Neill hope perceptive spectators would take from his play? One thing is certain above all others: He was deadly serious about this work that taxed him, he said, more than anything else he had done up to that time. (He wrote seven drafts of *Days Without End,* one more that he had for *Mourning Becomes Electra.*)

O'Neill, who had by now (1933–1934), made many public denials of personal faith, knew that writing *Days* would prove a risky venture. If it met with a hostile critical reception, as he predicted it would, he could complain about the "jackasses" who have no religious tradition to give them a background for understanding the hero's dilemma: "New York critics dwell in a too pseudo-sophisticated, self-consciously modern, wise-crack atmosphere to be able to judge objectively a play which treats religious faith as a psychological problem of to-day."[38] If, on the other hand, sympathetic critics (mainly Catholic) approved it, he could accept this compliment graciously and plead that he no longer had the gift of simple faith but wished he might recover it. It is clear that O'Neill was not only conscious of patrons' religious sympathies but would rely on these sentiments to gain approval. As he wrote to Macgowan, "I want it to open as soon after Christmas day as possible because then, if ever now, you catch people in a frame of mind to remember their past or present religious background."[39] No doubt his sentiments were honest, but the total effort required something of a tightrope performance.

The immediate foreground of the play would be Catholic, yes, but all Christian (and other) believers would get the point. He raised the issue with Winther: "Did you read H. T. Parker's criticism in the *Boston Transcript?* He was the best of all our newspaper critics and surely could not be charged with any Catholic bias. (He was, I believe, a complete agnostic.) His article would give you a true impression of the reaction in Boston (a New England non-Catholic Theatre Guild subscriber audience). *Days Without End* went over finely there."[40] It would be even better, of course, if approval came from a theater professional of more impressive credentials than the press reviewers. Superb, indeed, if the paragon were himself a great poet, playwright, and Nobel Prize winner, and a Protestant: "William Butler Yeats—no Catholic—cabled me and the Abbey Theatre people want to produce it immediately.[41] If a poet like Yeats sees what is in it, all my hard work on it is more than justified."[42] And he wrote to Russel Crouse that "Yeats is Yeats. Also, he isn't a Catholic. Whatever bias he might have in that line would, I think, be contra rather than pro."[43]

It seems that we are forced to conclude that O'Neill's very uncertainty about the meaning of *Days Without End* accounts for the dual reception—favorable responses from Christian sympathizers, confusion or vitriol from the "pseudo-sophisticates." However, even if such disparate reactions served his immediate needs, they do not illuminate the question of *O'Neill and faith*. Consider. If the play is not intended to show that the "miracle" is in some way related to the divine and to suggest that therein lies the answer to John's prayers, what are we to make of his behavior at the end? As he looks upon "*the face of the Crucified,*" and since he has "*at last surrender[ed],*" what are we to make of his ultimate state of mind? In spite of Carlotta's insistence to Saxe Commins that the end of the play "has nothing to do with *Christianity* or *prayer,*" did O'Neill expect the audience to suppose that Elsa willed the happy ending? that his characters are victims of their self-created illusions? Is the hero deceived in his own understanding? What then is the audience to infer? And how can the playwright speak of his protagonist as the "hero" if that character does not understand what has happened to him, if he is the victim of a religious opiate?[44]

It would be presumptuous in the extreme to suggest that *Days Without End* reestablished Eugene O'Neill for a moment in his childhood Catholicism. Nor is such a claim made here. Even so, it is important to underscore (1) what the play means in terms of its own logic and (2) what it seems to have revealed about O'Neill's own state of mind. To Winther, O'Neill had remarked that he wished "to keep my theme mystically true as an old miracle play and psychologically true as a *modern* miracle play."[45] It is not easy to know what he finally meant by "mystical." But he had also written to Bennett Cerf: "It is a play about a Catholic. It is an attempt to express what I feel are the life-preserving depths in Catholic mysticism—to be fair to a side of life I have dismissed with scorn in other plays."[46] His explanations suggest a man who was not entirely sure what he wanted to impart. In this his struggle reminds us of many another modern artist-*aliéné*. Santayana had remained something of a "Catholic atheist"; in *Long Day's Journey into Night* O'Neill evokes an image of the Irish mystic "who can never belong." But the text of the "play about a Catholic" tells us that O'Neill contradicted himself both in his remarks about his own spiritual dilemma and in what he said his play means when it stands without his gloss.

Days Without End has never served O'Neill well. Its New York failure ended his plan to complete a trilogy to be called "Myth Plays for the God-forsaken." The play has been dismissed as poorly conceived, stilted in language, and weak in character motivation. (One would have to work hard to learn when or where it was last produced.) Because it represents a low moment in the playwright's development, moreover, it seldom receives extended discussion, except as it is logged in assessments of the O'Neill canon.

But O'Neill himself never accepted the failure as just, in the way that he came to terms with other of his plays that received little praise. For a time he intended to keep *Anna Christie,* another "happy ending" play, from inclusion with his collected works. The poor receptions of *The First Man* and *Welded* disturbed him because his control of craft had been questioned. Even so, in the same period he had known major successes: *Beyond the Horizon, The Emperor Jones, The Hairy Ape.* By the early 1930s the great critical acclaim and box office records of several plays—*Desire Under the Elms, Strange Interlude,* and *Mourning Becomes Electra*—had greatly strengthened his confidence. The astonishing popularity of *Ah, Wilderness!,* produced only a year earlier than *Days,* suggested his mastery of the comedic as well as the tragic form. Herewith his reputation as the brooding black Irishman was somewhat softened. He was by now far less likely to be plunged into insecurity by hostile criticism.

Days Without End opened up the question of his own faith, so great a consolation to him in childhood. For Eugene O'Neill was a Catholic. That is, his religious background had formed his identity: "Once a Catholic always a Catholic." What else can that formula mean, if not identity? He had often proclaimed proudly that only Irish blood flowed in his veins. It was useful, of course, if Yeats ("no Catholic") approved his theme, but it was Catholic Dublin that made the European premiere of his miracle play a success.

Well, John Loving is not Daniel O'Connell. In fact, this hero's ethnicity can hardly be inferred. But, if it seems irrelevant, John's Catholicism isn't. Faith was the deepest issue in O'Neill's life. In the end it was the only question that mattered. *Days Without End* tells of faith's recovery, whatever O'Neill may have intended. He said he knew who would understand his play and its language: "Jesuits and Catholic theologians." He also knew who would not understand it: "the critical lads . . . [who created] such an idiotic storm of prejudice."[47]

In one way or another, each of the O'Neills had difficulty keeping the faith. We remember the other family members now chiefly because Eugene memorialized them. If he had not written his plays, their individual dilemmas would have been lost to memory. The triumph of his work has caused his own life and the lives of his parents and brother to become a source of endless fascination for men and women everywhere. Like his parents, Eugene found his greatest tragedy in living his own life. He never regained the beliefs that might have eased this sorrow. Yet the very fact that he could not give up the search suggests that he kept faith in the best way he could.

7 | Plays: Late Period (1939–1943)

The Iceman Cometh

THIS WORK STANDS as something of an anomaly in modern theater history. Generally acclaimed a masterpiece, it has received relatively few productions. Yet, if we reflect even briefly on this situation, no puzzle remains. Uncut, *The Iceman Cometh* rivals *Hamlet* in running time, a test of endurance contemporary audiences accept without enthusiasm. Nor do the play's tragic theme and unrelieved pessimism encourage producers who measure success by clicks of the turnstile. O'Neill himself, of course, was characteristically indifferent to conventional expectations. It is "a simple play," he remarked, that has "no plot in the ordinary sense. I don't need plot—the people are enough."[1] His people, however, appear to be little more than a collection of social rejects: losers, drifters, and has-beens. What could they say or do, one may ask, to hold the patrons' interest for four and a half hours. Small wonder, then, that few playgoers have seen *The Iceman* performed.[2]

The theme of sin and redemption does not at first suggest itself. "The inmates of Harry Hope's saloon," as O'Neill called them, live by an unspoken compact of reciprocity, an arrangement by which the individual tolerates the others' life lies in order that his own shaky self-deception will not be threatened. The logic of this accommodation appears to be nothing more than each person's self-serving acceptance of the group's *modus vivendi*.

Such is the low-voltage dynamism of their interaction. As Larry Slade, the house cynic, puts it cannily: "Don't you notice the beautiful calm in the atmosphere? That's because it's the last harbor. No one here has to worry about where they're going next, because there is no farther they can go. It's a great comfort to them. Although even here they keep up the appearances of life with a few harmless pipe dreams about their yesterdays and tomorrows . . . " (III, 587).

O'Neill was recalling the dark period when he had finished his sea voyages and had, nearly destitute, found shelter in a flophouse on the lower East Side. "It's not just one place perhaps, but it is several places that I lived in at one time or another—places I knew put together in one."[3] He drew chiefly on his memories of two such gathering spots: "Jimmy-the-Priest's" (James Conlon's bar on Fulton Street) and Tom Wallace's Golden Swan (the "Hell Hole") on 6th Avenue. This shadow world becomes Harry Hope's Raines Law hotel, the setting of *The Iceman Cometh*.

Here converge a minor legion of "ex-politicians, anarchists (recently out of jail or on their way in), gamblers, touts and pimps."[4] They are waiting for "Hickey," hardware salesman Theodore Hickman—raconteur and jolly good fellow, who comes by every year on Harry's birthday to treat the "gang" to a booze binge and general good time. He is eagerly awaited, both because he has always before entertained them and because the booze he supplies washes away all threats to their illusions. This time things will turn out differently, however. One of their company announces that she has spotted Hickey on the street. "And I kidded him. 'How's de iceman, Hickey? How's he doin' at your house?' He laughs and says, 'Fine.' And he says, 'Tell de gang I'll be along in a minute. I'm just finishin' figurin' out de best way to save dem and bring dem peace.' . . . [H]e was only kiddin'. But he was funny, too, somehow. He was different, or somethin' " (617–618).

Any attempt to portray such characters poses a considerable challenge to the artist. He must resist, on the one hand, the temptation to sentimentalize them; and he must avoid, on the other, leading the audience into an act of voyeuristic condescension. Each of these treatments is sure to degrade his characters. But O'Neill, having himself completed the hard-knocks curriculum, could describe this underworld without patronizing his "people." He could speak with the authority of experience: " . . . [A]ll I can say is that it is a play about pipe dreams. And the philosophy is that there is always one dream left . . . down there at the bottom of the bottle. I know because I saw it."[5] In recalling his acquaintances of that period, O'Neill offered this simple tribute: "The people in that saloon were the best friends I've ever known."[6]

Yet what value is served by producing this vivid rendering of pock-marked humanity? Whatever else may be inferred, one is mistaken if one reads O'Neill's meaning too narrowly, say, as an argument about the consequences of material poverty. Rather, the play grips us by its fidelity to a more generalized truth. Some years ago Gerald Weales made this perceptive observation: "In [*The Iceman Cometh*] O'Neill tells a story that is at once a meticulously motivated psychological drama and a generalized statement about the nature of man."[7] Lest we take comfort in a smug detachment from these residents of the lower depths, O'Neill sets about to capture us in the very nets that ensnare his characters. Seek not, his play tells us, to stand above these hapless symbols of Everyman: "Their weakness was not an evil. It is a weakness found in all men."[8]

A weakness found in all men. The phrase suggests a universal condition: fate, we might call it. In his vision of human nature, O'Neill stands with the great storytellers. Like Dostoevski, he permits his characters to feel a worthy (i.e., deserved) guilt, the *sine qua non* of the tragic condition. That presence—from Oedipus to Hamlet, from Lady Macbeth to (his) Electra—suggests potential dignity, a quality denied by narrow determinism. It is this view of human nature that elevates O'Neill's naturalism above that of a rigorously scientific school, which withholds any element of will or guilt except as conditioned response. Whence this fate derives has been the preoccupation of all tragedians.

* * *

We see in *The Iceman Cometh* that the ultimate basis for relationship remains fixed in the dynamics of the human family. The ancient patterns are retained but are played out in the larger community. The characters' violations of each other, magnified perhaps because they occur in a larger and more public setting, match the hurts in relationship (sin) that occur in all families. The dynamics of *Iceman* are suggestive of these conflicts. Indeed, important pairings in friendship and other ties are established from the start: Piet Wetjoen, "The General," and Cecil Lewis, "The Captain," former soldiers; ex-Anarchists Hugo Kalmar and Larry Slade; Harry Hope and Ed Mosher, brothers-in-law; Cora (a street walker) and Chuck Morello (her pimp), whose pipe dream is that they will someday settle down in conventional married life; Pat McGloin, ex-cop, and Willie Oban, law school graduate.

In several instances, however, O'Neill makes the familial bases of relationship explicit: husband-wife and father-son. In each case these (antecedant) connections explain the logic of the character's motive and action (*praxis*) and thereby affect the play's denouement. Hickey's relationship with his now-deceased wife, Evelyn, is the more obvious conjugal tie, but no less significant is Slade's long-abandoned liason with Rosa Parritt, a figure modeled on Emma Goldman.[9] Thus, an inference that Larry is Don Parritt's father seems inevitable. And, of course, Parritt has abandoned Rosa to the police. Travis Bogard suggests that each of these men experiences profound guilt for betraying his wife or mother.[10] At any rate, in charting the dynamics of these three relationships, O'Neill has produced his subtlest variations on the theme[11] of sin, guilt, and redemption.

As a boy Eugene O'Neill learned the definitions and classifications of sin in *The Baltimore Catechism*.[12] Here it was explained how one might know that he had been forgiven his offenses against charity. The priest was empowered to hear the confession, impose a penance, and grant absolution. Without debating the theological validity of sacramental cleansing, one might see certain psychological benefits deriving from such a ritual. The artist drew on his memory in creating the confessional episodes of *The Iceman Cometh*. But, in the context of the play the characters must forgive each other. It matters little whether they represent only, or even mainly, believing Christians. Indeed, no religious identification need obtain. If it can be said that sin constitutes an equivalent of O'Neill's "weakness," guilt constitutes a universal symptom. Recall Paul Ricoeur's definition cited in chapter 2: " . . . guiltiness is the burden of sin." Trapped in the malaise of their weakness, they might be tormented even further if no ritual of forgiveness were available. O'Neill's background and early training had given him an exceptional sensitivity to this modern dilemma.

The Iceman is often seen as O'Neill's ultimate statement of despair. Yet, for all his insistence on the theme of "hopeless hope," it is not the playwright's pessimism that gives the work its convincing depth. Nor is the play's impact to be accounted for by the sort of theatrical pyrotechnics he had sometimes practiced. On the contrary, the tragedy's power depends largely on its simplicity of language and surface action. Here we find dialogue unencumbered by stream of consciousness; we experience a naturalistic directness unconfused by masking, expressionistic devices, or Jungian symbolism. The simple and naked character, in elemental conflict, becomes once more the focus as had been the case in the dramatist's early sea plays.

Larry Slade claims only to be waiting for death, "a fine long sleep" (578). His pose of "old foolosopher"-in-residence allows him to play the role of detached observer. Yet his very need to comment suggests Larry's uneasy alliance with truth. His philosophic "detachment" serves only to shield his vulnerability. Once an agent in the turn-of-the-century anarchist movement, he now sneers at human nature: "When man's soul isn't a sow's ear, it will be time enough to dream of silk purses" (590).

Nevertheless, Slade shepherds his fellow lost souls. Indeed, O'Neill stresses his *"expression of tired tolerance giving his face the quality of a pitying but weary old priest's"* (574). Though he protests that he can no longer believe in the Movement or mankind, he is in truth a deeply compassionate man. Bound by the seal of secrecy, the "old priest" must hear every confession. Furthermore, his unconvincing detachment and claim of freedom from pipe dreams are to be severely tested in the day and a half covered in *The Iceman*. He is destined to collide with Hickey and Parritt, who will force him to see that he, too, lives a life lie. As the most cynical, of course, he is the most open to hurt.

The youthful anarchist-on-the-run, Don Parritt, seeks a hiding place at Harry Hope's. Having betrayed his own mother, for whom the Movement is a way of life, he knows that Slade had once been close to Rosa and therefore asks forgiveness of a man who had himself betrayed the cause. Larry Slade's pipe dream has been his detachment from all human loyalties in his wait for death. He will have to wait no longer. Death, the Iceman, cometh.

Enter Hickey, inveterate rounder and drunk. The son of a backwoods preacher, he has secularized his inherited gift for oratory and put it to the service of salesmanship. Now, recently reformed, he comes on a quasi-religious mission to deliver his gospel of death-to-illusions and thus to bring the "brothers and sisters" his "line of salvation." Hickey must let them have their way for a time. But, as he provides drinks, he hopes to force all to jettison their tomorrowism and seize the new day. If forced to live out their fragile dreams, he intends to tell them, they will inevitably fail but will no longer feel guilty for their life failures. Whether he believes what he says (whether, that is, he acts in charity toward them) or has simply rationalized his motive, all this will come clear soon enough. At the moment he must take on Slade, their louse-infested defender, who teaches that "the lie of the pipe dream" alone gives life.

*　*　*

It looks as if Hickey cares deeply for the residents of the Hope's hotel. But he no longer has viable relationships. Evelyn, his wife, has been dead now several months. Overly familiar with "de gang" and a bit frenzied, he combines an air of circus barker with that of the revivalist, calling them pals, *boys and girls, Brothers and Sisters*. Hickey claims that he wishes to restore their vitality. In truth, he is practicing a complex strategy of self-examination and self-evasion. While protesting that he means only to bring them peace, he hopes to dodge his guilt: his guilt for murdering Evelyn. Thus Hickey merely uses the "boys and girls." He must convince them, and himself, that bringing them peace will prove the efficacy of denying all guilt; he seems to have convinced himself that he is acting in their behalf. But, whatever he tells them about the peace he has experienced and wants to share with them, Hickey continues to bear a heavy burden of guilt. He has not escaped from Evelyn. In the end he cannot escape his spiritual ties to these old friends, nor can they escape theirs to him (as O'Neill had put it, the "weakness found in all men").

As Hickey turns the screws tighter on each of them, the brothers and sisters become testy. The earlier calm breaks up. All grow to hate him and to hope that he will be destroyed by his own misguided zeal. Harry Hope's place becomes a den of sullen failures, each prepared to tear the heart out of the others. His confidence weakened, Hickey is forced to test his own achievement of peace by reconstructing the manner of its evolution.

Compulsively ("I've got to tell you!") he rehearses with them how he delivered Evelyn of her pipe dream that he would someday reform. For years she had forgiven him his infidelity and binges. Unconsciously he had grown to hate her sweet charity: "There's a limit to the guilt you can feel and the forgiveness and pity you can take!" (715). So, to free her of the need to forgive him, Hickey (the Iceman/Death) murdered his wife in her bed. He had come to loathe her insufferable kindness. (In a similar way the derelicts have grown to resent his plan to "save" them.) In a brief flash of insight, Hickey recognizes his real motive for murdering Evelyn. Almost as quickly, he denies this truth.

A law of retribution seems to operate in human affairs: *sin is punished*. Sin always had to do with relationships: One could not injure or degrade another without degrading oneself. In the 1946 production interview O'Neill spoke of Hickey in a language that betrayed his (O'Neill's) own culture and training. It is worth recalling here the complete context of his remarks. Was the salesman a good man, he was asked.

> Raw emotion produces the worst in people. Remember, goodness can surmount anything. The people in that saloon were the best friends I've ever known. . . . Their weakness was not an evil. It is a weakness found in all men. . . .
> Revenge . . . is the subconscious motive for the individual's behavior with the rest of society. Revulsion drives man to tell others of his sins. . . . It is the Furies within us that seek to destroy us. . . .
> In all my plays sin is punished and redemption takes place.
> Vice and virtue cannot live side by side. It's the humiliation of a loving kiss that destroys evil.[13]

Hickey is taken off by the police at the end, presumably to face the electric chair. (So had Abbie and Eben been taken away by the sheriff for the murder of their baby.) Public knowledge of the sinner and his condemnation might have been O'Neill's meaning, but that seems unlikely. In his late plays the "sinner's" torment is often inflicted by conscience and the sin must be confessed. This is Hickey's punishment. In a mind ravaged like his, however, the possibilities for self-deception appear to be endless. His guilt is the engine that drives his compulsion to confess, yes. But, in having set out to "save" his brothers and sisters, Hickey has created a further complication. For now he has committed the fault of pride, which fosters another variety of pipe dream, one destructive of the community. In this case it is a self-engendered Messianic illusion whose vitality actually depends upon the *weakness* of others.

In O'Neill's universe the greatest sin is neither drunkenness nor adultery. It is, rather, to rob another of his hopeless hope. Such an act constitutes the most egregious violation of the person. To deny one his self-image is to strip him of his dignity and his interior life. In historical Christianity redemption has meant, not a denial of the sinner's weakness, but an acceptance of his total humanity through charity.[14] In a world where the Christian can no longer locate God, his impulses do not cease to be formed by his tradition. O'Neill's plays recall such a world. As noted earlier, each member of Hope's community defers to the other's life lie in order that she herself might not be hurt. Perhaps we can call this habit a kind of defensive altruism. Habit very often produces merely compulsive behavior, of course, but it can also foster health. This was the teaching of St. Thomas Aquinas, by way of Aristotle, who described virtue as *habitus.*

Some see in Harry Hope's birthday gathering a celebration, or even a parody, of *agape:* those present equal the number of guests at the Last Supper.[15] But Hope's friends ("de gang") join the party to keep alive their own faint sparks of tomorrowism, not to enact or mock the solemnity of a religious celebration. Here we discover souls so bruised and spiritually disfigured that the world no longer esteems them. Yet Hope's bar can also be seen as a retreat where men and women find something worthy in one another and where they can exchange a human word to lift the spirit.

Hickey has been operating on a different logic, however. His relentless campaign to bring them "salvation" derives not from mutual need but from a self-hatred born of the guilt Evelyn had made him feel. We are required, it seems, to make an important distinction between two kinds of guilt: that borne simply by being human (which, it can be argued, is very Christian), and that engendered by the knowledge that others pity us for being ourselves. This latter is degrading. Hickey's guilt carries disease to the corporate whole. Since he would rob the gang of their feeble illusions, Hickey represents a threat that must be eliminated. He endangers everyone's painfully wrought self-image. He must go.

The portrayal of Larry Slade, however, shows O'Neill's even profounder reliance upon a memory galvanized by Irish Catholicism. It is important to recall that Slade's own Catholic background has been established in the character description. Over the years his faculty for belief has been paralyzed, and his sense of lost faith has defeated him. He knows that men cannot escape the essential tragedy of life. Nevertheless, what Slade is he is: simultaneously house cynic and resident confessor: "I was born condemned to be one of those who has to see all sides of a question" (590). In a moment of crisis he is *re-*formed in the image of his cultural identity. This movement of character is staggering in its dramatic revelation, a stroke of creativity that places Eugene O'Neill, for a moment, at least, with "all the Olympians." Let us examine precisely what happens.

Don Parritt has been fairly mesmerized by the incantatory power of the salesman's long self-analysis. Hickey had sensed something of the boy's dilemma from the beginning: "No offense, Brother. . . . Haven't we met before some place? . . . I know damned well I recognized something about you. We're members of the same lodge—in some way" (624). Having heard (reluctantly) Parritt's confession, Larry gives a profane absolution: "Go! Get the hell out of life. God damn you, before I choke it out of you!" (720). Larry's pity, however, unlike Hickey's, has been impelled by his Christian nurture, not his philosophical pessimism.

After Larry hears Parritt's body hurtle to the ground, confirming the suicide, the playwright inserts a significant stage direction before his speech: ("*A long-forgotten faith returns to him for a moment and he mumbles*) God rest his soul in peace" (726). This is a superb insight, in every way the mark of O'Neill's cultural memory. In the moment of crisis, one "re-forms" along the lines of his earliest psychological self. Larry's genuine belief in what the line implies is not the point. What is important is what his gesture means: Men respond to trauma in terms of their elemental selves, in this case an identity formed by culture and religion. Residual faith and hope sputter for an instant in Larry Slade's response, only to die again forever. But it is in the heart of his character that O'Neill has touched upon a deep truth: one's early formation marks his identity indelibly.

One can hardly argue that Parritt's suicide constitutes a form of redemption. What, then, did O'Neill mean to convey by Slade's granting "absolution" to Parritt? It has drained Larry. In a way this has been his final "living" act; thereafter, he is dead. But in a wonderfully muted way Larry has given what surfaces but rarely in the human drama—selfless love. He takes on a portion of Parritt's guilt. But now, bereft of his pipe dream of detachment, he becomes "the only real convert to death Hickey made here" (727). Parritt's suicide, nevertheless, is not left to stand as a base human deceit, unmourned. And in this, Larry's response provides a further insight into O'Neill's psychological rapprochement with his culture's ideal of *caritas*. Women and men need a confessor to absolve their tragic failures.

Early in the play Larry had scorned the truth as irrelevant, as having "no bearing on anything." Yet he must come at last to live in the knowledge of it. His despair is terrible, but even here his language confirms his cultural origins: "Be God, there's no hope." (Con Melody slips into the brogue when all his pipe dreams have been dissolved in *A Touch of the Poet*.)

In his way he gives his life for his friend (perhaps, it is hinted, for his own son). Whatever his philosophy, Larry's deepest identity is Irish-Catholic. In the moment when his love is tested to the breaking point, he does not hold first to his flim-flam line. The wisecracks stop, the layers of cynicism and feigned detachment melt, and the mask falls away as Larry hears Don Parritt's body hit the ground. *"He half rises from his chair just as from outside the window comes the sound of something hurtling down, followed by a muffled, crunching thud. Larry gasps and drops back on his chair, shuddering, hiding his face in his hands"* (726). Stripped of all his defenses, a man's utterance will come not from his cynic's acid vat but from his heart: "God rest his soul in peace."

* * *

In a letter to the Corinthians, Paul instructs the small Christian community: "So faith, hope, and love abide, these three; but the greatest of these is love" (1 Cor. 13:13). This is the new law that marks the spirit of the New Testament. Eugene O'Neill could hardly claim the first of the Pauline virutes,

The Iceman being "a denial of any other experience of faith in my plays." Nor could he find consolation in the second. Larry Slade surely speaks for him: "Be God, there's no hope" (726).

O'Neill's portrait of the Raines-Law hotel recalls his days at Jimmy the Priest's on the New York waterfront and the Hell Hole near Greenwich Village. Like the men and women who lived there, he too had failed. He looked upon each of them as "the victim of the ironies of life and of himself."[16] They were not the debris of the cosmos but friends. He had taken compassion on their sufferings and had thereby attempted to restore something of their humanity.

Asked late in life if he had returned to the faith, O'Neill replied, "Unfortunately, no." Nor has the object here been to contradict his declaration. The aim has been to show, however, that he had found a measure of consolation in his Irish-Catholic heritage.

Long Day's Journey into Night

Tragedy, whose arch theme is loss, summarizes the terrible cost of human experience. This classic form teaches the message of fate: We will be defeated *in time*. Whatever is precious becomes all the more cherished as we perceive its vulnerability. In time our very lives will become museum pieces. Thus it is that memory itself constitutes both a benison and a curse, since it permits us to keep alive essences even as it galls us with the knowledge of death. By these certainties the strong as well as the timid are chastened, the wise as well as the foolish. If we scold ourselves for having squandered opportunities, we recognize that not even the greatest husbandry could have preserved what has been lost. One concedes but can never quite fathom the inevitability of this law. These lessons haunt us. Yet we know that tragedy also celebrates the privilege of human experience. Some, the O'Neills and Quinlans perhaps, saw themselves as members of a pilgrim church. To the pilgrim the end of the journey meant the harbor, salvation. Others, less certain about the end, may have seen themselves as waifs in the cosmos. In any case, one was not given a choice whether to make the journey. Thus fated, the traveler embarks with the resources at hand—faith and hope, a brave toast to "sunny days and starry nights," or even the shaky supports of tomorrowism.[17]

Long Day's Journey confirms the timeless mystery of loss. How perfect the play's fundamental image, the dying of the light. It compares with Shakespeare's sonnet 73 ("That time of year thou mays't in me behold") or Milton's "Sonnet on Blindness." The very metaphor suggests the theme of loss: loss of energy, illumination, creativity, warmth, love. As O'Neill's play begins in the light and promise of a new day, the audience cannot be criticized if it builds hopeful expectations. The stage directions indicate the day and season, *a morning in August,* just after breakfast. It could just as easily be the morning of July Fourth in the Miller household (*Ah, Wilderness!*). But in the tragedy the hope of this new day quickly fades, and the progressive decay of light brings to mind the coming on of death.

The setting in the family is also classic in its simplicity. But again the first promise is blighted. The Tyrones founder in malaise: sickness of soul and body, each member equally the victim of his and her own lost chances, each equally the plaything of heartless powers that devastate fair expectations. The natural grace of the family is at every moment strained, its vitality constantly threatened by warring tensions. "Here is a family living in a close symbiotic relationship, a single organism with four branches, where a twitch in one creates a spasm in another. [They are] chained together by resentment, guilt, recrimination; yet, the chains that hold [them] are those of love as well as hate."[18] If the characters bear little responsibility for the givens of their condition (*fate*), as partners in relationship they fulfill the other requirements of tragedy (*complicity*). Each fails the other, just as all have failed themselves. A burden of guilt is thereby incurred, the partial cost of sin. As always, however, paradox confounds us. For in wounding each other, all have become candidates for redemption.

O'Neill had not closed accounts with his parents and brother before they died. His father succumbed in 1920, his mother less than two years later, and his brother Jamie in 1923. In this undeniably autobiographical play, Eugene was paying his debt of love to "all *the four haunted Tyrones*." Here he registered "pity and understanding" for what he had done to them and they to him. He had found himself in the situation of many who survive parents and siblings but realize that necessary closure had never occurred. Such a dilemma is common enough, of course, and is addressed in various ways. Some seek the help of the analyst in coming to terms and working through guilt; others invoke the assistance of the clergy or a grief therapist. Most difficult are the cases where women and men simply carry on, but with the sense that things will remain forever unfinished.[19]

The Tyrones, like any other family, have been shaped in great part by historical forces and events. In this case the contributing impulses have been Ireland and the plague of famine and the attendant homesickness: Catholicism, ambitions, love, and marriage.[20] These givens, having produced the unit, account for common loyalties as well as conflicts within the group. Differences in personality both strengthen and undermine the members' interdependence. Thus the sins of the father, and mother, have been visited upon their sons. And by some law of reciprocity the sons, in their very existence, constitute both the reward and punishment the parents have earned. The conditions are classic in their ubiquity. For, as the father and mother recall their own parents with combined fondness and bitterness, so do their children respond to them with a mixture of generosity and anger. In *Long Day's Journey*, then, we have the ancient story of the family as its own savior and tormentor. The organism has considerable potential for mending its own wounds. In its most hopeful self-management, it may function as one philosopher has envisioned:

> . . . it is in the nature of things that the vitality and virtues of love develop first in the family. Not only the examples of the parents, and the rules of conduct which they inculcate, and the religious habits and inspiration which they further, and the memories of their own lineage which they convey, in short the educational work which they directly perform, but also, in a more general way, the common experiences and common trials, endeavors, sufferings, and hopes, and the daily labor of family life, and the daily love which grows up in the midst of cuffs and kisses, constitute the normal fabric where the feelings and the will of the child are naturally shaped.[21]

It is also possible, of course, that the family can be overwhelmed by these same dynamics. Even if its destiny could evolve propitiously, the family would remain locked together in their individual fates (Brustein's point). All is organic. The health or sickness of the body affects the members; the health or sickness of the member affects the body. It becomes us to grant this measure of determinism.

Long Day's Journey offers a splendid vehicle for testing these assumptions. Its simple plot hinges on two threats to individual, and therefore to family, health: Mary's regression into morphine addiction, and Edmund's developing case of tuberculosis. Before the harrowing day's end, each of the four Tyrones will be unmasked and his connections with the others severely tested.

* * *

The Tyrones have taken to their summer retreat on the [Long Island] Sound. James, immensely popular and a veteran actor, has accumulated a considerable fortune. Recalling the racking poverty of his youth, he has invested much of his wealth in the land. With immigrant parents and siblings, he had been driven to America by the mid-century famines of Ireland. By a most admirable dedication to craft, James had risen to the highest stratum of his profession. He married his beloved Mary, whose convent-bred innocence and piety he had hoped above all things to shield. But a shadow has long since fallen over the house of Tyrone. In giving birth to her third son, Mary was given morphine to diminish the pain of labor. Since that day she has been cruelly addicted and has suffered not only the addict's torment but also the humiliation of many confinements for cure. Although she loves James deeply, Mary blames him for bringing this curse upon them all by his unholy devotion to thrift. Indeed, his parsimony had caused him to seek out a physician who charged lesser fees. This lifelong habit has by now disaffected his sons. Not only do they blame him for their mother's agony, but they resent him for the constraints his frugality imposes on their pursuit of pleasure.

On his side James does not lack for complaints against his ingrate sons. Ever and always does he chide them for their profligate ways. Tyrone charges them with infidelity to their traditions and heritage: Ireland and Catholicism. He abhors their cynicism, their lack of filial respect, and their having both been "fired" from college. Especially does he condemn Jamie's pernicious influence on Edmund, ten years his junior.

> You've been the worst influence for him. He grew up admiring you as a hero! A fine example you set him! If you ever gave him advice except in the ways of rottenness, I've never heard of it! You made him old before his time, pumping him full of what you consider worldly wisdom, when he was too young to see that your mind was so poisoned by your own failure in life, you wanted to believe every man was a knave with his soul for sale, and every woman who wasn't a whore was a fool! (*LDJ*, 34)

Now Edmund, like Mary, feels the cold fingers of sickness on him, a sickness that can destroy his life. On this day he will learn whether he has consumption and, if he has, what will be done about it. The tensions mount as the morning and afternoon wear on. It soon becomes clear that Mary Tyrone has reentered the fog of her addiction. By evening, the men know well from experience, she will have slipped into a zone where they have no access to her. That terror is compounded by the suspense in waiting for the diagnosis of Edmund's condition. As the hours pass, father and sons spit fire at each other. At the same time each is moving more deeply into himself, is sinking under the influence of whisky and under the threat of collective disaster. The logic of this progression is brilliant in its persuasive power. After their earlier testiness, each Tyrone falls further into sad reverie and the recognition that he has lost the good life his talents might have earned. The terror suffered by each nearly crushes the figures we see on the stage.

*   *   *

Four sets of relationships operate in the Tyrone family. Of course, isolating any one for examination constitutes a somewhat artificial maneuver. As Brustein noted, each member acts and reacts as she or he is connected with the other three. All is organic. Even so, we can derive useful insights by focusing for a moment on the relationships in arbitrary sequence: mother-sons, father-sons, brother-brother, husband-wife.

That Mary Tyrone loves both her sons is a truth beyond dispute. But she does not love them without conflicting elements of ambivalence and guilt. Nor is the sons' love for her an affection without alloy. Indeed, this complexity of relationship is often magnified in Irish-Catholic families, where sons are trained to associate the mother with the Blessed Virgin Mary herself, the very ideal of purity. Irishman-litterateur Noel O'Hara offers an exceptionally helpful insight into this phenomenon.

> The portrait of Ella, and indeed her children's attitudes to her, reminded me in one way of my own time growing up in Ireland. I have often thought since that, technically, the Irish Church, in its attitude to the Blessed Virgin, was idolatrous. We were much closer to her, and she was much more important in our lives, than the Man himself. There was no devotion more widespread or passionate than the rosary. Novenas were a grand opportunity for a girl to ask her to help find her a husband, and the young fellows would try and soft talk her into getting them a good job in the Civil Service. . . . Anyhow I often thought how in those bleak years in Ireland, very large families and little money, and no thought of a woman going out to work, that the Virgin Mary must have been the surrogate romantic mother for the untold thousands of offsprings of mothers too overburdened to have any softness left over. So perhaps there was a deep psychological factor in the Irish devotion to her, which no doubt carried over into America. No doubt too it was a factor in Irish sexuality, in generations of convent educated wives up to this day, to say nothing of priest or brother educated husbands and fathers, inhibitions that are manifest in a variety of ways. Ella O'Neill is partially a product of the same influence. And Eugene's own dichotomous attitude to women, the double standard, can no doubt be traced back to Irish Catholic puritanism.[22]

That she is not virginal greatly complicates the sons' view of the father, of course. If the Oedipal complex operates more or less universally, in this cultural milieu what is normally difficult can become positively baroque. One has no reason to wonder, then, about O'Neill's having chosen Mary for the mother's name, particularly since his own mother had been so profoundly dedicated to the Virgin. Because she feels she has betrayed the Lady of Sorrows, Mary Tyrone also feels guilt for having betrayed her sons. (She does not seem to hold herself responsible for a similar betrayal of James. Why?) But she does not see Jamie and Edmund as equally deserving of her affection.

Jamie's words to and about his mother are harsher and more cynical than Edmund's. The older son's conflicts suggest the first set of complications. He has known about Mary's addiction for ten years longer than Edmund. He resents that Edmund is "Mama's baby, Papa's pet." Furthermore, outrageous as it seems, Jamie sees his father as "competitor" for Mary's affection. He feels, moreover, apparently with good reason, that he himself was long ago found guilty for having infected baby Eugene with a fatal case of measles. As Mary says to Tyrone, "*her face hardening:* I've always believed Jamie did it on purpose. He was jealous of the baby. He hated him. . . . He knew. I've never been able to forgive him for that" (87). At the same time she recognizes that she should not have left Jamie and Eugene in her mother's care in order to be with James on the road. The brilliant and poison-tongued Jamie, sensing her guilt, viciously cuts through her denials as she retreats to her room for "another shot in the arm" (75). The sins of anger, of lashing out against another's weakness, are always terrible in their effect. The venom he releases cuts scars deeper into the soul of the viper than into his victim's. His mask of Mephistopheles hides his otherwise naked and terrifying vulnerability.

The acid that runs through Jamie's veins has corroded his heart. His violations of those he loves most, sins of cruelty (*words, words, words*), have intensified his own pain almost beyond bearing. Since early childhood he has lived with fear and guilt; now he needs his mother more than ever, since he has not been able to grow up. One of the greatest questions in *Long Day's Journey into Night* is this: Who will redeem Jamie? It may be that in this play he is not, cannot be, saved by love. It may be that he is the object of love but cannot summon the courage to accept the gift.

Mary seeks to give comfort to Edmund by caressing him. She speaks with him tête-à-tête, as once she must have spoken with Jamie. She is solicitous about his "summer cold." As it is often the case in O'Neill, however, outward appearance is deceiving. Mary has a heart's grudge against Edmund too, just as she has against James and Jamie. To Tyrone she makes known that his birth stands as a kind of reproof to her, a punishment: "I was afraid all the time I carried Edmund. I knew something terrible would happen. I knew I'd proved by the way I'd left Eugene that I wasn't worthy to have another baby, and that God would punish me if I did. I never should have borne Edmund" (88). One wonders if any child can ever come unscathed through the dark maze of childhood.

We should always be open to a fresh view of things, however. O'Hara sees the background a bit differently.

> O'Neill [Edmund] had a lot going for him really, when I think of his young man's head on his mother's lap and the consoling him for his marriage to poor old Kathleen [Jenkins]. Of course we read novels and lives from our own childhoods, and many a boy I knew would have envied him such love from a mother, absent or not. And James, the Count, doesn't seem to have been such a bad old stick.[23]

In the family one suffers much from all the pushing and tearing that takes place. But the kisses come as frequently as the cuffs, a truth that makes the deliberate injuries such a burden to bear in the after-years. What Edmund wants most is that Mary not take the drug that day. And she wants desperately to provide that succor to him; she nearly promises the impossible, inspired by her vision of the Virgin.

> Now I have to lie, especially to myself. But how can you understand, when I don't myself. I've never understood anything about it, except that one day long ago I found I could no longer call my soul my own.
> *She pauses—then lowering her voice to a strange tone of whispered confidence.*
> But some day, dear, I will find it again—some day when you're all well, and I see you healthy and happy and successful, and I don't have to feel guilty any more—some day when the Blessed Virgin Mary forgives me and gives me back the faith in Her love and pity I used to have in my convent days, and I can pray to Her again—when She sees no one in the world can believe in me even for a moment any more, then She will believe in me, and with Her help it will be so easy. I will hear myself scream with agony, and at the same time I will laugh because I will be so sure of myself. (93–94)

When he sees that she has begun once more, he is willing to jolt her by pointing out that her habit has made "life seem rotten." Finally, driven by fear, anger, and frustration, he lashes out: "It's pretty hard to take at times, having a dope fiend for a mother!" (120).

The internecine character of these relationships fairly shreds the soul. Once we understand this situation, we need not wonder why it took O'Neill many years to "forgive" himself and the other "Tyrones." He knew how much Ella loved her Catholic faith. Agnes Boulton tells how, after her recovery from morphine addiction, Ella slipped away from the sleeping James each morning to attend Mass at a church close by the Prince George Hotel where they lived in the winters. And, when we know this, we know that O'Neill must have retained some affection for the Church: because his mother loved it, and his father did. If Ella O'Neill conquered her addiction, however, Mary Tyrone cannot be saved. *Long Day's Journey* does not permit such an inference. Indeed, all four characters are locked into the logic of the play. It will always come out the same, just as *Antigone* does, and *Hamlet* and *Lear.* Jamie will not reform; no words will call Mary back.

James Tyrone's grudges against Jamie are long standing. He has been repeatedly offended by his son's disregard for good taste and nearly all that James holds sacred, by his "loafing" and waste of talent, and by the bad example the older brother has set for Edmund. Tyrone describes Jamie's chief fault in Shakespearean imagery: "Ingratitude, the vilest weed that grows" and "How sharper than a serpent's tooth to have a thankless child." James wants credit for supporting his son and giving him endless chances. (How difficult it is to rise above our "good deeds.") Jamie, on the other hand, hates his father's stinginess and his insistence on taking the moral high ground: "I wouldn't give a damn if you ever displayed the slightest sign of gratitude" (32). But these two men fight it out in the open, each knowing precisely what the other thinks. Each knows, moreover, where the other is most vulnerable and strikes there unfailingly. For the most part their complaints against one another are real enough but are not especially complicated. In just one area does Jamie tread on sacred ground: his assertion that Tyrone loves his money more than he loves Mary. His proof is that James nearly sacrificed "Mama's" health in order to save a few dollars on the doctor bill. To Jamie such frugality was more an outrage than a sign of virtue.

James's relations with Edmund are subtler. He sees in Edmund not only Mary's finer sensibilities but her greater susceptibility to illness. The family knows that its youngest member lives under the threat of consumption. To survivors of the Irish famine, like James Tyrone, tuberculosis struck fear into the heart, for it was remembered as an almost certain sentence of death. Again he feels the pangs of guilt, for he had talked Mary into having this third child to take the place of stricken Eugene. Nor will Edmund let him off the hook. Like Jamie, he knows that his father will not send him to a private hospital: "Don't lie, Papa! You know damned well Hilltown Sanatorium is a state institution. Jamie suspected you'd cry poorhouse to [Doctor] Hardy and he wormed the truth out of him" (144). Even so, James and Edmund have a deep rapport because "I'm like Mama, I can't help liking you, in spite of everything" (142).

One of the greatest moments in O'Neillian drama takes place in the act 4 exchange between these two. It occurs when both are a little drunk and therefore even less inhibited than usual. Under the double stress of this terrible day, they have somehow made contact. The moment begins in lightness: the humor Edmund finds in Tyrone's claim that Shakespeare was an Irish Catholic. This levity is followed by their shared sorrow over Mary's addiction and Edmund's present danger. Their masks drop and each man sees the other briefly in a moment of unguarded truth. Each sees the human being who is his son or father. James's long *apologia*—about the paralyzing poverty of his youth, the suffering of his own beloved mother, abandonment by his father, and a confession that he betrayed his own talent for security—all touch Edmund: "It was at home I first learned the value of a dollar and the fear of the poorhouse. I've never been able to believe in my luck since" (146). Thus the son is moved to give his father the gift of his poetry.

Edmund begins by thanking James for sharing his sorrow. Because the usual distance between them has been bridged for once, he invites his father into his most intimate memory chamber. Such an act places one at great risk, of course; he lays himself open as he normally would not. It is not drink that has liberated his tongue, however; it is that variety of love that mends all the broken moments of the past: "I'm glad you've told me this, Papa. I know you a lot better now" (151). In language piercingly lyrical, O'Neill relates the story of Edmund's mystical experiences at sea. He tells of lying on the bowsprit, fusing into the spume and rhythms of the sea, "every sail white in the moonlight." Here, he says, he experienced a transport such as no drug can give, guilt-free and, for once, belonging to something outside time: "To God, if you want to put it that way." He tells his father that once the "veil of things" has been lifted, for a moment one becomes perfectly phased into the divine being at the heart of creation. But when the veil drops again and one becomes aware of his own awareness, one knows that he has been reclaimed by time and the misery of cosmic orphanhood. One will not share such moments, or try to, unless he trusts the other totally. For he permits his soul, his truest self, to become exposed to the other. James acknowledges the gesture by making an equally generous gift: "Yes, there's the makings of a poet in you all right" (154). In this miraculous instant of connection, father and son have been briefly redeemed, each blessed by the other's love.

No such moment can be shared between James and Jamie; the layers of defense are by now impenetrable. Again we wonder who will redeem Jamie. It will not be Mary, as the older son knows very well: "I suppose I can't forgive her—yet. I'd begun to hope, if she'd beaten the game, I could too" (162). She loves him, yes, but with such deep reservation that she reminds him, even without intending to do so, of his failures, his sins. Her natural affection for Jamie has been blighted by his inveterate neglect and thousand assaults on her sensibilities. Deepest wound: she can neither forget nor forgive his infecting baby Eugene so many years before. Every irresponsible act thereafter, his sins of omission and commission, merely reminds her of Jamie's selfishness. In her attitude toward this man, Mary Tyrone fails most glaringly to imitate her beloved model and namesake. Jamie, devoted to his mother in ways that cripple some men, has learned a bitter truth: her feelings for him can never be those of unalloyed grace. Her feelings for him are mixed: thus, something is forever held back.

If his redemption is to take place, it must be in connection with Edmund. But little time remains. Between Edmund's exchange with his father and Mary's coming in upon all three men in the play's final scene, Jamie has only brief minutes with Edmund. If he can muster courage to face the truth at all and confess his sins, it must be under these restricted conditions: "Not drunken bull, but in vino veritas stuff." Torn between self-hatred and a love for his brother, he confesses his envy in seeing Edmund succeed. He tells how he had set out "to make a bum of you. . . . Mama's baby, Papa's pet" (165). To make this gesture, even under the influence, has been agonizing. From the porch the old actor has also heard the confession. "*Edmund remains silent.*" Now Tyrone, in mixed charity and despair, tries to ring down the curtain on the tragic farce of his son's life. To Edmund: " . . . don't take it too much to heart, lad. He loves to exaggerate the worst of himself when he's drunk. He's devoted to you. It's the one good thing left in him" (167). Then it's over. James and

Jamie are back at each other's throats. Edmund tries fumblingly to mediate but to no good.

Enter Mary Tyrone.

* * *

In certain ways Mary is blessed in the very nature of her situation. For she lives with three adult men, each riveted to her in passionate devotion: her husband, a very model of fidelity; her sons, proud of her fragile beauty, aware that through her some gentleness attaches to their otherwise unlovely lives. In even the most prosaic cluster of mortals, a woman in such circumstances might come into her glory. But in the Catholic family, this veneration for her can border on idolatry. She is the vessel of honor: in the beginning the virgin lover and lifelong partner to husband; later the nonpareil feminine model to her sons. For these men, the sacrament of matrimony has sealed the conjugal union in holiness. (Of all the barbs delivered by his "ingrate" sons, none throws doubt on Tyrone's love for their mother.) In the Irish-Catholic family all characteristics of this beatification were intensified. The culture had nearly deified the wife-mother and equated her station with that of the Blessed Virgin Mary. This is why, when Edmund tells Mary what he felt on first learning of her addiction, his words carry such terrible resonance: "God, it made everything in life seem rotten" (118). All three Tyrone men had been brought up in the cult of Mariolatry. (It is worth recalling that James O'Neill's own mother was named Mary, a fact surely not lost on his playwright son.) At its least attractive, such veneration was made sentimental in portraits like those rendered in "Mother Machree." But the virtues praised were of constancy and compassion. In any case, Irish motherhood has been a powerful myth: the Sorrowful Mother becomes the Suffering Mother.

* * *

The union of James and Mary reminds all who have known them that love means fidelity. James, handsome and popular, had no doubt experienced many temptations to his virtue in the tawdry world of backstage romances. In a marriage of thirty-five years, moreover, indiscretions could never have been hidden. Mary loves him all the more for this, as she says to the second girl: " . . . there has never been a breath of scandal about him. I mean, with any other woman. Never since he met me. That has made me very happy, Cathleen. It has made me forgive so many other things" (105). Of course, the "other things" were real enough. Mary came to know very early that life with the matinee idol was not at all glamorous. Although she liked being with him, even on the road, the endless hours on rickety trains, the long nights in second- and third-rate hotels, the nearly inedible food all greatly lessened the pleasure of his company. She thought his background had prevented him from knowing how to make a fine home. But Mary recalls with greatest bitterness his having enlisted the services of the quack whose incompetence had led her into addiction. "I hate doctors! They'll sell their souls! What's worse, they'll sell yours, and you never know it till one day you find yourself in hell" (74).

The play records one day that represents hundreds, perhaps thousands, of others. Devoted to her as he is, James must chafe under Mary's constant reminders, often in front of their sons, of his lack of refinement and his inveterate miserliness. In their exchange James informs Edmund that her father's home wasn't quite what she liked to recall: "Her wonderful home was ordinary enough. Her father wasn't the great, generous, noble Irish gentleman she makes out. . . . [b]ut he had his weakness. . . . He became a steady champagne drinker, the worst kind. That was his grand pose, to drink only champagne. Well, it finished him quick—that and the consumption—" (137).

After so many years both have grievances. Yet in remaining faithful to their vow, Mary and James have found comfort. Their relationship has been tested endlessly by visitations of unfriendly fate and by their own imperfections, but in their tradition and culture they have found what alone redeems human frailty: the forgiving love of one for another. The power of this mystery deeply moved Eugene O'Neill. In creating the story of the Tyrones, he conquered his own ancient hostilities in an act of pity and forgiveness. He seemed, as it were, to become one with his family. As Travis Bogard wonderfully says, "In the agony of the others, it is possible, the playwright's identity was at last to be found."[24]

In the final, crushing scene all three men are paralyzed with a fear whose meaning we can infer: that they may not be able to recover Mary this time. She has come down to them and, in what she says and does, she pierces their hearts with the memory of what she has been to them: bride and lover, mother and confidante, gentle and wistful presence. So great has been her love for James Tyrone, so deeply has her soul entered his, that even in her remove from him Mary utters his name in the play's final phrase. As his private memories of her are stirred, each man recalls a Mary that is his alone. Yet, because she is one person whom they share, their memory is also collective. In the end each knows that he is forever trapped with her in the tragedy of time.

A Touch of the Poet

In 1943 O'Neill wrote to Sean O'Casey, "All I've done since Pearl Harbor is to rewrite one of the plays in my Cycle. *A Touch of the Poet*—(an Irish play, incidentally, although located in New England in 1828)."[25] Incidental or not, its Irishness convinced Dubliners when the play's English-language European premiere was given in the Theatre Festival in the fall of 1962. Eight of ten characters speak in a brogue not long removed from Erin. Old-world antagonisms between the Yankees and the immigrant newcomers simmer for a time and then flare in act 4. The protagonist Melody family, with roots in Galway, once owned a castle and estate.

Their privileged background has been greater in the description than in reality, however. Cornelius Melody's father, once a lowly shebeen keeper, made a fortune collecting rackrents, bought the estate, set up like a squire, and sent Con "off to Dublin to school, and after that to the College with sloos of money to prove himself the equal of any gentleman's son."[26] The younger Melody created an image of himself as the superior man, superior in all things important: as drinker, soldier, lover, and gentleman. He could bring it off with his good looks, his genuine courage, his charm and air of sophistication. Proud of his military record as a major in "His Majesty's Seventh Dragoons" fighting in Spain under Wellington, ex-Major Cornelius Melody has virtually become the mask he himself has fashioned. He has set himself apart from the peasant "scum," Irish and other, and attaches to himself Lord Byron's lyric, stunning in its anti-Jacksonian sentiment: "—I stood/Among them, but not of them." He has created a grand illusion. Until he is forced by undeniable defeat to admit that his life has been a sham, his most devoted admirer is the face that regards him from whatever mirror he looks into.

The sin-redemption theme is present in *A Touch of the Poet* in ways we have already seen: the tensions, conflicts, and love that derive from the dynamics of intimate relationships within the family. Of course, this is not the play's only theme and possibly not the central one. A constant emphasis of the sort that results in a study of this kind can distort an artist's intention. As a matter of justice and balance, therefore, we should remind ourselves of this truth from time to time. Nevertheless, three crucial relationships operate in the play: mother-daughter, father-daughter, and, by far the most significant, husband-wife.

In this play O'Neill has created a thoroughly engaging story of class conflict, ambition, and scheming, all carried out in order to protect or to achieve wealth and social position. As in most similar narratives, these goals are symbolic of deeper human needs and ends: the achievement of self-possession and respect, the sense that one controls one's own fate, the knowledge that one "belongs" in a grander order of things than what is implied by the mere topography of an Athens or Elsinore or Boston. Thus, the logic of the characters' behavior comes out of the background and realism of their situations.

In Ireland Con fell in love with the beautiful peasant girl, Nora, whose family lived on his family's Galway estate. Jamie Cregan, Melody's cousin and veteran with him of battles in Spain and Portugal, fills in some of the background. " . . . [H]e married her and then went off to the war, and left her alone in the castle to have her child, and nivir saw her again till he was sent home from Spain." Con was forced to resign from the army because he had seduced a Spanish nobleman's wife after the battle of Salamanca and had killed the husband in a duel to vindicate his honor. Although he loved Nora, Con found her peasant ways and brogue unappealing and infinitely below the quality that befitted him. "Then he raised what money he still was able, and took her and Sara here to America where no one would know him" (14).

Melody has never accepted the "degraded" station of his present circumstances. Although, as owner of a run-down tavern on a now discontinued stagecoach line, he looks down on the local Irish who provide what business he has. Con, "among them but not of them," attempts to play the role for which he feels he is by grace and gifts best suited, that of a gentleman and distinguished former officer in the royal service. He cannot afford the services of the bartender Mickey Moloy he has hired; he gives out free drinks to the Irish "scum" who pay him due respect; he shelters and feeds a fine mare, whose upkeep requires that wife and daughter perform scullery chores in his establishment.

In his character motivation O'Neill here achieves considerable success. The mainspring of motivation in a social drama is a character's desire to belong to and, if possible, to manipulate the social organism to one's own advantage. Thus, we expect to see characters who become involved in intrigues, petty or significant, and in attempts to achieve their personal ends. The proof of motivational validity is its truth to human nature; is the playwright's keeping alive in him or her some sense of guilt. This evidence reveals a character's awareness of his own capacity for self-degradation. Another word for this is shame. To the extent that this capacity lives in a character, he remains human, no matter how hateful he has become to himself or others. In *A Touch of the Poet* O'Neill realized this aim of his art as well as he ever would.

The women offer fine character studies. Nora, abused by Melody since the earliest days of their relationship, excuses his pretentions and bears his insults. Sara acidly mocks his claims to nobility by accentuating her brogue to remind him that he too came from peasant stock and to suggest that he makes a fool of himself before the Yankee gentry when he seeks to curry favor with them. But Sara herself is by no means without such ambitions. Indeed, she rivals Con in her pride. She too wants a place in the world; and she intends to get it. Resourceful and bold, Sara will use her craft and beauty to gain entrance into the local power elite. For some time, we gather, she has been nursing a young idealist and poet, Simon Harford, scion of the powerful merchant and town's first citizen, Henry Harford.

The ailing Simon is convalescing in an upper room of the tavern, tended to by Sara who loves him but who will not give herself to him for nothing. Recognizing in his daughter this will to power, Con Melody himself, even though he later calls her "common, greedy, scheming, cunning peasant girl," is forced to admire her spunk. Although Simon never appears on stage, Sara's scheme to achieve this Harford liaison draws every character into the main action. In this respect, the plot is seamless.

Only Nora Melody is moved to act and live without regard to her own advancement. Indeed, her virtue is so great ("Sure, there's divil a more loyal wife in the whole world" [174]) that O'Neill ran the risk of implausibility in creating her. But she does not bear the stamp of the type. She moves in her individual reality; her loyalties are solidly riveted in the facts of her personal history and situation. Nora possesses a capacity for self-effacement equal to Con's appetite for vainglory. Through two decades of marriage Con has ridiculed her origins and commitments, even her fidelity to him. In order to placate him, she rationalizes his early-morning drinking; even that elicits his venom.

> Well? I know what you're thinking! Why haven't you the courage to say it for once? By God, I'd have more respect for you! I hate the damned meek of this earth! By the rock of Cashel, I sometimes believe you have always deliberately encouraged me to—It's the one point of superiority you can lay claim to, isn't it? (36)

When he predicts that America will someday defeat England in another war, Melody identifies with his new country and heaps scorn on Ireland.

> NORA. Glory be to God for that! And we'll free Ireland!
> MELODY. (*Contemptuously.*) Ireland? What benefit would freedom be to her unless she could be freed from the Irish? (*Then irritably.*) But why do I discuss such things with you? (40–41)

Nora is berated by both Melody and Sara for her ties to Catholicism.

> NORA. Father Flynn tould me again I'd be damned in hell for lettin' your father make a haythen of me and bring you up a haythen, too.
> SARA. (*With an arrogant toss of her head.*) Let Father Flynn mind his own business, and not frighten you with fairy tales about hell.
> NORA. It's true, just the same. (27)

Here O'Neill demonstrates perfect pitch in recording both brogue and idiom.

Melody's offenses against charity are far greater than Sara's. Her insolence can be counted in large part against her youth, for she loves her mother deeply and usually apologizes for her own rudeness. Melody's unkind cuts are habitual and, one might say, constitute something of a character disorder. But he remains vulnerable to his own humanity, a trait that might be termed a character's saving grace: he retains the capacity to feel guilt. At this point in his life, however, Con Melody has but small reserve. When, lacking all fairness, he condemns Sara's planning to "trick" Simon to win high station, Nora reminds him of their sin in conceiving her. Nora touches a nerve. He twitches but immediately adjusts his mask and recovers and shows his irritation: "Damn your priests' prating about sin!" (61).

Nora pretends nothing of virtue and thereby achieves virtue. She scolds Sara for boasting of seducing Simon. Rather the daughter should feel shame.

> SARA. (*Proudly.*) Ashamed! You know I'm not! Haven't you told me of the pride in your love? Were you ashamed
> NORA. (*Weakly.*) I was. I was dead with shame. . . . [I]t's a mortal sin. God will punish you— (148–149)

*   *   *

We are well advised to give a wide berth to those who wrap their deeds in the flag of high principle. They often deceive themselves, as they intend to deceive others. Melody's variety is the most egregious, for he uses his own family as pawns in his game to seek advantage. When Sara refuses to play her part in his scheme to advance his social position by accepting a sum that Harford will surely settle on his son and Sara, Con is surprised at her failure to see the propriety of his intentions.

> Simon is an elder son, the heir to his father's estate. No matter what their differences in the past may have been, now that Simon has decided to marry and settle down his father will wish to do the fair thing by him. He will realize, too, that although there is no more honorable calling than that of poet and philosopher, which his son has chosen to pursue, there is no decent living to be gained by its practice. So naturally he will settle an allowance on Simon, and I shall insist it be a generous one, befitting your position as my daughter. I will tolerate no niggardly trader's haggling on his part. (111)

This sort of flesh trading is precisely the principle of greed that O'Neill saw had already corrupted America. Such hypocrisy posing as both courtly wisdom and good business was to be the key to his analysis of American greed in the cycle of plays that *A Touch of the Poet* would advance: *A Tale of Possessors, Self-Dispossessed.* He talked about this problem long after he had given up any hope of finishing the cycle.

> Some day, this country is going to get it—really get it. We had everything to start with—everything—but there's bound to be a retribution. We've followed the same selfish, greedy path as every other country in the world. We talk about the American Dream, but what is that dream, in most cases, but the dream of material things? I sometimes think that the United States, for this reason, is the greatest failure the world has ever seen. We've been able to get a very good price for our souls in this country—the greatest price perhaps that has ever been paid—but you'd think that after all these years, and

all that man has been through, we'd have sense enough—all of us—to understand the whole secret of human happiness is summed up in that same sentence (from the Bible) which also appears in the teachings of Buddha, Lao-tse, and even Mohammed.[27]

Only the simple Nora, without agenda or sinister motive, owns up to her own sins. Yet in the end she alone can be said to conduct her life unfailingly on principles of honesty and love. She seeks to fool neither herself nor others. To her a pledge is a pledge. She is simple but not simpleminded. In fact, Nora has a terrible knowledge of the gravity of her deeds. "It's because I'm afraid it's God's punishment, all the sorrow and trouble that's come on us, and I have the black tormint in my mind that it's the fault of the mortal sin I did with him unmarried, and the promise he made me make to leave the Church that's kept me from confessin' to a priest" (138). As she tells Sara, "It's little you know of love. . . .

> It's when you don't give a thought for all the if's and want-to's in the world! It's when, if all the fires of hell was between you, you'd walk in them gladly to be with him, and sing with joy at your own burnin,' if only his kiss was on your mouth! That's love [*caritas*], and I'm proud I've known the great sorrow and joy of it! (25)

Whether or not Nora has sinned by the letter of the law, she has kept faith with its spirit: to provide for the happiness of others.

If Nora's conscience has been formed by her Jansenist Irish training, she appears to be the only character committed to any moral law. Melody's sense of justice, such as it is, has to do only with himself: with gaining revenge for his fall from grace and with achieving status equal to that of the Yankee Harfords. Nora, in a rare moment of bitter resentment, remarks to Sara: "Has he ever cared for anyone except himself and his pride? Sure, he'd never stoop to think of me, the grand gentleman in his red livery av bloody England! His pride, indade! What is it but a lie? What's in his veins, God pity him, but the blood of thievin' auld Ned Melody who kept a dirty shebeen?" (138). Sara is willing to let her ends justify her means. When she plans to tell Simon of her talk with his mother, she says: "I've got to be as big a liar as she was. I'll have to pretend I liked her and I'd respect whatever advice she gave him" (88). Nor do Deborah and Henry Harford operate on principles of fairness and certainly not out of regard for a law of love. On her visit to Simon, Deborah warns Sara that her son is a dreaming idealist but one who will turn into an arch materialist like all the Harford men. She claims, in this honesty, to be acting out of duty but she knows only the reflex of duty. Her gesture lacks a generosity that could ennoble her motive. She is the whited sepulchre. Henry Harford sends his attorney to Melody with a guarantee of three thousand dollars if the shebeen keeper will move to Ohio with wife and daughter and thus will pledge that Sara will never again tempt Simon to disgrace himself in a marriage to an Irish peasant. And, of course, Melody's toadies—Cregan, Dan Roche, Paddy O'Dowd, and Patch Riley—will serve the major in any way, so long as they are assured of access to the premises and of an ample supply of free liquor.

*   *   *

The play's great magnet character, however, is not Nora. Cornelius Melody fascinates us in his psychological complexity. If he is at bottom as vulnerable as Dion Anthony, Con's mask is harder. In certain personality traits, he may be closer than any other O'Neill character to Brutus Jones, the "emperor" of an inconsequential West Indies island. The surface, especially the trappings of power and authority, means everything to him: the military uniform, the whip or swagger stick, dueling pistols, the spoken deference of his colleagues or underlings. Image is his be-all and end-all. The ex-major literally lives by the lie.

Even so, he is striking, this handsome and seductive illusionist who can completely bedazzle both women and men. To achieve his end, he will manipulate and wheedle; he will do whatever may be required to gain the appearance of control. But the years have drained this inveterate poser of the capacity to care deeply for the welfare of family and friends. Something is dormant in him, or undeveloped. We hear early in the play from his cousin and comrade-in-arms, Jamie Cregan, that Con's father had been "but a thievin' shebeen keeper" who had hardly got settled in his new money "when his wife died givin' birth to Con" (11). To be without memories of his mother, to be without those mother-son entanglements, is a condition not typical of the O'Neill protagonist: Eben Cabot, Dion Anthony, Charles Marsden, Orin Mannon, John Loving, Simon Harford, Jamie and Edmund Tyrone. At any rate, we see repeatedly how he hates the "scum" and "riffraff," finds Nora's untidiness and manners disgusting, Sara's brogue coarse, Harford's pompous attorney a lickspittle and lackey. He is contemptuous of the very idea of the democrat that Andrew Jackson appeals to in this year of 1828. Melody sees himself as superior to the "rabble."

We confront in Con Melody a most curious personality type: the man who is psychologically complex but has almost no spiritual density. His facade has become his reality.

> *Wearing the brilliant scarlet full-dress uniform of a major in one of Wellington's dragoon regiments, he looks extraordinarily handsome and distinguished—a startling, colorful, romantic figure, possessing now a genuine quality he has not had before, the quality of the formidably strong, disdainfully fearless cavalry officer he really had been.* (88)

Ultimately his vanity renders him hollow. We think of similar cases: Wilde's Dorian Gray or Balzac's M. Vautrin. Such a type displays impressive surface control but, like other O'Neill characters, he has invested heavily in the life lie. However, Melody's relationships with others differ critically from, say, Larry Slade's or Jamie Tyrone's. These latter, in their very ambivalence, are pulled toward compassion. They sense division within themselves and act, finally, because they are moved by love. But Con Melody is his own and only center and focus. Perhaps Fitzgerald's miraculous description of Jay Gatsby (appropriately amended) comes close to defining him: *he sprang from his Platonic conception of himself.* That, of course, is a romantic explanation. In America, we tend to speak with greater approval of the "self-made man." In another way, we might say that Con Melody is beyond good and evil. The very idea of sin is meaningless to him.

Offended by Henry Harford's arrogant offer to buy him off, Melody sets out with Corporal Cregan to force the Yankee to apologize or "I'll put a bullet through him, so help me, Christ!" (124). But these heroes of Talavera are drubbed by Harford's men, because the ever-hated police do just as their counterparts in Ireland have done so often: side with the rich and the power brokers against their brothers and sisters in poverty. Melody is beaten senseless and sent home thoroughly humiliated, his uniform torn to filthy tatters. The outward signs of his authority now in shreds, he kills his mare, that other symbol of the gentleman's livery. He begins to speak in the broadest brogue, as he thinks befits the son of a Galway pub owner. Major Melody is dead and the shell that is now Con Melody speaks of him to Nora as someone who poses no threat now to her gentleness. "So let you be aisy, darlint. He'll niver again hurt you with his sneers, and his pretindin' he's a gintleman, blatherin' about pride and honor, and his boastin' av duels in the days that's gone, and his showin' off before the Yankees, and thim laughin' at him, prancin' around drunk on his beautiful thoroughbred mare—" (168).

His image of himself was all that Cornelius Melody had truly loved. That destroyed, he is absolutely lost. We cringe before this spectacle, for the defeat of a man's illusion is not a thing beautiful to behold. Thus does Sara sob and thereupon wonder, " . . . why should I cry, Mother? Why do I mourn for him?" (182). There is nothing Nora can do for Con: he has long since lost the capacity to be redeemed by love. But Nora is self-redeemed. Of this pair, only she has the ability to receive love (which is something different from taking love). This finally is the crucial difference between them: Nora has not only the power but the desire to give love. Indeed, this is her *modus vivendi*, that quality of soul Aquinas may have had in mind when he defined virtue as *habitus*. To give is part of Nora's character. Thus, she will humor Con, if that will provide him any comfort. Yet in her honesty she knows that her power to help him is limited because she knows his limitations. "God pity him, he's had to live all his life alone in the hell av pride" (181).

More Stately Mansions

The family into which we are born has much to do with what we become. So, of course, have the church, the nation, and the social class. O'Neill's plays tell us this again and again: *All God's Chillun Got Wings; Desire Under the Elms; Ah, Wilderness!; Long Day's Journey into Night; A Touch of the Poet; More Stately Mansions; A Moon for the Misbegotten.* The institutions of our world encourage our loyalties and virtues but also our prejudices and hatreds. Such conditioning is not absolute in its power to form us, however. If it were, the human person would be no more than a mindless automaton, of no interest except in the workings of its mechanism. For, if the laws of an unqualified determinism were to be invoked, no character in a play could sin or feel guilt, except as a sort of Pavlovian puppet. Nor could the character be redeemed by a human act. There would be no mystery of personality, nothing of conflict within the spirit or psyche. O'Neill knew from experience the soul-searing imprint of family, ethnicity, and church. But he also understood that characters conceived in a narrow determinism cannot surprise us by growing into something worthier or lesser than they were in earlier states. In *More Stately Mansions* these beliefs are wonderfully exemplified and O'Neill's Irish Catholic memory is deeply stirred.

Yet anyone who writes about this play is bound to feel a twinge of uneasiness. It is well known that the author had tucked a note into a surviving copy of the typescript: "Unfinished Work. This script to be destroyed in case of my death!"[28] Nevertheless, the text of this play represents O'Neill's longest work. If the unexpurgated version were staged,[29] its running time would exceed that of either *Strange Interlude* or *Mourning Becomes Electra. More Stately Mansions* is the sequel to *A Touch of the Poet.* It was designed to be part of an eleven-play cycle called "A Tale of Possessors Self-Dispossessed." The cycle would have "trace[d] the saga of the Harford-Melody family's pursuit of wealth and power from their arrival in the New World in 1755 to the year 1932."[30]

O'Neill's purpose was to track the evolution of the national soul as it became ensnared in the nightmare of greed and corruption that is sometimes called the American Dream. But this fascinating theme by no means indicates O'Neill's only interest in *More Stately Mansions.* Another theme is the plight of the artist who turns aside from his vocation to serve the demands of love. The dreamer-poet Simon Harford reminds us of earlier examples of the type: Robert Mayo and Dion Anthony. A third major conflict is the Strindbergian struggle for dominance between male and female O'Neill had already treated in *Welded, Desire Under the Elms,* and *The Great God Brown.* Not only do we sense a pulsing of ambivalent attraction between mother and son in *Mansions,* but we see that, in order to compete, the wife is willing to play both her conjugal role and that of mother, nurse, and mistress. The battle between Simon's mother and wife to possess the son and husband nearly destroys him. Each victory is the result of an attempt by one to move the other off the board like a spent checker. The reader himself becomes exhausted by their ceaseless maneuvering and release of psychic energy.

Thus, the possible approaches to *More Stately Mansions* seem endless. In this study of O'Neill's plays the emphasis has fallen on character relationships. This focus, of course, generally implies individuals connected by kinship or marriage. But, since each woman and man lives an inner, private life that she cannot share (even if she wished to), no relationship can ever be entirely fulfilling or complete. Perhaps O'Neill, who was striving in this play as in others to understand the secret of a satisfactory relationship, achieved a profound insight: one must grant the other party her spiritual mystery and not seek to possess her. One cannot indulge the will to power without disfiguring himself. This, I think, is the more general reading O'Neill makes of the American psyche. In this he was only a good Emersonian: the attempt to possess the person or the mystery of anything destroys its integrity: "Things are in the saddle/And ride mankind."

Before endeavoring to make a close examination of the central relationships in *More Stately Mansions,* let us look briefly at the givens of the larger plot and attempt to understand what each character is seeking. The time is 1832, near the end of Andrew Jackson's first term as U.S. President. The scene is the Melody tavern; the occasion is that of Cornelius Melody's wake. Con's widow, Nora, hopes to pay off her late husband's debt of two thousand dollars and thereafter to enter a convent. As a death-bed favor to Nora, who had been the very model of fidelity and love, Con "came back to the Faith before he died. . . ."[31] Sara and Simon arrive with their three sons and Sara pregnant with the fourth. In the young Harfords the Irish line has been grafted onto the Yankee strain. Simon the dreamer of the earlier play, has convinced Sara to give Irish names to at least half the children: hence two will be called Ethan and Jonathan, the other two Wolfe Tone and Owen ("Honey"). Sara, shamed by her peasant origins, scolds Nora for letting the neighbor women keen; she wishes "to free herself from her innate Irishness and to merge with mainstream American culture and society. She is perhaps the only O'Neill character to break through the isolation barrier and diligently compete for the American Dream."[32] The idealistic Simon, who is quite sympathetic to the plight of Ireland and of the Irish in America, convinces Sara that they can and should pay off the Melody debts. If this situation suggests that the sins of one generation are visited on the next, the far greater theme of the play is the corruption of America in its greed and lust, the unholy pollution of the fertile land that the first American enjoyed. The full implications of this theme will be played in *More Stately Mansions:* as early as the 1830s, then, the culture of rapaciousness fouls the relationships in the American family.

That Simon, who has "a touch of the poet," has natural talent for business is not surprising. His father, Henry Harford, is a powerful Yankee merchant. Harford has disowned his elder son, however, for the disgrace of his marriage to low Irish stock. Simon's business acumen turns out to be more curse than benison. He is so soon successful that his poet's focus is blurred. He becomes seduced by his own gifts for money-making and his capacity to dominate his competitors. For a time Simon vacillates. On the one hand, he purchases the "worthless" farm where his earlier cabin-retreat still stands and where he had hoped to write a book on the rights of man, an argument sympathetic to Rousseau's belief in man's natural goodness. But Sara, ambitious and acquisitive, does little to encourage these proclivities in her husband. As she says to Nora, "He doesn't talk about that anymore, thank God! I've laughed it out of him! I've told him you can make new laws but you can't make new men and women to fit them, so what's the use of dreaming! I've said, even if he could make it come true, it would be a coward's heaven he'd have, for where is the glory of life if it's not a battle where you prove your strength to rise to the top and let nothing stop you" (41).

Upon the death of Henry Harford, with whom Simon has not spoken since his marriage, it is discovered that Harford and Company stands on the brink of bankruptcy. The staid Harford had uncharacteristically gambled with his company's credit. A great opportunity arises when Simon's mother, Deborah, and his brother, Joel, come to ask that Simon save the company from disaster. Sara and Simon see a way to make an immense fortune that will buy servants, carriages and groomsmen, estates, and ever more stately mansions.

Driven and talented, Sara and Simon make a formidable business force. She encourages his capacity to dominate opponents without pity on the battlefields of trade and commerce. She learns from him "to skin" an opponent: "Remember what I've impressed on you so often in the past year. This office is no garden of dreams. It is a battlefield of reality, where you must face the fact of yourself as you are—and not as you dream you ought to be—where one eats or is eaten" (240). All earlier dreams for social justice and equality among men are forgotten in the new Harfords' financial pillaging and savored victories over their unpitied rivals. Their operational philosophy becomes Napoleonic: divide and conquer. Their *modus operandi* reverses the Darwinian dictum: weakness is an evil; strength is a virtue. The logic of Sara's willingness to accept this jungle ethic has been foreshadowed in her words to Nora at the funeral: ". . . . where is the glory of life if it's not a battle . . . ?"

* * *

O'Neill is like Shakespeare in the sheer complexity of his characters and in the depth of his penetration into their psyches. *More Stately Mansions* is especially difficult to treat, however, because it combines dramatic techniques. While O'Neill employs a powerful realism in his critique of American greed, he also makes occasional use of characters as symbols. Deborah and Sara are sometimes made into a single force, Woman: Deborah recalling Nina Leeds as she uses the male for her own needs; Sara a version of Cybel as a kind of earth mother. O'Neill returned to the workshop again to find an old tool of expressionism: in act 3, scene 3, he reactivates the interior monologue, a technique used in *Strange Interlude*.

On early consideration it appears that *More Stately Mansions* offers three central relationships for examination: those of mother-son, mother-in-law and daughter-in-law, and wife-husband. In this study an adult relationship has been one in which at least one partner accepts moral responsibility for his acts, especially as his behavior has harmful effects on the other person. Another way of putting this is to recognize a possibility for sin in a relationship and, by extension, the possibilities for guilt, atonement, and forgiveness. A whole or complete character is one capable of sin, guilt, and redemption. Judged by these criteria, only one such relationship exists in *Mansions*, that of Simon and Sara. In the other relationships, at least some of the time, the characters are fractured, incomplete; in this, they tend to stand more as symbols than as persons.

Deborah Harford's response to life has been to retreat rather than to engage. Because she finds human nature to be essentially sordid, she has created an imaginary world, a dimension of dreams and fantasies. Here she can avoid occasions for human intercourse, episodes which she finds vulgar and dispiriting. Deborah has seen and hated in her husband, and in most men, an insatiable lust and desire for wealth and power. Thus, over the years she has peopled her fantasy world with kings and queens, emperors and empresses, in which she is courted and waited upon, a world where she may dismiss the low and vulgar with a simple gesture of disapproval. Deborah dresses in white, the sign of her spiritual virginity and superiority. She spends endless hours in her garden and summerhouse. One cannot miss the parallel to the garden of innocence. Of course, while that garden was beautiful, it did not remain perfect: the first sin was committed there. Deborah Harford's garden is denatured. All that is wild or that implies the bestial is muted or disguised by a superimposition of eighteenth-century geometric order. Nothing that suggests the natural is permitted in these sacred precincts. So vivid can these illusions become that neither "intruders" nor Deborah herself will know with certainty if she distinguishes her imaginary life from her real life.

All that ties her to time, she hates, for time reminds her that she shares the vulnerability of human nature. This dimension forces the recognition that all grow old, and ugly, and *in time* pass away. She explains to Simon.

> While you are still beautiful and life still woos you, it is such a fine gesture of disdainful pride, so satisfying to one's arrogance, to jilt it. But when the change comes and the tables are turned and an indifferent life jilts you—it is a repulsive humiliation to feel yourself a condemned slave to revengeful Time, to cringe while he lashes your face with wrinkles, or stamps your body into shapelessness, or smears it with tallow-fat with his malicious fingers! *[anticipating his protest]* Oh, I realize that I am hardly as bad as that yet. But I will be, for I constantly sense in the seconds and minutes and hours flowing through me, the malignant hatred of life against those who have disdained it. But the body is least important. It is the soul, staring into the mirror of itself, knowing it is too late, that it is rejected and forever alone—seeing the skull of Death leer over its shoulder in the glass like a roué in a brothel ogling some life-sick old trull! (61)

Whatever connects her to the laws of time she eventually comes to hate. This surely includes her magnate husband, who used her for carnal pleasure. She even hated the resulting possession of her body by the baby. Therefore, even before his birth, Deborah hated Simon and later practiced mischief on his child's heart by bringing him into her garden but denying him full access to her private world. She made it seem beautiful to him by reading poems and reciting stories of magical creatures. All of this appealed to his dreamer-poet's nature. But she denied him full access to the one place he wished to be with her.

In the garden of her estate is Deborah's *sanctum sanctorum,* a summerhouse whose red laquer door symbolizes the entrance into a secret world. Both as child and adult, Simon has been refused admission. Later, after he has made a fortune by directing the Harford Company but also by denaturing himself, he comes to her garden for succor. She rejects him for the final time, enters the red door alone, and denies him herself forever. Literally she pushes him away so that he falls, is injured, and loses the memory of the experience for many years. Deborah used Simon and thereby hurt him.

Her white dress has been the sign of Deborah's purity and her unapproachability. She has used Simon as a toy. In this she reminds us of Nina Leeds, who absorbs what she wants from men with but little care for their spiritual needs. Unlike Nina, however, Deborah stands always on the border of madness. Thus, she is denied full moral development and maturity, yet the effect on Simon is that he is made to feel incomplete and unworthy. In this sense he is also denied full development of personality and moral imagination.

Deborah has hated from the beginning the idea of Simon's attraction to the "common Irish biddy," even from the time of her first meeting with Sara in Melody's Tavern. She ridiculed the Melodys' low peasant origins and scoffed at any claims to aristocracy that Con Melody and now Sara have pretended. Sara's four children are the Irish "slut's brats," no mark against Deborah's own heritage.

As her son, the child-dreamer-poet, has saved the Harford Company and thereby has preserved her security, Deborah has paradoxically grown to hate his surrender of innocence as necessary to enter the battle for money and power in the world of "hogs." As he has given up his intention to write a book that would rescue men from their greed, a philosophy she always found naive, Deborah lays much of the blame to Sara, whose "lusts" Simon has agreed to satisfy. And, indeed, these desires have been real enough in Sara, who has wanted equal station and power with her "betters." She has come to accept two principles of the power struggle by which Simon has won an empire for her: only the ruthless survive; and, more indicative of the monsters they have both made of themselves, "I am good because I am strong. You are evil because you are weak" (243).

Both women wish to control Simon. But the son and husband comes alive to this fact and even recognizes that, in their plan to manage him, one of the women was bound to lose to the other. He lets Deborah know this. "By God, there have been times when, as I watched you together in the house at night, she would seem to steal all identity from you and absorb you! Until there was but one woman—her!" (185). On yet further reflection, Simon sees that they have no genuine affection for one another. In knowing their game, he can take control of them as he takes control of his own life: "—two women—opposites—whose only relation derives from the relationship of each to me—whose lives have meaning and purpose only in so far as they live within my living—henceforth this is my home and I own my own mind again!—I am a free slave-owner" (201).

O'Neill makes Deborah and Sara represent two sides of Woman: the life of the creative imagination (Deborah); the lure of flesh and all things fertile (Sara). In their desire to "master" Simon, they have formed a kind of pact in which they will use Woman's full range of powers to seduce and subdue him. They are powerful. Moreover, the mere fact that Simon understands their plan does not provide him with an antidote against their potions. He endeavors to pit them against each other because, if their lethal pact is successful, he will be driven to madness.

To the extent that Deborah and Sara represent aspects of Woman's nature (Nina and Cybel), they do not share a relationship with each other. In this respect each is an abstraction, an element in the compound of Woman. In her near insanity, Deborah has hardly developed a conscience. She stands as a kind of amoral nonentity. Sara has permitted herself to league with Deborah and has become, like her mother-in-law, a sort of mask, one manifestation of Woman. Although they go through the motions of human intercourse (Deborah is "granny" to the Harford boys, Sara practices the domestic arts with Deborah), the women do not trust each other. They are adversaries in the struggle to absorb Simon, to possess him. And indeed to him they have become symbols of what is both attractive and intimidating in feminine nature. But he must choose one. He would be mangled in the battle of opposites to own him.

*   *   *

Whereas the connections between Simon and his mother begin in her resentment of his intrusion into her private world and her final rejection of him as a citizen of it, Sara and Simon's relationship to each other begins and ends in love. In their story Eugene O'Neill's sin-and-redemption theme comes to the surface. In plotting their paradise lost and reclaimed, his Catholic memory is energized.

In 1828 the young idealist Simon Harford had attempted to live a simple life in harmony with the rhythms of nature. He had built a cabin in the countryside where he hoped to write a kind of blueprint for the ideal human community. Early in his marriage, when he has not yet succumbed to "hoggishness," he meets his mother in her garden and rehearses a theme she had often heard from him.

> To be truly free, we must start all over again. In a free society there must be no private property to tempt men's greed into enslaving one another. We must protect man from his stupid possessive instincts until he can be educated to outgrow them spiritually. But at the same time, we must never forget that the least government, the best government. . . . In my book I will prove this can easily be done.

Deborah replies, "Ah, yes, if only men—and women—were not men and women" (58).

Simon based his concept on Rousseau's vision of men and women freed from the hardscrabble struggle to survive. Having fallen ill, he was nursed back to health by Con Melody's daughter. All this was revealed in *A Touch of the Poet,* although Simon never appears in that play. (But he is much talked about.) It is also revealed that Sara, who truly loved him, had permitted relations that precipitate the birth of their first son, Ethan. Of course, the generous

Simon had married her, an act which was detested by Deborah and that resulted in his being disinherited by Henry Harford.

As husband and father himself, Simon has had to support his young family and thereby has come upon his talent for making money. At this point, early in *More Stately Mansions,* he has arrived at a crossroads. Simon experiences a deep ambivalence: he still has a fondness for his dream of making a better world, even as his appetite for wealth and power has been activated. Simon forgets his book as he strives to please Sara by achieving ever higher standards of material success. In remarks to her mother, Sara reveals more than she knows, remarks that make plausible her response to Simon's plight near the end of the play. "Sure, when he's himself, there's no one takes more joy in getting ahead. If you'd see his pride sometimes when he comes home to tell me of some scheme he's accomplished [*She laughs.*] Oh, he's a queer mixture. [*then intensely*] And I love him, every bit of him! I love him more than ever any woman loved a man, I think. I'd give my last drop of blood to make him happy!" (41).

Nothing stops Simon. So ruthless does he become that he can take a perverse pleasure in destroying his opponents. Having made Sara an active partner who can dispatch a weakened rival with equal relish, both become "hogs." Simon devises a game wherein she will come to the office to win pieces of property and financial control of the company. Her part is to make her body available to him as payment. She has become a whore, selling herself in exchange for profit. Thus they have used and hurt each other.

O'Neill, by now a keen student of human psychology, understood the dynamics involved in such wasteland diversions as this man and woman practice at this stage of their relationship. They have become denatured, their marriage an ugly parody of Simon's earlier dream of men and women liberated from the need to own each other. But the games become too much for the dormant poet who lives in the body of the monster. At home, forced to choose between the sides of Woman that confront him in the persons of Deborah and Sara, he feels himself falling into sickness and madness. He retreats into his mother's garden and pleads to be taken with her through the red door of the summerhouse into the zone of peace and sleep. If she will admit him to her illusory other world, he will escape the lust Sara now represents and he will walk into the enchanted land where his fairy-mother is empress.

The moment has arrived when the value of Sara's love, once proclaimed in pride to Nora, will be tested. She will be forced to confront her own part in her own and her husband's undoing. Here is no game. What she must give of herself for Simon is her *self*. Coming into the garden, she calls out to Simon's mother, who seems ready to establish ownership over him, "For the love of God! For the love of your son, Deborah! You can't! And don't you see there's no need now! You can have him back without—I'm telling you I'll give him up

to you! I'll go away! I'll leave him to you! I'll never trouble you again. You'll
be rid of me! And that's all you've wanted, isn't it? So, for the love of God,
stop—!" (292).

Sara owns that it was her tricks and greed that first diverted Simon from
his noble path and ushered him into the pit where dog eats dog, the muck field
where human values are trampled. She is willing to release him and to raise
their children in poverty, if Deborah will take her victory but spare Simon from
entrance with her into a world of insanity. Deborah gloats:

> You are welcome to the farm. I am glad you at last realize what you are and
> where you belong. A stupid peasant tilling the soil, her bare feet in the earth,
> her gross body stinking of sweat, a dumb brainless, begetting female animal
> with her dirty brats around her! [*jeeringly*] But what becomes of your grand
> estate, and the ridiculous Irish dream castle in Spain? (293)

In a gesture that imitates the goodness of her mother, now many years dead,
Sara responds quietly: "If I'm humbled, it's by myself and my love, not by
you."

Deborah chooses to keep her world secret. She rejects her son, pushes him
so that, when he stumbles, he falls backward down the steps. Deborah suggests
that her willingness to release him to Sara proves the mother's higher love,
superior to that proffered by "a greedy, money-grabbing merchant and . . .
peasant slut of a wife" (295). In fact, however, she wants no intrusion into her
private world. She drives Simon from her in pride and selfishness. Conversely,
Sara's willingness to give him up springs from a motive of self-abnegation and
generosity.

Some may see Sara's gesture as an implausible *volte-face*. It is not that. Nor
is it a sign of miraculous intervention. Granted, her behavior may appear unusual, but it is natural enough. The explanation of what we do, and fail to do,
often derives from deep memory: that is, from remembered model gestures that
surface in moments of great stress or calls for sacrifice. This is different from
saying that our behavior has been programmed response to stimulus. Sara's
model is Nora, who also served her husband in his weakness. She showed the
value of supporting a loved one's dream, even when the dream itself was hurt-
ful. It would be incorrect, however, to call Nora's lifetime generosity to Con
Melody an illustration of spineless self-effacement. Her goodness was a habit
(Aquinas's virtue, perhaps), in this case love. If we can see Sara's brave gesture
as an act connected to her mother, then we can see in Con Melody's daughter
not only a spirited personality but a personality capable of growth. In this
description of human motivation, we have at least one argument for the possibility of redemption: the love of one generation is visited upon another. Sara
is thus able to extend this benefit to her husband, whom she has injured. This,
I believe, makes mystery itself plausible.

I have said that the playwright possessed in great measure a moral imagination. If the reader finds this declaration worthy, it may be agreed that O'Neill stands with other geniuses as an artist of great vision. As to the merits of the unfinished cycle, Travis Bogard speaks with considerable authority.

> That Eugene O'Neill could not complete the historical cycle as it was designed is one of the greatest losses the drama in any time has sustained. . . . It was a work of astonishing scope and scale. Theresa Helburn rightly called it a *comedie humaine*. Nothing in the drama, except Shakespeare's two cycles on British history, could have been set beside it. The two plays that have survived reveal something of the power of life that beat in it, but they show only vestiges of what its full plan realized would have provided: a prophetic epitome of the course of American destiny.[33]

A Moon for the Misbegotten

In this final discussion[34] (O'Neill's own last play), we confront something of a new situation. In no earlier work had the issue of sin and redemption been more prominently set forth. In none had the fact of his guilt been so openly acknowledged by the protagonist. Nor had O'Neill ever before dramatized the dynamics of confession more directly or skillfully. It is true that in his tremendous monologue in *The Iceman Cometh,* Hickey stumbles into confession and carries Don Parritt with him. But, excepting Slade, there were no sympathetic listeners: "Who the hell cares?" In *Long Day's Journey* Jamie Tyrone, after revealing his resentment of Edmund to Edmund, remarks, "Feel better now. Gone to confession. Know you absolve me, don't you, Kid?" (167) But the moment owed its authority (his denial notwithstanding) to "'in vino veritas' stuff." Of course, Jim Tyrone's[35] confession in *Misbegotten* (1923) differs fundamentally from Jamie's in *Journey* (1912) because there is literally no one left to make amends to. Mary Tyrone is dead.

In *A Moon for the Misbegotten* the sin-and-redemption theme is deftly managed. The very words the characters use describe the teachings that remained forever alive in O'Neill's Catholic memory: *sin, guilt, confession, forgiveness, peace, Virgin birth.* Strangest of all conditions is that, for once, neither party in the relationship has ever injured the other, or wished to. Thus, the Josie-Jim exchange is uncluttered by a history of injuries that degrades nearly all relationships: grudges, animosities, envy, and resentment. In other O'Neill works subplots provide resonance to the main plot: for example, Don Parritt's story of betrayal and the many instances of Tomorrowist pipe dreams in *The Iceman Cometh;* Mary's addiction and Edmund's consumption in *Long Day's Journey.* But in *A Moon for the Misbegotten* many wonderful inclusions have no part in the present discussion: the humor of the Phil-Josie mock war, the T. Stedman Harder episode, or Hogan's attempt to trick Jim Tyrone into a compromising situation with Josie. " . . . Hogan is held off-center. O'Neill is writing what is essentially a love story, a thing he has not done since *'Anna Christie,'* and Hogan, like old Chris, must move aside for the misbegotten lovers."[36] Here we have a straight-out issue of guilt: Jim has committed a reprehensible act and he knows it. The memory of his sin is wrecking his life; indeed, his guilt is causing him to drink himself to death.[37]

In this play we have a variation on the central theme of this study. The usual pattern has been, however, that those who have violated but loved each other can also participate in each other's spiritual renewal. But, since *A Moon for the Misbegotten* presents protagonists who are innocent of hurting one another (at least in any grave manner), we wonder how Jim and Josie can fulfill the criteria thus far established. Jim knows himself to be guilty of an act of extreme human insensitivity, one that would scandalize even the hardened cynic. He has violated the memory of his own beloved mother. Because she is dead, moreover, Mrs. Tyrone can no longer perform an act of ritual forgiveness and thereby relieve him of his guilt. Jim requires a *mediatrix*[38] (a word that may suggest a hint of chauvinism in today's gender-sensitive climate, but an expression that once carried powerful connotations in the catechism).

* * *

Jim Tyrone, in his early forties, is a habitual cynic and boozer. He has paid for his life's truancy with his health, both physical and emotional. Retaining *"the ghost of a former youthful, irresponsible Irish charm,"*[39] his mask and manner now repel the very people who might give succor to his troubled soul. A man of immense talents now crumbled, he employs his wit in mockery of his own failure. To gain release from pain he requires a partner who will not be defeated by his efforts to defeat himself.

O'Neill presents only the sketchiest account of Jim's early years. What we are given, moreover, is not a very attractive portrait. We learn almost nothing of his childhood, except that he developed his ne'er-do-well style and self-destructive patterns very early. Jim recalls his father, "a true Irish gentleman" by most accounts, as "a lousy tight-wad bastard" (128). To Phil Hogan, the tenant who farms the land Jim inherited from old Tyrone, he recalls the time he was expelled from his Jesuit college for a prank he committed in his senior year. In many ways he has not yet grown up and recounts the incident with sophomoric glee. He had brought "a tart from the Haymarket to visit me [and] introduce[d] her to the Jebs [Jesuits] as my sister. . . . "

> It was a memorable day in the halls of learning. All the students were wise and I had them rolling in the aisles as I showed Sister around the grounds, accompanied by one of the Jebs. He was a bit suspicious at first, but Dutch

Maisie—her professional name—had no make-up on, and was dressed in black, and had eaten a pound of Sen-Sen to kill the gin on her breath, and seemed such a devout girl that he forgot his suspicions. (*He pauses*) Yes, all would have been well, but she was a mischievous minx, and had her own ideas of improving on my joke. When she was saying good-bye to Father Fuller, she added innocently: "Christ, Father, it's nice and quiet out here away from the damned Sixth Avenue El. I wish to hell I could stay here!" (*Dryly*) But she didn't, and neither did I. (39)

He makes a joke of this, of course, as he says the "bum racket" of life makes everything. But the episode is more humorous in the telling (and endless retellings, no doubt) than it could have been in fact. Jamie O'Neill, who was actually forced out of Fordham in his brilliant senior year,[40] offered the model for this stunt. The elder O'Neills had been mortified by the deed, for this caper had been his most egregiously mindless up to that point. In this he might have known that he had trampled their sensibilities. Perhaps it did not bother him if the "tightwad" had been offended, but he could not have tossed off his mother's hurt that easily. Indeed, it is his final abuse of her dignity that is at the heart of Jim Tyrone's misery in *A Moon for the Misbegotten* and that is the mainspring of the play's "action."[41]

Jamie had apparently made something of a recovery after the death of his father. He was no doubt energized by Mary, who had conquered her morphine addiction so tragically dramatized in *Long Day's Journey into Night*. When James, Sr., died and no longer stood between Jim (as he had been called at school) and his mother, the younger man had her finally to himself. (As is so often the case in O'Neill's late plays, we find it difficult to separate Tyrone family experience from that of the O'Neills.) Jim had been happy for the first time in years. He even began to imitate her recovery:

When Mama died, I'd been on the wagon for nearly two years. Not even a glass of beer. Honestly. And I know I would have stayed on. For her sake. She had no one but me. The Old Man was dead. My brother had married—had a kid—had his own life to live. She'd lost him. She had only me to attend to things for her and take care of her. She'd always hated my drinking. So I quit. It made me happy to do it. For her. Because she was all I had, all I cared about. Because I loved her. (*He pauses*) No one would believe that now, who knew—But I did. (146)

They had traveled to California together to sell some of James's property. But Mary suddenly became ill and fell into a coma. "I went crazy. Couldn't face losing her. . . . I got drunk and stayed drunk." Mary came out of the coma just long enough to recognize his condition: "She saw I was drunk. Then she closed her eyes so she couldn't see, and was glad to die" (147). In a stupor of booze, frantic and frightened, Jim had to accompany the body back to the East Coast. His memory of what he did on this journey has produced the greatest guilt and shame he has ever known. But he had compounded the guilt he felt for disappointing his mother. In a gesture of incredible obscenity, he further sullied his mother's death dignity by remaining drunk and taking a miserable prostitute ("a blonde pig") into his roomette: "I bribed the porter . . . and that night she sneaked into my drawing room. . . . So every night—for fifty bucks a night—" (149). As he confesses this to Josie, later, even she feels revulsion: "Oh, how could you! (*Instinctively she draws away, taking her arms from around him.*)"

When there no longer exists a medium of forgiveness, where will a man find absolution? If as a child he had believed in the efficacy of sacramental confession, the "Mephistopheles" of later years no longer has available to him that agency of grace. Fallen beneath the weight of his own cynicism, he requires forgiveness but lacks a belief in the existence of any authority to purge him.

Josie Hogan is, in her way, a character equally grotesque. No more than Jim Tyrone is she likely to evoke easy pity. Hulking and "freakish," she has put abroad the rumor that she possesses a nearly mythic sexual appetite. Because in her massiveness she cannot play the coquette, she enhances her image as its opposite. This reputation gives her a kind of notoriety. In fact, the ploy is her mask, a face-saving defense against having to take credit for virtue she does not possess, credit that she does not deserve. To some extent the legend has taken. Early in the play her skittish and "primly self-righteous" brother Mike scolds her for scandalous behavior: "You've never cared about your virtue, or what man you went out with. You've always been brazen as brass and proud of your disgrace" (9). In fact, she is nothing of the kind, and Jim Tyrone sees behind her pretense.

These misbegotten souls know their own kind. Neither Jim nor Josie believes in the image the other projects. Not that she is unaware of his weaknesses. He makes several passes during the long night. But she knows that he cannot really enjoy the hideous jokes he makes about himself. Josie sees the terror and self-loathing that are hidden behind his facade of Broadway sport.

Nor is she above scheming to get Jim into her bed and to be "caught" with him. Jim Tyrone kids Josie, as is his style, about being "my Virgin Queen of Ireland," but these are mere high jinx. She is willing to be of greater service to him. Although she is miffed when she thinks he has forgotten their plan to spoon in the moonlight, he comes late and they spend the long night until dawn together. In that meeting nothing happens and everything happens. Her virtue is preserved and he receives the benison of her grace. What is given and taken is something greater than mere carnal experience; he is able to draw on the treasure of compassion that he knows is stored in her heart. The play has every possibility for breaking apart into saccharine bathos. But by some alchemy and art, O'Neill keeps that from happening. Moreover, he lifts the play from its beginnings in farce onto the high plane of drama.

But *A Moon for the Misbegotten* puts the audience to a hard test. Perhaps this is true of all of O'Neill's late plays except *A Touch of the Poet*. After the considerable humor of act 1, we face a demanding two-act working up to confession, followed by a brief denouement (act 4). The protagonist, although he is quick with a quip, is not especially prepossessing. Jim Tyrone staggers under the knowledge of his own wasted life: he can look back on no deed of his own that was brave or honorable. Perhaps this common condition constitutes precisely the problem audiences nowadays experience in seeing the modern character as tragic: Willy Loman, Blanche DuBois, Larry Slade, and so on. If Macbeth turns into a monster, he has also fought valiantly and spoken Olympian poetry. If Hamlet quivers in cowardice, he stands nevertheless as the greatest Renaissance intellectual of tragedy. But what to do with that character whose booze-and-broad exploits on the transcontinental express mark the hero's great fall? Well, of course, this was *not* the sin but merely its tawdry outward sign. Still, the play can tax our patience. In terms of what the characters have to say about their own histories and prospects, we find little of intrinsic importance. If we are unacquainted with the O'Neill family history, we have not even those connections to keep in mind. As Bogard observes, "As a theatrical work, *A Moon for the Misbegotten* is one of O'Neill's most difficult plays. . . . [It] is doomed to failure without superb acting."[42]

The problem centers on Jim. In the inelegant parlance of our time, he is a loser. In him we behold the final stage of *fin de siècle* mordancy. His favorite poet, Dante Gabriel Rossetti, like his peers Dowson, Swinburne, and Wilde, was never wholly in fashion. Jim's tragedy has already occurred, in the death of his youth, which he can hardly recall, and in the death of his here lamented mother. He sees both her and himself as victims of her husband, his father, the ogre Tyrone. But his manner of commemorating these losses calls forth neither beautiful language nor worthy philosophy. His are throw-away lines and acid barbs directed at life and at himself, words that rob even grief of its possible nobility. He is a sad man who has been unable to confess his sadness, for that would make him even more vulnerable. Yes, he needs a miracle worker.

* * *

O'Neill's achievement quite disarms us. We expect no *volte-face*. Everything points to Jim's spiritual demise, his soul the victim of its own lethal cynicism. But no. Sensitive beyond expectation to the soul's suffering, Josie responds to his need out of her own suffering and love. We have here not the majesty of Raskolnikov's terrible pride and the simplicity of Sonia's charity.

That story was a vehicle of massive theme. But we do have similar dynamics: the scar of self-indulgence succored by uncomplicated pity. In this pure light of the moon, Jim releases the burden of his self-contempt to that one party he knows will not abuse his confession. "You won't believe it could have happened. Or if you did believe, you couldn't understand or forgive—(*Quickly*) But you might. You're the one person who might. Because you really love me" (145). Thus it happens that the cradle of Josie's embrace becomes his confessional. The seal of this revelation will not, he knows, be broken.[43] If later Josie tells her puzzled father the outcome of the night's exchange, that is no violation. For she reveals not the intimacies but the mystery of a "virgin who bears a dead child in the night, and the dawn finds her still a virgin. If that isn't a miracle, what is?" (160).

In a scene that is altogether convincing, Jim must at first deny what he realizes has happened. Since he has learned to trust his secret to no one, since he had years ago adjusted his mask for life, he feels in the new dawn's light the instant threat of his nakedness. So he responds as if by autonomic reflex that what has taken place did not take place: "I don't know what you're talking about. I don't remember—" Josie, craftily, will not challenge him: "All right, Jim. Neither do I then. Good-bye, and God bless you" (174). Her withholding censure is itself an act of love, for she thereby gives just that proof of fidelity his now-shriven soul requires. All signs being fair, he can accept the moment of his own redemption.

Josie has stood as Jim's surrogate mother. Only his mother could forgive him of the monstrous obscenity he had committed. But Mary Tyrone is dead. For that reason Jim has been without confessor and therefore without absolution. Josie Hogan's act of love has been truly selfless. Had she thought to gain advantage from the moment, to ply the trade of voyeur posing as the golden-hearted prostitute, she would surely have upset the gentle balance of the evening. But her holding him through the night has been painful. Moreover, she must now bear the knowledge of another's guilt. This is never easy, and it is why deep lovers exchange something far more mysterious than the gratifications of momentary exhilaration. Josie has shared Jim's mystery, the privilege of knowing him as only he has known himself. The price has been considerable. She has had to sacrifice the sexual, and perhaps conjugal, benefits of relationship. In her words we hear echoes of Abbie in *Desire Under the Elms*, but the dynamics are different. It is through sexual union that Abbie had brought Eben to terms with himself and his mother's *presence*. Here the denial of sexual union brings Jim to terms with himself and his mother's *absence*. Josie now speaks with the authority of his mother.

> JOSIE. (*Throws her arms around him and pulls him back—tensely.*) No! You won't go! I won't let you! (*She hugs him close—gently*) I understand now,

Jim, darling, and I'm proud you came to me as the one in the world you know loves you enough to understand and forgive—and I do forgive!

TYRONE. (*Lets his head fall back on her breast—simply.*) Thanks, Josie. I knew you—

JOSIE. As *she* forgives, do you hear me! As *she* loves and understands and forgives!

TYRONE. (*Simply.*) Yes, I know she—(*His voice breaks.*)

JOSIE. (*Bends over him with a brooding maternal tenderness.*) That's right. Do what you came for, my darling. It isn't drunken laughter in a speakeasy you want to hear at all, but the sound of yourself crying your heart's repentance against her breast. (*His face is convulsed. He hides it on her breast and sobs rackingly. She hugs him more tightly and speaks softly, staring into the moonlight.*) *She* hears. I feel her in the moonlight, her soul wrapped in it like a silver mantle, and I know she understands and forgives me, too, and her blessing lies on me. (152–153)

In standing for his mother, Josie has known him as he had hoped his mother could. And she has blessed his guilt.

O'Neill had once called *Days Without End* "a miracle play." The phrase comes far closer to describing *A Moon for the Misbegotten*.

Epilogue

On DECEMBER 2, 1953, a hearse bearing the corpse of Eugene O'Neill eased into the mid-morning Boston traffic. Its destination was Forest Hills Cemetery, Jamaica Plain. No requiem Mass had been sung. No prayer would be said at graveside. Carlotta Monterey O'Neill, now his widow, later remarked, "I carried out every wish of Gene's to the letter. . . . He wished no publicity . . . nobody to be at his funeral . . . no religious representative of any creed or kind. . . . "[1] She had kept her word.

*   *   *

How inscrutable are the forces that shape our lives. When we are twenty, we cannot know what joys will have quickened and sorrows pierced our hearts in the decades to come. Even when the scroll has been at last unrolled, our modest histories will remain to us unfathomable. Indeed, the random changes wrought by time cause us to wonder at the immensity of life's mystery. In this O'Neill was like all others, even if he felt more keenly the gravity of his experience.[2] He could not have guessed, for example, when he saw her last in 1918, what would happen to Dorothy Day or to himself over the next thirty-five years. Nor could she have foretold what persons and events would touch their lives. But it is impossible to suppose that O'Neill, who kept track of everything from World Series scores to the rise of Mussolini, was unaware of the Catholic Worker Movement and *The Catholic Worker*. What did he make of it all? Why did he never, so far as the record shows, write or visit her? We know that Dorothy Day often recalled the early Greenwich Village years and her friendship with O'Neill. In her way she had also kept faith with him.[3]

> . . . the candle flickering in the wind caught my eyes, and the lines "flickering tapers" came to my mind and I thought of Gene, and his sad death, a death expected for some years but tragic in its loneliness. He died "out of the Church." He did not have the last rites. He was not anointed. He did not receive Viatecum (*sic*). He did not make peace with God, the "practicing Catholic" would say. And I thought of our obligation to pray for the dead. It is one of the works of mercy, "to pray for the living and the dead."

... When I spoke to my spiritual director, an old Spanish priest at the Church of Our Lady of Guadalupe on Fourteenth Street about this, and asked that question, "What good does it do [praying for the dead?]," he answered, "There is no time with God. There is neither past, present or future. The prayers which you say today are capable of giving him that moment at death, that grace to open his heart, his mind to God, to hold out his arms, to accept the forgiveness of sins, the redemption that Jesus Christ came to bring."

So as I thought of the glimmering tapers, and that poem of Francis Thompson, and Gene and his reciting it to me in the back room of Wallace's saloon, I prayed for him with love and fervor, and at the same time was shocked at the sudden feeling that I had of the terrible risk, the danger, so likely of Gene's refusing that redemption, of turning from that light[,] even at that last dread moment. I can see his somber eyes and bitter mouth now and hear that tragic monotonous grating voice. And even with his heart full of love and longing for "that way and truth and light," that Jesus, that man-god, I can see him turning from Him as an illusion, as too good to be true. . . .

Since he brought to me such a consciousness of God,—since he recited to me *The Hound of Heaven,* I owe him my prayers. There is no time with God and I would be sinning against hope, faith and charity if I did not believe that my prayers, and whoever else is praying for the soul of Gene, are not heard.

There is another who I know is praying for him and that is Archbishop Francis [*sic*] [later Cardinal] Cushing of Boston[4] archdiocese.[5]

In this book I have offered an idea. I have suggested that, as man and artist, Eugene O'Neill retained a Catholic sensibility. If this presence was not so demonstrable as his blood type, it was something equally constant. He recognized this truth. Yet he struggled for fifty years and never reentered the Catholic mainstream. As a boy Eugene had found the church beautiful but austere: "Religion is so cold," he once said to a classmate at St. Aloysius. Thereafter, he felt himself abandoned by those he longed for most: Mother and God. Down the years he became certain, in spirit and blood, that he had been betrayed. No doubt the whole notion became quite complicated and, therefore, very Irish. If he felt himself to be a victim, however, O'Neill must occasionally have wondered if he had not himself been guilty of betrayal. Does this not explain why he was mesmerized by *The Hound of Heaven* and, in reciting it, mesmerized others?

> ... a Voice beat
> More instant than the Feet—
> "All things betray thee,
> Who betrayest Me."

> I was heavy with the even,
> When she lit her glimmering tapers
> Round the day's dead sanctities.

Such material as this falls properly into the category of biography, of course. But what impact did this Catholic sensibility have on his plays, on theme and characterization?

✻   ✻   ✻

If God is dead, as Nietzsche proclaimed and O'Neill repeated, would the habit of seeing things in the light of Catholic experience and training become irrelevant? Would the power of one's moral imagination be canceled or found useless? What does it mean anyhow, moral imagination?

Historically, the philosopher and critic have spoken of the artist as one who possesses, in uncommon measure, the faculty of imagination. The artist can visualize (*imagine*) a world that is "more real than reality." In asserting this, the philosopher is not practicing a kind of verbal legerdemain. She or he is not playing at words without regard for the truth. *More real than reality,* one supposes, is that state or condition Aristotle had in mind when he argued that the storytellers give us a truth greater than that given by the historian.[6] The historian, trained to hew to the facts, surely does not lack imagination. Thus, she may interpret the data and thereby exercise imaginative judgment; however, the facts alone determine what may fairly be interpreted. But in the end fiction is more real than reality, is more truthful than history, because it always and everywhere obtains. We can put it this way: great fiction maintains fidelity to human nature. That is what we have in mind when we call a work of art timeless and universal.

Add to this idea of imagination the qualifier *moral.* Of course, the greatest storytellers have not been moralists in the narrow sense of the term—self-righteous, inflexible, meanly dogmatic. Rather, they have given a view of human nature, even in its sinfulness or pathology, that celebrates human bravery and the capacity to suffer profitably. Their own experience is no doubt their greatest guide to truth. Strindberg and Dostoesvski come to mind. For such artists, the experience of guilt can be healing as well as crippling. O'Neill belongs in this company. "In the history of the theater perhaps only Strindberg, one of his idols, told as much about himself as this lapsed Catholic, who so often stepped into the confessional to write his plays."[7]

If his plays are forgotten, it will not be because they are dated and topical.

"His plays are neither social sermons nor contemporary satire," said Richard Dana Skinner. "They are more like parables."[8] A moral imagination does not, indeed cannot, refuse to judge, for it comes to terms with laws and movements that, when set into motion by human will, do not permit a character to become mere victim. The importance of fiction and drama rendered in the light of such an imagination rests in this: character is made participant in its own destiny. "O'Neill characters do not escape the consequences of their deeds. The proud are humbled or destroyed. The possessive lose the objects of their desire. The connection between evil and disaster is direct, internal as well as external, and, in the true dramatic sense, inevitable."[9] Thus, even if the artist agreed with Nietzsche's conclusion, his Catholic sensibility and moral imagination were not necessarily made irrelevant. This imagination can be given birth by various forms of acculturation. In Eugene O'Neill's case, the faculty seems to have been shaped by his Catholic background and experience.

In the early stages of his research, Louis Sheaffer[10] sought the assistance of Sr. Madeleva, poet and president of St. Mary's College, South Bend. He was grateful that she, like so many others, was willing to contribute what she could to filling in the playwright's spiritual portrait.

> I was pleased that you referred to O'Neill as "a great and unhappy man," for your description gave me the impression that perhaps we share to some extent the same view of O'Neill. Although he never returned to the Church, I see him as a deeply religious person at bottom who lost his way, due to unfortunate external experiences in his early life, and never succeeded in finding his way home again. Among many indications of his deep-rooted religious feeling, one of his favorite poems, as you probably know, was "The Hound of Heaven," which he knew by heart and used to recite to friends during late unhappy hours in Greenwich Village.[11]

To women and men like O'Neill, life is tragic and therefore ennobled. *Hurrah!* Whatever else this idea may have meant, it suggested that one must suffer. Still, such a view places the human heart at the center of the things. Life might be meaningless, but it is not worthless. In accepting this paradox, O'Neill distinguished himself from rank-and-file modernists and absurdists. To him, the tragedy of time was to be found in the individual's spiritual dislocation. Of course, to be abandoned meant to suffer, for it implied that one had been abandoned by Someone, or someone. If this were not so, betrayal meant nothing. Can we not infer, then, that guilt is fixed in the nature of things? Recall Jim's response to Ella, who wonders whether God will forgive her: "Maybe He can forgive what you've done to me; and maybe He can forgive what I've done to you; but I don't see how He's going to forgive—Himself" (II, 341).

O'Neill wished to be "an artist or nothing," as he said in his application letter to George Pierce Baker in 1914. By no means did he see himself as a "Catholic" writer. If that attitude did not please church authorities, then let the chips fall, as he indicated to Bennett Cerf, who had advised him to seek endorsements from church officials to bolster the Random House sales of *Days Without End*.

> *It is not Catholic propaganda!* If, after it comes out, the Church wants to set the seal of its approval on it, well that's up to them. But I don't give a damn whether they do or not—and I certainly will not make the slightest move to win that approval in advance. . . .
>
> I don't think you know the prelates, and their feeling about my work, and the use of Church themes in the theatre, as well as I do. . . . No! As far as the Church is concerned, hands off! Let the play speak for itself without any advance comment on that part of its subject from you or the Guild or me. And then let the Church like it—or lump it.[12]

None of this meant that he gave up all claim to religious questions, however, including those of God's existence or the issues of sin, guilt, and redemption.

When he died, few Catholic newspapers and magazines commented on O'Neill's life and art. One did: a brave journal of opinion established and operated by laymen and women. In noting his death, the eulogist did not mention the word "Catholic." It does not seem likely that O'Neill would have felt slighted.

> There are not many American writers whom one can call, with some certainty, "great." Among the novelists—Hawthorne, Melville, Henry James, Faulkner and Hemingway. Among the poets—Poe, Whitman, Hart Crane, Pound, and T. S. Eliot. Among the dramatists—Eugene O'Neill.
>
> In the drama, O'Neill's name stands alone. Experimenter and craftsman, prober of our national dreams and our national frustrations, he created a body of work which is the American theater's chief claim to respect throughout the world.
>
> Now Eugene O'Neill is dead and with him a part of America's greatness has surely died. But the influence of art cannot be measured. It extends for generations. It becomes tradition. What Eugene O'Neill gave to America is now part of America's tradition. We are grateful for it, and for his genius. May he rest in peace.[13]

APPENDIX

The Immigrant Church Press and the Catholic Writer, 1920–1950

CATHOLIC INTELLECTUALS HAVE been forced, no less than their "secular" peers, to confront the confusion and faith crises of the modern world. Yet, as we look back at the decades 1920–1950, European and American Catholic intellectuals appear to have faced the challenges differently. The former seemed more poised, more confident in their independence. Perhaps these writers and artists found the example of John Henry Newman more accessible: Leon Bloy, Charles Peguy, G. K. Chesterton, Evelyn Waugh, François Mauriac, Jacques Maritain, Graham Greene, and so on. European Catholic writers apparently suffered less insecurity than did their American brothers and sisters. That is, as artists, they remained recognizably Catholic. Even so, Pius X's condemnation of modernism had devastating effects in both Europe and the United States. This is why John Tracy Ellis called *Pascendi Dominici Gregis* (1907) "the harshest and most negative language employed by a papal encyclical in this century."[1]

The origins of modernism may be found in a movement toward intellectual freedom among Protestant and Catholic theologians in the second half of the nineteenth century. New emphases in research and scholarship had revolutionized those fields of study where the institutional church might be expected to declare proprietary interests: archaeology, scripture studies, Egyptology, biblical exegesis, philology, and psychology. In these disciplines, as in certain of the natural sciences, time-honored investigative methods were being reexamined in light of the new findings. Staid assumptions about unchangeable truth were now being challenged by new critical approaches to the study of history and culture. Scholars had begun to look at history as a process, dynamic and organic, not necessarily as a continuum governed by fixed laws. If such views were to become ascendant, the church might be forced to see itself in the way that all other institutions did, as an evolutionary entity subject like the others to the laws of time and space. The implications were grave in Catholic circles: the church's very teaching authority could be called into question.

Scholasticism itself, the philosophical method approved by the church as the *via regia* to truth, had indeed been challenged. Threats, visible and potential, had begun to unsettle the keepers of tradition in Rome. Ancient doctrines of Catholic Christianity might themselves be opened to new interpretation: matters such as the divinity of Jesus or the teaching on papal infallibility. What had been thought inadmissible might be reconsidered: for example, subjective religious experience as an avenue to truth (smacking as it did of Protestant antiauthoritarianism); or lay participation in defining doctrine.

In acknowledging the revolution in the ranks, Rome acted firmly and finally to condemn the threat. In 1907 Pius X promulgated two withering denunciations of modernism. In July came the decree *Lamentabili Sane Exitu,* a syllabus of errors found mainly in the works of Alfred Loisy and George Tyrrell. On September 8, the Pope circulated his encyclical, *Pascendi Dominici Gregis,* in which he identified the sixty-five errors of modernism. (The movement might just as well have been called progressivism or liberalism.) The chill that fell upon the new movement was lethal, for the church had seen a "Protestant" threat in the trend toward intellectual independence. It perceived a leaning toward a personalist interpretation of Scripture, a drifting away from papal authority as old as the Reformation.

* * *

It may be that the American church felt the need to prove itself loyal to Rome, given the contemporary ideals of progress and the relative isolation of the U.S. church from the Vatican. At any rate, the roster of church authorities and journals that rode herd on American Catholic writers was formidable.

One might wish to consult Arnold J. Spaar's excellent study, *The Catholic Literary Revival in America, 1920–1960* (1985). Jesuits and Jesuit-trained commentators (e.g., Calvert Alexander and Daniel Lord, S.J., the indefatigable pamphleteer), promoted "a renaissance of Catholic literature," even as they torpedoed the flagships of modernist intellectualism—Darwin, Freud, Nietzsche, Bertrand Russell—and the American writers—Theodore Dreiser, James T. Farrell, Sinclair Lewis, H. L. Mencken, and Eugene O'Neill.[2]

Francis X. Talbot, S.J., named literary editor of the Jesuit journal *America* in 1923 and editor-in-chief in 1936, and Michael Earls, S.J., professor of literature at Boston College, were stalwart defenders of "wholesome" literature. Talbot was something of a literary workaholic, editing three important journals in the late 1930s: *America* (1936–1944), *The Catholic Mind* (1936–1944), and *Thought* (1936–1940). Talbot, and others, sought to encourage Catholics to produce fiction and poetry worthy both as literature and as Catholic apologetics. Many commentators attempted to muffle what they heard as voices of cynicism and pessimism. (In the 1950s the brilliant radio and television personality, Msgr. [later Bishop] Fulton J. Sheen[3] continued to attack those he saw as defeatist intellectuals.) The Catholic journals joined the debate. Talbot, Earls, Daniel Lord, and James F. Kearney were regular contributors,

Jesuits all. Elizabeth Jordan, the drama critic for *America* from 1922–1945, was also a frequent commentator.

The subject of "Catholic" literature was altogether worthy of discussion, of course. Unfortunately, the quality that characterized much of this criticism was its posture of embattled defensiveness, a quality that one analyst later said characterized too much of the Catholic point of view. There developed, he wrote, a kind of "martial attitude forced upon American Catholics by their nineteenth-century experience and the related partial segregation of Catholics from American cultural developments. . . . "

> There is a kind of vicious circle involved. Our defensiveness inhibits the development of a vigorous intellectual tradition. Our lack of such a tradition keeps our contribution small and leaves us occupying fewer positions of importance in American life than our numbers warrant. This in turn makes us resentful and increases defensiveness, thereby reinforcing the original cause of our difficulties.[4]

The "revivalists" championed sunny literature that would create an optimistic view of modern life. Many of the writers from the 1920s and 1930s who were approved have been forgotten since 1950. "The years between the wars are a veritable desert, even for writers who might claim momentary celebrity. One has to vigorously shake the trees of both memory and corporate history to find the meager harvest of Theodore Maynard, Sr. Madeleva, Aline Kilmer, and Leonard Feeney—names long submerged by collective embarrassment. (Alongside these names are the vastly more substantial apostate writers F. Scott Fitzgerald, Theodore Dreiser, Eugene O'Neill, and James T. Farrell)."[5] We could include among the lesser talents the names of other American Catholic writers of this period celebrated by Talbot, Earls, Alexander, and others: Edith O'Shaughnessy, Kathleen Norris, Sr. Eleanore (like Sr. Madeleva, a poet who taught at St. Mary's College, Notre Dame). If these were the best and the brightest of that era, it seems that the criteria endorsed by the Catholic literary revival encouraged varieties of shallowness, skittishness, and pietism. It was not that Fathers Talbot, Lord, Kearney, and Fulton Sheen later, lacked intellectual gifts; they were very well read men. The problem was that their disapproval of certain writers could easily be interpreted as the official position of the church. Eugene Kennedy, in an arresting passage that mixes compassion with acid, put the matter this way:

> The immigrant Church of the twentieth century, which prided itself on a unity and sense of purpose doubly bound to Roman authority, was particularly hard on poets and writers—on Catholics like F. Scott Fitzgerald and Eugene O'Neill and converts like Ernest Hemingway—who unsentimentally peered into the broken heart of the twentieth century. . . . The immigrant Church was hardheaded and literal, preferring undistinguished and senti-

mental renderings of Catholic piety to any possibly unsettling invitation to ambivalence in the interpretation of life. It preferred a fluent apologetics to its main business of religious mystery, Fulton Sheen and "Lovely Lady Dressed in Blue" to O'Neill and *Long Day's Journey into Night.*[6]

Few Catholic intellectuals were willing to defend those writers named by Kennedy. One who had the courage to defend them, however, was George N. Shuster, Notre Dame graduate (1915), and early editor of *Commonweal.* Before his graduate school days at Columbia, he was chosen, somewhat as Knute Rockne had been asked to teach chemistry and coach football, to profess English at his alma mater (1919–1923). It was a mistake. William Halsey tells of a searing incident in which Shuster placed a title by D. H. Lawrence (*The Rainbow*) on his freshman syllabus. The prefect of religion, Rev. John F. O'Hara, C.S.C., saw the book on the reserve shelf "and proceeded to tear it up. . . . Shuster left Notre Dame as a result of the incident and was not to return until 1961" in the Hesburgh presidency.[7] Critic, teacher, or artist-intellectual, what was one to do? Some, like Shuster, stayed inside the institution to do what they could. Others left—some in sadness, others in bitterness. "In the 1920s George N. Shuster, who for over a generation has been an outstanding Catholic figure in American secular education—an almost lone figure, as a matter of fact— looked in vain for genuine intellectual and artistic accomplishment among American Catholics and concluded that 'Catholics have not even done what might reasonably have been expected of them to foster letters, speculation and the arts.' "[8]

Such faith-defenders as Francis Talbot and Daniel Lord, however, feared secular skepticism, and fear makes shaky ground on which to fight. Although they hoped to effect a literary revival, they offered little specific guidance as to how this might be achieved. Insisting on a program so poorly defined suggested both *hubris* and uncertainty of ends. " . . . [F]or all their insights into the modern philosophical and cultural crisis," says Arnold J. Sparr,

> a certain smugness characterized much of American Catholic intellectual and philosophical life during the post World War I era. Doubt was interpreted not as an opportunity for growth, but scorned as a sign of weakness. Indeed, many American Catholic cultural leaders between the wars seemed to gloat over Catholicism's own philosophical and moral certainty in contrast to the confusion, drift, and doubt outside the scholastic world.[9]

*   *   *

It was this strain of anti-intellectualism, then, that had serious implications for modern artists in general and for Eugene O'Neill in particular. It was their modernist proclivities that were looked upon as a force for evil by the Catholic Church. One wonders if O'Neill, who admired *Dubliners,* might not have found in Joyce's stories a confirmation of his own views. For he came to see most institutions as moribund and most of men's shrines as decayed vessels of culture.

To the extent, however, that his sensibilities had been formed in the bosom of church and family,[10] O'Neill retained something like an immunity to the full fever of the antiauthoritarian movement in modern art. Moreover, since he was not much of a spokesman for any agenda other than his own, his name is sometimes omitted in surveys of modernist writers of the 1930s. Still, O'Neill's plays show that he was always conscious of the presence of sin and the power of guilt as a force in tragedy, although the *Catholic Encyclopedia* does not give him much credit for that: "The degree to which O'Neill's early Catholicism affected his work is debatable; his awareness of sin and guilt is Jansenistic rather than Catholic."[11] It is a nice question how many pre-Vatical II Irish were not more Jansenistic than "Catholic." One does not have to be the playwright's defender to question the encyclopedia entry. Whatever may be said of his personal life, O'Neill maintained a high regard for the sanctity of relationship, a regard that he had learned from his parents and their religion.

The hierarchy's uncertainty about the efficacy of a free literature did little to encourage trust or a sense of their own worth among Catholic writers in the middle decades of the twentieth century.

Notes

Prologue

1. Croswell Bowen, with Shane O'Neill. *The Curse of the Misbegotten: A Tale of the House of O'Neill* (New York: McGraw-Hill, 1959), 309 (emphasis mine).

2. Ibid., 316.

3. Edwin H. Cady, *The Light of Common Day: Realism in American Fiction* (Bloomington: Indiana University Press, 1971), 205–206.

4. Richard B. Sewall, "Eugene O'Neill and the Sense of the Tragic," in *Eugene O'Neill's Century: Centennial Views on America's Foremost Tragic Dramatist,* ed. Richard F. Moorton, Jr. (Westport, Conn.: Greenwood Press, 1971), 5.

5. Ibid., 6.

6. Joseph Wood Krutch, introduction to *Nine Plays by Eugene O'Neill: Selected by the Author* (New York: Random House, 1954), xvii.

7. Lionel Trilling, introduction to *The Emperor Jones, Anna Christie, The Hairy Ape, by Eugene O'Neill* (New York: Random House, 1937, 1964), x.

8. William D. Miller, *Dorothy Day: A Biography* (New York: Harper-Row, 1982), 117–118.

9. Oliver M. Sayler, *Our American Theatre* (New York: Brentano's, 1923), 42.

10. Karl Schriftgriesser, "Interview with O'Neill by Karl Schriftgriesser," *New York Times,* 6 October 1946, sec. 10: 1.

11. Karl Menninger, *Whatever Became of Sin?* (New York: Hawthorn Books, 1973), 229.

1. The Lad, the Rebel, the Artist

1. It is interesting to observe how other prominent Americans have looked upon their Irish-Catholic inheritance. George M. Cohan turned the tables on his heritage. He made himself into the very personification of America, the Yankee Doodle Dandy. Joseph P. Kennedy complained about a reference to him as an Irishman: "I was born here. My children were born here. What the hell do I have to do to be called an American?" (quoted in William V. Shannon, *The American Irish: A Political and Social Portrait* [New York: Macmillan, 1963], vi). These men are probably not typical of the pilgrims who make the annual trip from the U.S. back to "the ould sod."

2. O'Neill wrote to James T. Farrell in July of 1943: " . . . I want to recom-

mend a book published in the U.S. some six months ago, *The Great O'Neill* by Sean O'Faolain. If you haven't already read it, you will find it worth your while. It is a biography of Hugh O'Neill but also a study of Irish history in Elizabethan times. I learned from it a lot of Irish past I had mislearned before. You know what most Irish histories are like — benign Catholic benediction-and-blather tracts, or blind jingo glorifications of peerless fighting heroes, in the old bardic fashion. Hugh O'Neill, as O'Faolain portrays him in the light of historical fact, is no pure and pious archangel of Erin, but a fascinatingly complicated character, strong, proud and noble, ignoble, shameless and base, loyal and treacherous, a cunning politician, a courageous soldier, an inspiring leader — but at times so weakly neurotic he could burst openly into tears (even when sober!) and whine pitiably that no one understood him. In short, Shakespeare might have written a play about him." See *Selected Letters of Eugene O'Neill,* ed. Travis Bogard and Jackson R. Bryer (New Haven: Yale University Press, 1988), 545 (hereafter referred to as *Selected Letters*).

3. Jack English, "Can a Catholic Write a Novel?" *The American Mercury* 31 (January, 1934): 94.

4. Eugene O'Neill, *Long Day's Journey into Night* (New Haven: Yale University Press, 1956), 77 (hereafter called *LDJ* in citations).

5. When the parent actually believed, moreover, that life so organized promoted virtue, it should not be surprising that he would, like James O'Neill, write to the president of Notre Dame about signs of rebellion in his adolescent son (James O'Neill, Jr.) and ask the school's help in checking negative manifestations in the lad's character.

6. The line evokes Milton's phrase, "that one Talent which is death to hide," which itself is an allusion to Jesus' parable in Matthew 25:14-30.

7. Eugene O'Neill was baptized on 1 November 1888 at the Church of the Holy Innocents, 128 W. 37th St., Manhattan. The sacrament was conferred by Rev. M. J. Doherty and the sponsors (godparents) are indicated on the "Certificate of Baptism" as John O'Neill and Annie Connor. (The names of Fr. Doherty, John O'Neill, and Annie Connor are new in O'Neill studies, I believe.)

8. Louis Sheaffer, *O'Neill: Son and Playwright* (Boston: Little, Brown, & Company, 1968), 268. Volume 2 of Sheaffer's work on O'Neill is *O'Neill: Son and Artist* (Boston: Little, Brown, & Company, 1973).

9. Arthur Gelb and Barbara Gelb, *O'Neill* (New York: Harper and Row, 1974), 219.

10. Doris Alexander, *The Tempering of Eugene O'Neill* (New York: Harcourt Brace, 1962), 5.

11. Eugene's middle name marks his father's admiration for William Ewart Gladstone (1809-1898), British Prime Minister, who favored Home Rule for Ireland. James O'Neill, of course, remained throughout his lifetime an ardent supporter of Irish causes.

12. Gelb and Gelb, 88.

13. Sheaffer, *O'Neill: Son and Playwright,* 67.

14. Alexander, *The Tempering of Eugene O'Neill,* 24.

15. Sheaffer, *O'Neill: Son and Playwright,* 69.

16. John Cogley, *Catholic America* (New York: Dial Press, 1973), 202-204.

17. Sheaffer, *O'Neill: Son and Playwright,* 76–77.

18. Eugene O'Neill, *Selected Letters,* 370.

19. Mary B. Mullett, "The Extraordinary Story of Eugene O'Neill," *The American Magazine* 94 (November 1922): 34.

20. Sheaffer, *O'Neill: Son and Playwright,* 115.

21. Gelb and Gelb, *O'Neill,* 172.

22. See Susan Glaspell, *The Road to the Temple* (New York: Frederick A. Stokes, 1927); Helen Deutsch and Stella Hanau, *The Provincetown: A Story of the Theatre* (New York: Farrar and Rinehard, 1931); Robert K. Sarlos, *Jig Cook and the Provincetown Players: Theatre in Ferment* (Amherst: University of Massachusetts Press, 1982).

23. Glaspell, *The Road to the Temple,* 218.

24. Ibid., 254.

25. Sarlos, *Jig Cook and the Provincetown Players,* 161 and Appendix, 169–180.

26. Deutsch and Hanau, *The Provincetown,* 89.

27. Havel was the model for Hugo Kalmar and Goldman the inspiration for Rosa Parritt in *The Iceman Cometh.* Goldman thanks O'Neill for a volume of plays in a letter to Stella Cominsky in *Nowhere at Home: Letters from Exile of Emma Goldman and Alexander Berkman,* ed. Richard Drinnon and Anna Maria Drinnon (New York: Schocken Books, 1975), 8.

28. Five years after O'Neill's death, Agnes Boulton published reminiscenses of her life with him, calling the book *Part of a Long Story: Eugene O'Neill As a Young Man in Love* (London: Peter Davies, 1958). Boulton tells of their 1917 meeting in the Hell Hole, the Provincetown friends and the Greenwich Village scene, their marriage and relations with O'Neill's parents, and the birth of their son, Shane Rudraighe, in Provincetown in 1919.

29. Boulton, *Part of a Long Story,* 45.

30. Bowen, *The Curse of the Misbegotten,* 309.

31. Shriftgriesser, "Interview with O'Neill," 1.

32. Sayler, *Our American Theatre,* 42.

33. Among his gallery of characters, Larry Slade in *The Iceman Cometh* probably comes closest to reflecting O'Neill's own ambivalence about human nature. Slade is based on an old anarchist friend of the Provincetown days, Terry Carlin, something of a philosopher-in-residence. Slade speaks of men in a combined cynicism-lyricism.

> I was born condemned to be one of those who has to see all sides of a question. When you're damned like that, the questions multiply for you until in the end it's all question and no answer. As history proves, to be a worldly success at anything, especially revolution, you have to wear blinders like a horse and see only straight in front of you. . . . As for my comrades in the Great Cause, I felt as Horace Walpole did about England, that he could love it if it weren't for the people in it. The material the ideal free society must be constructed from is men themselves and you can't build a marble temple out of a mixture of mud and manure. (III, 590)

34. Peter Maurin became the greatest inspiration in Dorothy Day's life. Again

and again she credited him with planting the seeds that grew into the Catholic Worker Movement and its penny newspaper, *The Catholic Worker.*

In the early 1930s he heard about Dorothy Day from George Shuster, then editor of *Commonweal.* Unflinching in his pacifism, Maurin believed in nearly absolute adherence to the spirit of the Christian gospel. "Be for the other fellow," he said, "what you are teaching him to be." A reader of Jacques Maritain and Nicolas Berdyaev, he preached a doctrine of "gentle personalism." To Dorothy Day, Peter Maurin was a holy man, a saint, and a teacher.

35. In 1949 *The Catholic Worker,* which had no financial power whatever, took a stand in favor of the United Cemetery Workers, Local 293, of the International Food, Tobacco and Agricultural and Allied Workers Union of America. Its members, gravediggers in Calvary Cemetery, struck against the Trustees of St. Patrick's Cathedral. Francis Cardinal Spellman and the board took a very hard line against the cemetery workers. In fact, Spellman broke the strike by forcing students from St. Joseph's Seminary (Dunwoodie, Yonkers) to work as scabs. In April Dorothy Day in the *Worker* wondered why " . . . a Cardinal, ill-advised, exercised so overwhelming a show of force against a handful of poor working men. It was a temptation of the devil to that most awful of all wars, the war between the clergy and the laity." Day and others from *The Catholic Worker* marched outside the Cardinal's residence where they distributed leaflets. (See Miller, *Dorothy Day,* 404–405, and John Cooney's *The American Pope: The Life and Times of Francis Cardinal Spellman* [New York: Time Books, 1984], 187–195.)

36. Boulton, *Part of a Long Story,* 42.

37. Ibid., 79.

38. Francis Thompson (1859–1907) was born in Lancashire and died in London of tuberculosis at age 47. He might be grouped with the *fin de siècle* poets O'Neill admired (Wilde, Dowson, Swinburne, Rossetti, et al.), but they tended to be rather mordant. Thompson is more properly placed with the larger group of mystics of any period, for he simultaneously sought the divine and hoped to escape from it. He had failed to gain entrance into or succeed in the more conventional professions: medicine, the military, even salesmanship.

Thompson had nearly died of his opium addiction in 1888, having lived as a derelict in the streets and alleys of London. He was rescued by the intervention of an Evangelical minister. The poet was cured and lived for a year thereafter with the monks of Storrington Priory before returning to London in 1890.

"The Hound of Heaven" was published in 1890. Its style and theme are quite out of vogue today. The poem receives only modest attention in literary histories. *The Catholic Encyclopedia* includes the following observation:

> Thompson is generally thought of as a Catholic poet whose verse seems florid and ornate by modern standards, but his "mysticism" and his vision of nature are supported by a hard core of objectivity and accurate theology. Love and poetry itself are his other subjects. [In C. T. Dougherty, "Francis Thompson," in *New Catholic Encyclopedia* (Washington, D.C.: Catholic University of America Press, 1967), 14: 139].

39. William D. Miller, *All Is Grace: The Spirituality of Dorothy Day* (Garden City, N.Y.: Doubleday, 1987), 13–14 (emphasis mine).

40. Notes by Stanley Vishnewski on "Conversations with Dorothy Day,"

1978, Dorothy Day-Catholic Worker Collection Series W-12.3, Box 3, Marquette University Archives. [Stanley Vishnewski was a 17-year-old Lithuanian boy who joined the Catholic Worker Movement in 1932. See Dorothy Day's *Loaves and Fishes* (New York: Harper & Row, 1963, 1983), 24.]

41. Dorothy Day, "Told in Context," unpublished ms. (circa 1958) Dorothy Day-Catholic Worker Collection Series D-3, Box 7, Marquette University Archives.

42. Doris Alexander, *Eugene O'Neill's Creative Struggle: The Decisive Decade, 1924–1933* (University Park: Pennsylvania State University Press, 1992), 191.

43. Garry Wills, "The Saint of Mott Street," *New York Review of Books* 36 (21 April 1994): 45–48.

44. Dorothy Day includes the following reflection in *Loaves and Fishes,* 70:

> So many sins against the poor cry out to high heaven! One of the most deadly sins is to deprive the laborer of his hire. There is another: to instill in him paltry desires so compulsive that he is willing to sell his liberty and his honor to satisfy them. We are all guilty of concupiscence, but newspapers, radio, television, and battalions of advertising men (woe to that generation) deliberately stimulate our desires, the satisfaction of which so often means the deterioration of the family. Whatever we can do to combat these widespread social evils by combating their causes we must do. But above all the responsibility is a personal one. The message we have been given comes from the Cross.

45. Vishnewski, "Conversations," entries 41, 42, 43, and 44.

46. Day, "Told in Context," 6.

47. Mel Piehl, *Breaking Bread: The Catholic Worker and the Origin of Catholic Radicalism in America* (Philadelphia: Temple University Press, 1982), 13.

48. Travis Bogard, *Contour in Time: The Plays of Eugene O'Neill,* rev. ed. (New York: Oxford University Press, 1988), 367.

49. In *The Eugene O'Neill Companion* (Westport, Conn.: Greenwood Press, 1984), 483, Margaret Ranald records that *More Stately Mansions* was written between 1935 and 1941. The surviving manuscript, dated 1938, was left incomplete and unrevised. Karl Ragnar Gierow's shortening of the lengthy manuscript was edited by Donald Gallup, curator emeritus of the rare books and manuscripts collection in the Beinecke Library of Yale University.

2. Catholic Memory, Classic Forms

1. Cady, *The Light of Common Day,* 51 (emphasis mine).

2. Deutsch and Hanau, *The Provincetown,* 191–192.

3. Cady, *The Light of Common Day,* 24.

4. George Santayana, "A General Confession," in *The Philosophy of George Santayana,* ed. Paul Arthur Schilpp (Evanston, Ill.: Northwestern University Press, 1940), 7.

5. George Santayana, *My Host the World,* vol. 3 of *Persons and Places* (New York: Scribner's, 1953), 11.

6. Day, "Told in Context," 6.

7. George Santayana, *Poems: Selected by the Author and Revised* (New York: Scribner's, 1923), 91.

8. Santayana, "A General Confession," 7–8.

9. O'Neill, *Selected Letters,* 332.

10. John Henry Raleigh, *The Plays of Eugene O'Neill* (Carbondale: Southern Illinois University Press, 1965), 88, and Frederic I. Carpenter, *Eugene O'Neill,* rev. ed. (Boston: G. K. Hall, 1979), 187.

11. Raleigh, *The Plays of Eugene O'Neill,* 88.

12. Francis Thompson, *The Poetical Works of Francis Thompson* (New York: Scribner's, 1913), 1: 107.

13. Miller, *Dorothy Day,* 110.

14. Boulton, *Part of a Long Story,* 280.

15. William J. O'Malley, S.J., "Idiocies for Our Time," *Notre Dame Magazine* (winter 1991–92): 78–79.

16. Lionel Trilling, introduction to *The Emperor Jones, Anna Christie, The Hairy Ape,* by Eugene O'Neill, xviii–xix.

17. Egil Tornqvist, *A Drama of Souls: Studies in O'Neill's Supernaturalistic Technique* (New Haven: Yale University Press, 1969), 11.

18. Arthur Hobson Quinn, *A History of the American Drama from the Civil War to the Present Day,* rev. ed. (New York: F. S. Crofts, 1936), 2: 199.

19. Edward L. Shaughnessy, *Eugene O'Neill in Ireland: The Critical Reception* (Westport, Conn: Greenwood Press, 1988), 105.

20. Quoted by Thomas Werge in "GKC to the Rescue," *Notre Dame Magazine* 23 (Winter 1994–1995): 23.

21. Jacques Maritain, *Education at the Crossroads* (New Haven: Yale University Press, 1943), 25.

22. Joseph Wood Krutch, *The Modern Temper: A Study and a Confession* (New York: Harcourt Brace Jovanovich, 1984), 87.

23. John Tully Carmody and Denise Lardner Carmody, *Contemporary Catholic Theology,* rev. ed. (New York: New York University Press, 1961) [emphasis mine].

24. Ibid., 94.

25. Chester C. Long, *The Role of Nemesis in the Structure of Selected Plays by Eugene O'Neill* (The Hague, The Netherlands: Mouton, 1968), 13.

26. Paul Ricoeur, *The Symbolism of Evil,* trans. Emerson Buchanan (New York: Beacon Press, 1967), 103.

27. Thomas E. Porter, *Myth and Modern American Drama* (Detroit: Wayne State University Press, 1969), 14–15 (emphasis his).

28. Ibid., 254.

29. O'Neill, *Selected Letters,* 195.

30. William Kennedy, *Ironweed* (New York: Viking, 1983), 216.

31. Ricoeur, *The Symbolism of Evil,* 7.

32. Gelb and Gelb, *O'Neill,* 877.

33. Our culture does not foster the habits of reflection and meditation. The American has made a place for religion, but he often allots time for the Sunday morning service, just as he does for daily exercise, banking on Thursday, and golf on Saturday. The virtue of the American is his efficiency and capacity for organization. A willingness to examine complex psychological and moral issues does not fit easily into this system of priorities.

34. Thomas Porter contributes a useful observation in this connection.

There is, I think, in the popular Irish-Catholic tradition considerable mixing (Chalcedon's term) of Christ's "two natures." That is to say, Christ is "God-man" in ways that make him superhuman. So being "human" as such gets a bad rap. Augustine is adamant about Christ's being human, sin excepted. From this perspective, it seems to me that sin is always an attempt to *escape* humanness, to play God or to assimilate the animal. That the human being is inherently or essentially sinful (after the Fall) is the position of the Reformers. I am not arguing that any respectable theologian would buy either doctrine, but that popular belief, especially among the Irish, frequently featured both. When we say that "sin is always punished," we might well mean that the inhuman act or attitude always has dire consequences for our human condition. (Personal letter, 28 July 1994)

35. Cady, *The Light of Common Day*, 24.

36. Mullett, "The Extraordinary Story of Eugene O'Neill," 34.

37. It is interesting to note similarities in the Nietzsche and O'Neill biographies. (This implies, I think, that it is even more useful to note their differences.) Each man seemed to have, whatever his protestations to the contrary, a religious inclination or mindset. That is, each man was obsessed by the question of God and his relationship to human beings. Both gave up the Christian faith in adolescence: O'Neill at thirteen; Nietzsche, the son of a Lutheran pastor, at eighteen. The playwright's "Hurrah!" is, no doubt, patterned on the philosopher's "tragic optimism" (learned from the Greeks). Each man came to feel a stranger in Time: " . . . Nietzsche felt homeless: 'From first to last,' says Frau Foerster [his sister], 'we find the sense of loneliness, of having no home, of being strongly drawn towards Nature' " (Eric Bentley, *A Century of Hero-Worship: A Study of the Idea of Heroism in Carlyle and Nietzsche with Notes on Other Hero-Worshipers of Modern Times* [Philadelphia and New York: Lippincott, 1944], 104).

38. Tornqvist, *A Drama of Souls*, 12.

39. Krutch, introduction to *Nine Plays*, xxii.

40. *The Letters of George Santayana*, ed. Daniel Cory (New York: Scribner's, 1955), 302.

41. O'Neill, *Selected Letters*, 195.

42. Krutch, *The Modern Temper*, 80, 83.

43. Krutch, introduction to *Nine Plays*, xxi.

44. Krutch, *The Modern Temper*, 84.

45. In " *'Modernism' in Modern Drama*" (Ithaca: Cornell University Press, 1953), 121, Krutch observes, "All the characters in [*Winterset*] are in one way or another 'modern'; this means that no one is sure that he knows what Justice is, that it exists outside his own mind, that it is more than the mores of his group, or that any sensible man would sacrifice any real advantage in the interest of such an abstraction."

46. *New Catholic Encyclopedia*, 6: 849. (I have emphasized the phrase "human nature," for I realize that not all persons accept as reality the condition so named.)

47. I owe this insight to Thomas E. Porter, who steered me to the further discussion in Ricoeur. One is staggered by that philosopher's treatment of the subject in *The Symbolism of Evil,* especially chapters 1, 2, and 3 ("Defilement," "Sin," and "Guilt").

3. Church Authority, Artistic Freedom, and the Search for God

1. George Santayana, *The Winds of Doctrine: Studies in Contemporary Opinion* (New York: Scribner's, 1913), 188.

2. The late John Tracy Ellis, for many years Professor of Church History at the Catholic University of America, was widely honored as teacher and writer. Nothing else that he did, however, is likely to eclipse the impact of his provocative critique, *American Catholics and the Intellectual Life* (Chicago: The Heritage Foundation, 1956). In it Fr. Ellis focused on what he saw as a pervasive and paralyzing presence of Catholic *anti*-intellectualism. Coming when it did, but a few years before Vatican Council II (1962–1965), Ellis's pronouncement challenged the complacency of mid-1950s Catholic assumptions about the higher life of the mind. Scrupulously evenhanded, Fr. Ellis had taken cognizance of the peculiar difficulties that an immigrant church had faced. But those conditions did not excuse certain failures, he argued. The contemporary state of things was shameful: in certain ways, egregiously so.

3. Ellis, *American Catholicism and the Intellectual Life,* 17–18.

4. Eugene Kennedy, "What Do Catholic Novelists Do?" *U.S. Catholic Historian* 6 (spring/summer 1987): 249–251.

5. Santayana's astute observation in *The Winds of Doctrine*, page 200, may have relevance here. "Serious poetry [and] profound religion (Calvinism, for instance) are the joys of an unhappiness that confesses itself; but when a genteel tradition forbids people to confess that they are unhappy, serious poetry and profound religion are closed to them by that." Here was an arresting idea: Joy might come in expressing one's sorrow. Perhaps this sentiment is not so different from O'Neill's "Life's a tragedy. *Hurrah!*"

6. Margaret Mary Reher, *Catholic Intellectual Life in America: A Historical Study of Persons and Movements* (New York: Macmillan, 1989), 123.

7. William M. Halsey, *The Survival of American Innocence: Catholicism in an Era of Disillusionment, 1920–1940* (Notre Dame, Ind.: University of Notre Dame Press, 1980), 125. (Halsey's usually just criticism fails here. He does not perceive Skinner's full merits.)

8. O'Neill, *Selected Letters,* 535.

9. *The Legion of Decency* was founded under the direction of the Catholic Bishops of the United States in the spring of 1934. Among its chief architects were Martin J. Quigley, publisher of film magazines and an influential Catholic layman, and Daniel A. Lord, S.J. The Legion eventually established its own rating criteria by which films were classified on a scale ranging from A-1 ("morally unobjectionable for general patronage") to C ("condemned"). See Quigley, *Decency in Motion Pictures* (New York: Macmillan, 1937).

10. Eugene Kennedy, *Tomorrow's Catholics, Yesterday's Church* (New York: Harper, 1988), 54.

11. A quite helpful record of O'Neill criticism in Catholic journals of opinion from 1930 through the 1960s may be discovered in *Catholic Periodical Index,* published by the Catholic Library Association, Haverford, Pa.

12. Reviewed by "A. T. P." of *All God's Chillun Got Wings* in *America* 31 (17 May 1924): 115–116.

13. Skinner produced what may be the closest thing to a "Catholic" survey

of O'Neill in a period (mid-1920s through mid-1930s) that was critical both in the playwright's development and in Catholic intellectual history. Thus, Skinner's book-length study, *Eugene O'Neill: A Poet's Quest* (New York: Russell and Russell, 1935, 1964), undertaken with the "poet's" approval, may have softened somewhat the negative Catholic consensus on O'Neill. This was just one year before the American was awarded the Nobel Prize for Literature.

14. Richard Dana Skinner, "The Moods of O'Neill," *Commonweal* 1 (10 December 1924): 133.

15. Skinner, *Commonweal* 3 (10 February 1926): 384 (emphasis mine).

16. James F. Kearney, S.J., "The Lost Ideal," *America* 35 (24 July 1926): 355.

17. Elizabeth Jordan, "Mr. O'Neill's Dramatic 'Stunt,' " *America* 38 (25 February 1928): 490–491.

18. Elizabeth Jordan, letter to Francis X. Talbot, S.J. (13 November 1931), Georgetown University Archives.

19. Euphemia Van Rensselaer Wyatt, "O'Neill and His Miracle," *The Catholic World* 138 (March 1934): 729.

20. Wyatt, "Who Against Hope Believed in Hope," *The Catholic World* 164 (November 1946): 168–169.

21. George N. Shuster, *The Catholic Church and Current Literature* (New York: Macmillan, 1930), 100–101.

22. Ibid., 101.

23. Louis F. Doyle, "Mr. O'Neill's Iceman," *America* 76 (30 November 1946): 241–242.

24. Jerry Cotter, "Dramatic Nihilism," *Sign* 26 (December 1946): 18.

25. Skinner, "Eugene O'Neill's Dynamo," *Commonweal* 9 (27 February 1929): 489.

26. Ibid., 489–490.

27. Don Brophy and Edythe Westenhaver, *The Story of Catholics in America* (New York: Paulist Press, 1978), 103.

28. Shannon, *The American Irish,* 262.

29. Skinner, *Commonweal* 15 (11 November 1931): 46–47.

30. Ibid., 47.

31. Jordan, "Mr. O'Neill and Others," *America* 46 (28 November 1931): 404–405.

32. James Hennesey, S.J., *American Catholics: A History of the Roman Catholic Community in the United States* (New York: Oxford University Press, 1981), 236.

33. O'Neill, *Selected Letters,* 426.

34. Stephen Whicher, "O'Neill's Long Journey," *Commonweal* 63 (16 March 1956): 614–615.

35. O'Neill, *Selected Letters,* 311.

36. Quoted in Travis Bogard, *Contour in Time,* 316–317.

37. O'Neill, *Selected Letters,* 225.

38. O'Neill, *The Great God Brown,* in *The Plays of Eugene O'Neill,* vol. 3 (New York: Random House, 1955), 264. Volume 1 includes *Strange Interlude; Desire Under the Elms; Lazarus Laughed;* and *Ile.* Volume 2 includes *Mourning Becomes Electra; Ah, Wilderness!; All God's Chillun Got Wings.* Volume 3 includes *Beyond the Horizon; The Great God Brown; Days Without End; The Ice-*

man Cometh. A first citation to a play will be indicated by a roman numeral, followed by a page number (e.g., II, 425). Thereafter, only page numbers will be given within parentheses.

39. Eugene O'Neill, quoted in Barrett Clark, *Eugene O'Neill* (New York: Robert M. McBride & Company, 1926), 105.

40. Ibid., 104.

41. Ibid., 105.

42. Ibid.

43. O'Neill saw the problem but, it seems, less in philosophical terms than as a technical failure. He felt that the masks used in the first production were not well made and therefore failed to communicate his meaning. The passage below is excerpted from his letter to Benjamin De Casseres, in *Selected Letters*, 246.

> I quite understand the masks confusing you when you saw it [*The Great God Brown*]. They were never right and we had neither the time nor the money to experiment and get them right before we opened—the old story that prevents anything really fine from ever being done in the American theatre! When you read what I wanted those masks to get across—the abstract drama of the forces behind the people—as it suggested in the script you will remember more clearly how wrong they were. They suggested only the bromidic, hypocritical & defensive double-personality of the people in their personal relationships—a thing I never would have needed masks to convey. They became an unnecessary trick. Perhaps I was demanding too much, and it can't be done—but I'm sure with the right masks my meaning would get across, that the play would be mystic instead of confusing—and I'm sure, given the money and time, the right masks could have been made.

44. Bogard, *Contour in Time*, 277.

45. Clark, *Eugene O'Neill*, 104.

46. O'Neill, *Selected Letters*, 288.

47. Ibid., 209.

48. Margaret Ranald, *The Eugene O'Neill Companion*, 366.

49. O'Neill, *Selected Letters*, 245 (emphasis mine).

50. Clark, *Eugene O'Neill*, 119.

51. O'Neill, *Selected Letters*, 204.

52. Clark, *Eugene O'Neill*, 113.

53. Bogard, *Contour in Time*, 304.

54. O'Neill, *Selected Letters*, 332.

4. Plays: Early Period (1916–1923)

1. Eugene O'Neill, *Ile*, in *The Plays of Eugene O'Neill*, vol. 1, 549. (All passages from volumes, 1, 2, and 3 will, on first citation, be given with a roman numeral followed by a page number. Each subsequent citation from the same play will be cited with page numbers only, in parentheses. For further information, see note 38, chapter 3.)

2. Ranald, *The Eugene O'Neill Companion*, 325.

3. Louis Sheaffer (in *O'Neill: Son and Playwright*, 385) and Michael Man-

heim (in *Eugene O'Neill's New Language of Kinship* [Syracuse: Syracuse University Press, 1982], 16) make a similar point.

4. Bogard, *Contour in Time,* 119.

5. In O'Neill only those characters still interacting can be redeemed. Thus Andrew cannot be forgiven by his now-dead father, James Mayo. Theodore Hickman can no longer forgive or be forgiven by Evelyn. If the case be made that Eben Cabot is redeemed by his dead mother, I should say that the argument is specious. He is forgiven, if at all, and his value reestablished, through his relationship with Abbie Putnam. Jim Tyrone of *A Moon for the Misbegotten* cannot be forgiven by his mother, Mary, for she too is dead. If he is to receive "absolution," it must be through mediation of some other agent.

6. Bogard, *Contour in Time,* 191.

7. A fundamentalist reading of the first sin of man and woman recalls Adam and Eve's original act of disobedience, recorded in the book of Genesis. The "moment" is said to have occurred when the parents of all who have followed ate the forbidden fruit from the Tree of Knowledge. When God discovered this transgression of his law, he cast them out of paradise into the land east of Eden, where they would work for bread, suffer the pain of childbirth, and endure the ultimate humiliation of death. Their children (that is, all who would enter history) were to inherit their guilt: the sins of the parents would be visited on all later generations. Perhaps a more modern or sophisticated interpretation of this story is that all women and men, as in their very nature, have inherited the burden of guilt and a natural inclination to sinfulness. Inevitably, therefore, the human condition has been to suffer, and the world itself has become a valley of sorrows.

8. O'Neill, *Selected Letters,* 195.

5. Plays: Middle Period (1924–1933)

1. Bogard, *Contour in Time,* 208–209.

2. Ibid., 213–214.

3. O'Neill, *Selected Letters,* 194.

4. Robert Brustein, *The Theatre of Revolt* (Boston: Little, Brown, 1964), 335.

5. O'Neill, *Selected Letters,* 558.

6. O'Neill, "Working Notes and Extracts from a Fragmentary Work Diary," in *American Playwrights on Drama,* ed. Horst Frenz (New York: Hill and Wang, 1965), 3.

7. Ibid.

8. Normand Berlin, *Eugene O'Neill: Three Plays* (London: Macmillan, 1989), 54.

9. Krutch, introduction to *Nine Plays,* xxii.

10. Porter, *Myth and Modern American Drama,* 14 (emphasis his).

11. O'Neill, *Selected Letters,* 368.

12. Ibid., 193 (emphasis mine).

13. Euphemia Van Rensselaer Wyatt, "Agamemnon Turned Puritan," *The Catholic World* 134 (December, 1931): 331.

14. The guilt Orin feels, not only for driving Christine to suicide but for his overall obsession with her, may humanize him somewhat. See in Bogard, *Contour*

in Time, 348: "Orin's long written confession, which relates the history of the Mannons' crimes, has something of the same motivation [as Ezra's confession to Christine]—the psychoanalysis of a family which may lead to purgation."

15. Ibid., 347.

16. O'Neill, in *American Playwrights on Drama,* 14.

17. O'Neill, *Selected Letters,* 390.

18. O'Neill, in *American Playwrights on Drama,* 3–4.

19. Berlin, *Eugene O'Neill: Three Plays,* 56.

20. O'Neill, *Selected Letters,* 390.

21. Porter, *Myth and Modern American Drama,* 51.

22. Again Bogard makes a helpful remark about the moral weight of the play, *Contour in Time,* 349: " . . . O'Neill, while accepting modern psychoanalytic theory, still holds to the idea of crime and punishment that he inherited from the source in legend. In tragedy, human crime is punished by the Gods who control human destiny. A divinity shapes the end."

I should not wish to argue the point, except to say that O'Neill may have inherited his idea of sin and punishment as much from Irish Catholicism as from the Greek tragedians.

23. O'Neill, in *American Playwrights on Drama,* 6.

24. Gelb and Gelb, *O'Neill,* 762.

25. Bowen, *The Curse of the Misbegotten,* 315.

26. Had it not been convincingly positive, *Wilderness!* would never have appealed to Cohan, the Yankee Doodle Dandy, who played Nat Miller. Many observers, including members of the Theater Guild who produced it, were nonplussed when the playwright suggested casting the song-and-dance man for the part of Richard's father. They were even more surprised by Cohan's acceptance. This turn of events must have amused the author. Cohan was wary of "intellectuals" (members of the Guild?), just as O'Neill was often uncomfortable in the presence of the professional *cognoscenti.* Indeed, Cohan suspected that O'Neill "might try to pull some of that highbrow stuff," and he was pleased to discover a "regular" fellow of the theater who "wasn't born on the corner of Forty-third Street and Broadway for nothing," (in Sheaffer, *O'Neill: Son and Artist,* 419).

27. O'Neill, *Selected Letters,* 409.

28. In *The Plays of Eugene O'Neill,* (Carbondale: Southern Illinois University Press, 1965), 77–79, John Henry Raleigh has thrown light on O'Neill's use of songs and song titles. He notes that most of the numbers were of recent vintage or were well known in the period: "Mighty Like a Rose" (act 1), 1901; "In the Sweet Bye and Bye" (act 2), a nineteenth-century Salvation Army hymn, sung by Uncle Sid; "Dearie" (act 2), 1905. Let us recall that parents and children were probably not so divided in their musical tastes at the turn of the century as they have since become. In act 2, when Richard visits the prostitute in the backroom of the bar, Belle complains to the bartender that the player piano keeps playing the same tune: "Say, George, is 'Bedelia' the latest to hit this hick burg? Well, it's only a couple of years old! You'll catch up in time! Why don't you get a new roll for that old box?" In fact, the song was published in 1903. The point is that all these items lend authenticity to the background.

29. O'Neill, *Selected Letters,* 421.

30. O'Neill in a letter to Saxe Commins, quoted by Doris Alexander in *Creative Struggle,* 177, 301.

31. See Alexander, *Creative Struggle*, 175–177.

32. If we examine the play for its autobiographical content, we can hardly find a richer discussion than Doris Alexander's. Of course, one would anticipate an emphasis on such parallels in a study called *Eugene O'Neill's Creative Struggle* (1992). This book also takes considerable interest (pp. 175–177) in the artist's life. But the immediate focus in the present examination of *Ah, Wilderness!* is the play's impact on audience and reader. That is, what meaning does the play convey as drama or literature, whatever connections it may have with O'Neill's personal experience? In this way of looking at it, we discover not precisely a message but rather a strong insight into the importance of human relationships.

33. O'Neill, *Selected Letters*, 423.

6. The "Catholic" Play: *Days Without End* (1934)

1. Brooks Atkinson, review of *Days Without End, New York Times,* 14 January 1934, sec. 9:1.

2. Elizabeth Jordan, "The New Plays," *America* 50 (27 January 1934): 404.

3. Ibid., 405.

4. Patrick F. Scanlan, review of *Days Without End, Brooklyn Tablet* 13 January 1934.

5. Raleigh, *The Plays of Eugene O'Neill*, 137.

6. Bogard, *Contour in Time*, 329.

7. Sheaffer, *O'Neill: Son and Artist*, 412.

8. Ranald, *The Eugene O'Neill Companion*, 163.

9. Virginia Floyd, *The Plays of Eugene O'Neill: A New Assessment* (New York: Frederick Ungar, 1985), 415, 418.

10. Virginia Floyd, *Eugene O'Neill at Work: Newly Released Ideas for Plays* (New York: Frederick Ungar, 1981), 149.

11. O'Neill, *Selected Letters*, 442.

12. Gerald B. Donnelly, S.J., "O'Neill's New Catholic Play," *America* 50 (13 January 1934): 346–347.

13. Daniel Lord, S.J., to Martin Quigley, 27 December 1933, Georgetown University Archives.

14. Eugene O'Neill to Martin Quigley, 7 January 1934, Georgetown University Archives.

15. Jordan, "The New Plays," 404.

16. Edward L. Shaughnessy, "Masks in the Dramaturgy of Yeats and O'Neill," *Irish University Review* 16.2 (autumn 1984): 205.

17. Carlotta O'Neill, in *"Love, Admiration and Respect": The O'Neill-Commins Correspondence,* ed. Dorothy Commins (Durham, N.C.: Duke University Press, 1986), 158.

18. Donnelly, "O'Neill's New Catholic Play," 346.

19. In *"The Theatre We Worked For": The Letters of Eugene O'Neill to Kenneth Macgowan,* ed. Jackson R. Bryer, with the assistance of Ruth M. Alvarez (New Haven: Yale University Press, 1982), 207–208.

20. Skinner, review of *Days Without End, Commonweal* 19 (19 January 1934): 327.

21. Skinner to Michael Earls, S.J., 11 January 1934, Archives of the College of the Holy Cross.

22. In *O'Neill: Son and Artist,* 425, Louis Sheaffer tells of the reflections of a Rev. George B. Ford, who had been invited to meet the O'Neills at the Skinners' one evening, an occasion when *Days* was discussed.

> Father Ford, unlike Skinner, did not get the impression that O'Neill was wavering back to his former faith. "We never discussed religion per se that night. He simply narrated the story for my general reaction. Two or three times after that, Carlotta called and said Eugene wanted to talk with me, asked me to hold on, then came back to the phone and said he wouldn't. She always added, 'I hope you understand.' I don't know whether she wanted him to talk with me and he balked at the last minute, or whether it was his idea and he changed his mind."

23. O'Neill, *Selected Letters,* 208.

24. Skinner to Michael Earls, S.J., 22 January 1934, Archives of the College of the Holy Cross.

25. Skinner to Michael Earls, S.J., 28 January 1934, Archives of the College of the Holy Cross.

26. In *Creative Struggle,* 191, Doris Alexander provides insight into O'Neill's evolving attitude toward divorce. He had come to terms with his father, who had died in 1920, and had come to admire James's splendid example of fidelity to Ella Quinlan. Eugene himself, of course, had been twice divorced.

> O'Neill's model of enduring love had been his father's love for his mother, and hers for him. His father had been "a husband to marvel at," faithful through all the agonies of his wife's addiction. O'Neill had seen his father's ideal of service in his loving care for his wife and had read it when he was eight in his father's Christmas story for the 1896 *Dramatic Mirror.* It had been a true story of helping a desperate little girl who had mistaken him for a Catholic priest in which he had pointed up the moral that "life is really worth living" not merely for one's own sake but "through the fortunate circumstances which enable one to come to the assistance of a fellow-being." This became O'Neill's own ideal, for he saw adultery "as the great sin against love." (p. 196)

27. O'Neill, *Selected Letters,* 432.

28. In *"As Ever, Gene": The Letters of Eugene O'Neill to George Jean Nathan,* ed. Nancy L. Roberts and Arthur W. Roberts (Rutherford, N.J.: Fairleigh Dickinson University Press, 1987), 155.

29. Skinner, "The Critics and *Days Without End,*" *Commonweal* 19 (26 January 1934), 358.

30. Skinner to Michael Earls, S.J., 14 February 1934, Archives of the College of the Holy Cross.

31. O'Neill, *Selected Letters,* 433.

32. Sheaffer, *O'Neill: Son and Playwright,* 87.

33. Francis Thompson, in *The Poetical Works of Francis Thompson,* 1: 108.

34. In deference to Catholic sensibilities and to insure verisimilitude, O'Neill went a long way to assure authenticity of tone and detail. In the 1930s church regulations concerning adultery and divorce were strictly enforced. *Days Without End* registers the orthodox positions: *"as the great sin against love"* (emphasis mine).

Perhaps more interesting is O'Neill's scrupulosity with regard to authenticity of stage properties. He took extreme care in obtaining the crucifix used in the final scene, before which John prostrates himself and Loving slumps defeated. Sensitive to possibilities for a maudlin interpretation of the scene, he tried to avoid vulgarity in the design of the icon. Therefore, he sought the advice of the Liturgical Arts Society, a group of Catholic laymen who were "concerned . . . with making the church building a more appropriate setting for Christian worship." Its members were mainly architects, sculptors, musicians and other distinguished and influential professional men. The Society recommended the services of Adam Dabrowski, a New York sculptor whose work pleased O'Neill immensely. He wrote to the editor of *Liturgical Arts:*

> When it was necessary to procure a crucifix, sympathetically executed, and appropriate to the spirit of the last scene of my play *Days Without End* at present running at the Henry Miller Theatre, it was suggested that your Society might be able to help. May I express herewith my deep gratitude for the help extended in this matter. The crucifix which was designed and executed in wood by Mr. Adam Dabrowski of New York is a beautiful thing, a true work of art, and it adds immeasurably to the dramatic and spiritual quality of the final scene of my play. (O'Neill to Maurice Lavanoux, 10 January 1934, Archives, Hesburgh Memorial Library, University of Notre Dame)

35. O'Neill, *Selected Letters,* 432.
36. Floyd, *A New Assessment,* 420.
37. In *"The Theatre We Worked For,"* 208.
38. O'Neill, *Selected Letters,* 432.
39. Ibid., 423.
40. Ibid., 433.
41. To be entirely fair we should note that, whether O'Neill knew it or not, the Abbey Theatre had fallen out of favor with the Catholic hierarchy in Ireland at this time.

> Suggestions had surfaced that the National Theatre had taken on an anti-religious bias, a serious charge against any government-sponsored enterprise in Ireland. William Butler Yeats then received a timely suggestion from Patrick McCartan, a Dublin-born physician who was living in the United States. McCartan had just seen O'Neill's "Miracle play" and recommended that the Abbey produce it and thereby thwart its detractors. . . . Thus, both theatre and playwright were well served. The Abbey [gave] the European premiere [of *Days*] and gained forgiveness for its offenses against piety. O'Neill, rescued from his drubbing at the hands of the Broadway critics, had been invited by Yeats himself to come to Ireland. (Shaughnessy, *Eugene O'Neill in Ireland,* 64–65.)

42. O'Neill, *Selected Letters,* 430.
43. Sheaffer, *O'Neill: Son and Artist,* 432.
44. This catalog of questions is rhetorical in nature, to be sure, yet I feel that the reader deserves some commentary with regard to them. The "miracle" is a miracle only to those (O'Neill et al.) who choose to believe in it. The skeptic retains her right to view the intervention as a suggestion that he has been recalled from apostasy. Carlotta O'Neill's protest to Saxe Commins notwithstanding (see note 17, this chapter), the resolution of *Days Without End* can lead the audience

to only one conclusion: the play has everything "to do with Christianity [and] prayer." Finally, either the hero is duped by his own need for a "pipe dream," or, O'Neill implies, John Loving has found *doctrinal* redemption.

The evidence suggests that the "Catholic play" underscores O'Neill's own fear and guilt feelings and that he sought desperately some sign of divine forgiveness.

45. O'Neill, *Selected Letters,* 433.
46. Ibid., 426.
47. O'Neill, in *"The Theatre We Worked For,"* 207.

7. Plays: Late Period (1939–1943)

1. Bowen, *The Curse of the Misbegotten,* 308.
2. Because *The Iceman Cometh* makes such strenuous demands on both the acting company and the audience, few directors and established theaters have undertaken the risks certain to be incurred in its mounting. (I am thinking particularly of English language productions.)

The Abbey Theatre has given two exceptionally successful productions. In 1972 Sean Cotter directed Vincent Dowling in the part of Hickey and Philip O'Flynn as Larry Slade (design by Voytek). In 1992 the Abbey undertook *The Iceman* with Brian Dennehy as Hickey. In 1985 Jason Robards re-created the role of Hickey on Broadway, but nothing could eclipse the 1956 revival directed by José Quintero (565 consecutive performances in Circle in the Square Theatre, Greenwich Village), in which Robards may have given the definitive realization of the hardware salesman.

Greatest access to this play has probably been realized through John Frankenheimer's 1974 film version in which that director chose Lee Marvin to play Hickey (to mixed reviews). All in all, however, the cast was quite brilliant: Frederick March as Harry Hope, Robert Ryan as Slade, Jeff Bridges as Parritt, and Bradford Dillman as Willie Oban.

3. Bowen, *The Curse of the Misbegotten,* 310.
4. Gelb and Gelb, *O'Neill,* 284.
5. Bowen, *The Curse of the Misbegotten,* 310.
6. *"The best friends I've ever known."* For years O'Neill had contributed more than anyone now can know to the monthly support of his old friend from the anarchist days, Terry Carlin. Carlin, the model for Larry Slade, was seventy-nine and was dying in Boston when *Days Without End* opened there. He rallied briefly when he heard "Gene" would be coming to see him during rehearsals. But, we learn in Sheaffer, *O'Neill: Son and Artist* (427), "O'Neill never did appear or telephone; he probably was deterred less by the weather [heavy snowfall] than by reluctance to see his old crony in a decrepit state."

About the time of the first *Iceman* production (1946), Mary Eleanor Fitzgerald ("Fitzi"), friend to Emma Goldman and secretary to the Provincetown in its early days, called O'Neill for help. She had checked into Mount Sinai Hospital but could not pay the admission deposit. He sent her a check immediately for $100. Carlotta always disapproved of these "blood-suckers, thieves, bastards, scum— and bohemians." (See Dorothy Commins, *What Is an Editor? Saxe Commins at Work* [Chicago: University of Chicago Press, 1978], 68–70.)

7. Gerald Weales, "Eugene O'Neill: *The Iceman Cometh*," in *Landmarks of American Writing*, ed. Hennig Cohen (New York: Basic Books, 1969), 354.

8. Bowen, *The Curse of the Misbegotten*, 309.

9. See Winifred L. Frazer's useful study, *E.G. and E.G.O.: Emma Goldman and "The Iceman Cometh"* (Gainesville: University Presses of Florida, 1974) for the most complete discussion of this subject.

10. Bogard, *Contour in Time*, 422.

11. José Quintero makes a cogent statement about the play's sophisticated form. He is quoted by Edwin Joseph McDonough in *Quintero Directs O'Neill: An Examination of Eleven Plays of Eugene O'Neill Staged by José Quintero in New York City, 1956–1981*, Diss. no. 8614525 (Ann Arbor: University Microfilms International, 1985), 36.

> It resembles a complex musical form, with themes repeating themselves with slight variations, as melodies do in a symphony. It is a valid device, though O'Neill has often been criticized for it by those who do not see the strength and depth of meaning the repetition achieves.
>
> My work was something like that of an orchestra conductor, emphasizing rhythms, being constantly aware of changing tempos, every character advanced a different theme. The paradox was that for the first time as a director I began to understand the meaning of precision in drama—and it took a play four and a half hours long to teach me, a play often criticized as rambling and overwritten.

12. According to *The Baltimore Catechism* (which Eugene O'Neill had studied as a child) "sin is any willful thought, desire, word, action, or omission forbidden by the law of God." This was *actual* sin, as distinguished from *original* sin. Of course, O'Neill grew light years in sophistication beyond this level of understanding. Yet this was his grounding, an education in making distinctions: actual from original, *venial* from *mortal* sin, commission from omission. One developed, even as a child, a way of discussing matters grave beyond one's years: linguistic habits, some might say; conditioned scrupulosity, others will charge. But, as exaggerated and even lethal as this emphasis on guilt could be, one learned at any rate not to devalue his natural connections with others.

13. Bowen, *Contour in Time*, 309.

14. Indeed, it may be argued that even Evelyn's forgiving Hickey was destructive because by this she continually robbed her husband of his feeling of self-worth. Forgiveness without charity stings. "Christ," he shouts, "can you imagine what a guilty skunk she made me feel! If she'd only admitted once she didn't believe any more in her pipe dream that someday I'd behave. . . . Can you picture . . . all the guilt she made me feel, and how I hated myself!" (*Iceman*, III, 713). For all her long-suffering, abject "saintliness," Evelyn was subtly destructive: "I got so sometimes when she'd kiss me it was like she did it on purpose to humiliate me, as if she'd spit in my face" (715). Was her virtue more apparent than real? Evelyn's forgiveness served only to remind Hickey of his "weakness," what O'Neill said was found in all men.

15. See Cyrus Day, "The Iceman and the Bridegroom: Some Observations on the Death of O'Neill's Salesman," *Modern Drama* I (May 1958): 3–9. Here is a

brilliant contribution to O'Neill studies. Even so, I think the analogy to the Last Supper is perhaps too inventive.

16. Lawrence Langner, *The Magic Curtain: The Story of a Life in Two Fields, Theatre and Invention* (New York: Dutton, 1951), 378.

17. Biographers and literary critics claim to revere nothing so much as detached and objective commentary. Yet the critic occasionally does well to abandon the role of unbiased commentator. In the case at hand, the author's claimed detachment would constitute hypocrisy.

18. Robert Brustein, *The Theatre of Revolt*, 350–351.

19. As artist, O'Neill had available an option most men and women cannot invoke: he could include himself in the dynamics of reliving one day with his parents and brother. He could *re*-present them all by the power of his art and see them more clearly through the lens of his moral imagination. Like the other Tyrones, he would be neither better nor worse than he had been. But now, having been liberated from the anger and terror of the moment, he could give them a new grace. The creation of this *day* could be defended on the grounds of "faithful realism." Into the day would be absorbed the distilled essence of each haunted Tyrone: a phenomenon "more real than reality."

20. The Tyrones' immersion in an Irish-Catholic ethos is, of course, a given in *Long Day's Journey into Night*. The evidence of this cultural presence is revealed at every turn. James, for example, confesses that he is "a bad Catholic in the observance, . . . " Mary's many references to the Blessed Virgin provide another rivet to traditional belief, although she never speaks of her devotion except in soliloquy or in the ending moments of the play, when James and their sons have lost contact with her.

I am aware of no critic, however, who has pointed to the absence of religious objects among the furnishing and fixtures of the Tyrone household: a crucifix or a holy picture on the wall, the statue of a saint, a flickering votive light such as we might see in one of O'Casey's Dublin plays. Such iconography was ubiquitous in the pious Catholic household of the period. Considering O'Neill's meticulous attention to detail, this omission is striking. The stage directions are quite explicit, for example, about what volumes should be included in the small bookcase (whose authors James disapproved) and "*the large, glassed-in bookcase with set of Dumas, Victor Hugo, Charles Lever, three sets of Shakespeare, the World's Best Literature in fifty large volumes, Hume's History of England . . . and several histories of Ireland*" (*LDJ*, 11). A picture of Shakespeare hangs on the wall.

One can only suppose that the Tyrones held it to be in dubious taste to flaunt their faith by such open displays of piety. These items were visible, if at all, only in the precincts of the bedroom. But such fastidiousness or reticence would not have been typical.

21. Jacques Maritain, *Education at the Crossroads*, 96–97.

22. Noel O'Hara, personal letter to the author, 14 October 1993.

23. Ibid.

24. Bogard, *Contour in Time*, 451.

25. O'Neill, *Selected Letters*, 546.

26. O'Neill, *A Touch of the Poet* (New Haven: Yale University Press, 1957), 12.

27. Bowen, *The Curse of the Misbegotten*, 313.

28. Martha Gilman Bower, ed., introduction to Eugene O'Neill's *More Stately Mansions: The Unexpurgated Edition* (New York: Oxford University Press, 1988), 17.

29. For an account of earlier texts used in the (1962) Stockholm and (September and November 1967) Los Angeles and New York productions of *More Stately Mansions,* see Bower's introduction, 4.

30. Bower, introduction to *More Stately Mansions,* 12.

31. O'Neill, *More Stately Mansions,* 37. (Further citation of passages are keyed to this edition.

32. Bower, introduction to *More Stately Mansions,* 6.

33. Bogard, *Contour in Time,* 369.

34. Except for a handful of outstanding productions, *A Moon for the Misbegotten* has not received favorable reviews. Nor has it been placed in the literary pantheon along with *Long Day's Journey into Night.* Indeed, O'Neill's wife so disliked the play that he himself became discouraged about it. The dissenters have had their say. Let that go. The challenge here is to do justice to the deep calms of act 3, moments in modern drama that defy fair characterization. I hope in this final discussion to place a strong rivet in the seam of my argument.

35. It is interesting to note O'Neill's use of *Jamie* (Tyrone) in *Long Day's Journey* and *Jim* in *A Moon for the Misbegotten.* In the family, of course, he was called by the diminutive to distinguish him from his father, who was called Jim by most of his friends. Outside the family and in his own circle the son is called by the pal-like name of Jim.

36. Bogard, *Contour in Time,* 453.

37. Jim Tyrone's situation is analogous to Don Parritt's in *The Iceman Cometh,* each man having betrayed his mother. But Tyrone's is the more moving, for he is, with Josie Hogan, the "misbegotten."

38. Margaret Ranald also uses this word in *The Eugene O'Neill Companion,* 299.

39. O'Neill, *A Moon for the Misbegotten* (New Haven: Yale University Press, 1957), 12.

40. For an account of James H. O'Neill's career as a student (at Notre Dame [Minim Division], Georgetown [Prep], and Fordham [St. John's Prep and St. John's College]), see Edward L. Shaughnessy, "Ella, James, and Jamie O'Neill," *The Eugene O'Neill Review* 15, no. 2 (fall, 1991): 5–92.

41. See Francis Fergusson, introduction to *Aristotle's Poetics,* trans. S. H. Butcher (New York: Hill and Wang, 1961), 8. Here is an excellent interpretation of the idea of action in drama. " . . . [A]ction (praxis) does not mean deeds, events, or physical activity: it means, rather, the motivation from which deeds spring. Butcher puts it this way: 'The *praxis* that art seeks to reproduce is mainly a psychic energy working outwards.' . . . It may be described metaphorically as the focus or movement of the psyche toward what seems good to it at the moment—*a movement-of-spirit,* Dante calls it."

42. Bogard, *Contour in Time,* 451–452.

43. What should take place in sacramental confession is not a sadistic humiliation of the penitent, but an act of love. The confessor "hears" the self-accusations. He bestows upon the penitent his counsel and blessing, absolution (forgiveness), and penance (in paraphrase: "Do this. Go and sin no more"). The

psychology is, or ought to be, constructive, supportive, dynamic (give-and-take, question-answer), and reassuring ("Your sins are forgiven").

O'Neill, trained in an earlier mode, might not have approved the post–Vatican II deemphasizing of personal confession.

Epilogue

1. Sheaffer, *O'Neill: Son and Artist,* 671.

2. No critic has been more perceptive than Travis Bogard in describing the effect of these pressures on O'Neill. Indeed, the very title of his book, *Contour in Time,* constitutes one of those minor *coups* of creative genius. It serves Professor Bogard's intention, which is to trace "the course of his life in art."

3. Nothing in O'Neill's life suggests greater contrast than his brief relationship with Dorothy Day and his marriage to Carlotta Monterey. Day came to espouse a Christian-socialist philosophy of charity, poverty, and service to the poor. Her name has become an international symbol for pacifism. She has been recommended for sainthood by many admirers.

Mrs. O'Neill had developed patrician mannerisms and tastes. As the years went by, Carlotta became bitterly critical of O'Neill's friends from the Greenwich Village period, both for their politics and their "vulgarity." Carlotta's growing anti-Semitism must have embarrassed Eugene profoundly, for he had had many Jewish friends in and out of the theater: Emma Goldman, Michael Gold, Max Eastman, Irving Berlin, among others. Most distressing in this regard was Carlotta's behavior in O'Neill's last years, when she turned on his longtime friend, colleague, and editor, Saxe Commins.

In general she disliked the friendships he had made in his Provincetown and "Anarchist" days, before she knew him well. Perhaps it is not surprising, then, that O'Neill seems not to have regained contact with Dorothy Day in later years. He had good reason to fear how Carlotta Monterey might have treated his old friend.

4. When she heard that O'Neill was sick, Dorothy Day apparently asked Richard Cardinal Cushing to send a priest to see him. At any rate, Fr. Vincent Mackey (of St. Cecelia's parish, Boston) did attempt to see him, as Rev. Thomas J. Daly, Executive Director of the Boston Synod, makes known in the following communication.

> I remember one occasion in which Monsignor Vincent Mackey, now deceased, spoke about his intervention at the old Shelton Hotel on Baystate Road when Mr. O'Neill was dying in November 1953. [Louis Sheaffer (*O'Neill: Son and Artist,* 669) gives the priest's name as Mackay.] Father Mackey mentioned the fact that he knew that he was in residence there. Father Mackey knew one of the housekeepers at the hotel who informed him where Mr. O'Neill was lodging. Father Mackey then went over to the hotel but was not able to gain entrance because of his wife and her attitude toward him. I do know that she called later to say she was more than upset about his intervention. She assured him that if there was any change in his attitude toward the church she would be in touch but under no circumstances was he to make another intervention. (Personal letter, 10 August 1992)

5. Dorothy Day, "Told in Context."

6. See *The Poetics* 9.1–9.

7. Sheaffer, *O'Neill: Son and Playwright,* 79.

8. Richard Dana Skinner, *Eugene O'Neill: The Poet's Quest,* 2.

9. Ibid., xii.

10. O'Neill's biographer, Louis Sheaffer, fairly staggers us with his insights. A Jew, Sheaffer reminds all that women and men can step across the threshold of differences in religious and ethnic background and into the sitting room of shared humanity.

11. Louis Sheaffer to Sr. M. Madeleva, 19 February 1961, St. Mary's College Archives.

12. O'Neill, *Selected Letters,* 426 (emphasis his).

13. "Eugene O'Neill," editorial, *Commonweal* 59 (11 December 1953): 250.

Appendix

1. Quoted in Arnold J. Sparr, *The Catholic Literary Revival in America, 1920–1960,* diss. no. 8513483 (Ann Arbor: University Microfilms International, 1985), 141.

2. We should distinguish immediately between *"Catholic" modernism* and the more universal but less formal movement of *literary modernism.* They were very different phenomena.

Literary modernism achieved its zenith in the first three decades of the twentieth century. In its rejection of traditional literary forms and western values, it was characterized by a spirit of skepticism and antiauthoritarianism. The literary modernists, influenced by the discoveries of Sigmund Freud and Carl Jung, emphasized the roles of the unconscious mind and intuition as ways to discover reality. Luigi Pirandello, James Joyce, T. S. Eliot, Thomas Mann, and William Faulkner were its chief proponents. Perhaps the most succinct description of the impact of this movement on European and American drama was given by the late Joseph Wood Krutch in *"Modernism" in Modern Drama* (Ithaca, N.Y.: Cornell University Press, 1953).

For a comprehensive history of the modernist "heresy" defined and condemned by Pius X (especially in its implications for the American Catholic Church), see R. Scott Appleby's study, *"Church and Age Unite!": The Modernist Impulse in American Catholicism* (Notre Dame, Ind.: University of Notre Dame Press, 1992).

Both varieties of modernism connect importantly with the life and art of Eugene O'Neill.

3. Msgr. Sheen, who possessed a histrionic flair and a magnetizing voice, often lectured in the prelate's full regalia, with black cape. He frequently ended his performance with the recitation of a singularly maudlin poem by Mary Dixon Thayer, "Lovely Lady Dressed in Blue."

4. Thomas F. O'Dea, *American Catholic Dilemma: An Inquiry into the Intellectual Life* (New York: Devin-Adair, 1958), 40.

5. Paul R. Messbarger, *Fiction With a Parochial Purpose: Social Uses of American Catholic Literature, 1884–1900* (Boston: Boston University Press, 1971), 153.

6. Eugene Kennedy, *The Now and Future Church,* 62–63.

7. William M. Halsey, *The Survival of American Innocence,* 93.

8. O'Dea, *American Catholic Dilemma,* 5.

9. Sparr, *The Catholic Literary Revival in America,* 153.

10. No doubt James O'Neill's disapproval of his sons' radicalism was a disapproval of their modernism, whether or not Tyrone can be imagined to have known that term. He would very likely have applauded the Pope's edicts.

11. L. Brady, "Eugene O'Neill" in *The New Catholic Encyclopedia,* 10: 697.

Index